- THE FIRST HORSEMAN -
GOD'S CHOSEN SERVANT

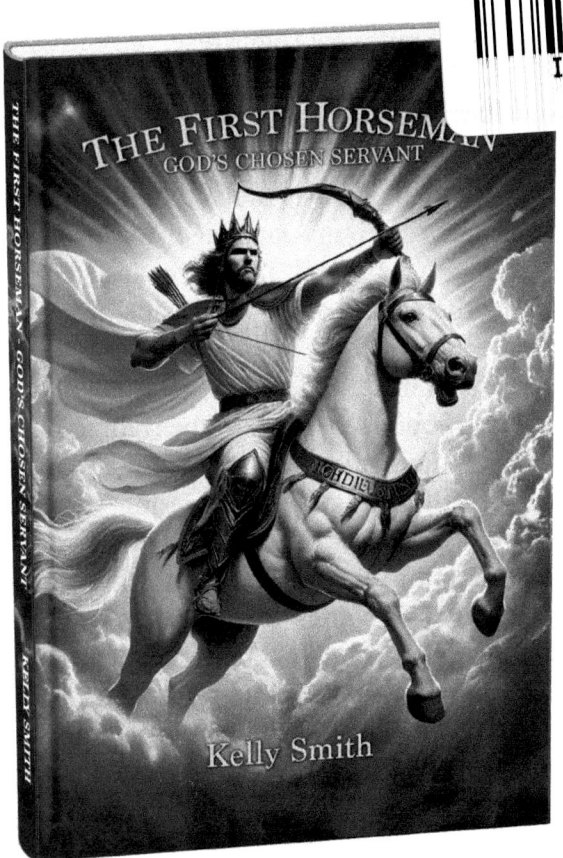

AUTHOR: KELLY SMITH

Copyright Notice
for All Purchasers

© 2025 Kelly Smith. All rights reserved. July 24, 2025

This publication is protected under the copyright laws of the United States and international treaties. No part of this book may be reproduced, distributed, shared, transmitted, stored in a retrieval system, or translated into any language, in any form or by any means—electronic, mechanical, photocopying, recording, or otherwise—without the prior written permission of the author.

The PDF contains embedded security measures that enable us to trace unauthorized copies. We reserve the right to pursue full legal remedies against individuals or entities who reproduce, distribute, or share this PDF without explicit permission.

It is disappointing that we must include this warning, particularly for readers who profess faith, integrity, and a desire to do what is right before God. Sharing this without permission is theft, pure and simple. We invite all readers to honor the sacredness of the revelations herein by respecting the rights and labors of the author.

If you feel inspired to share this message, please direct others to purchase their own copy using our special Affiliate Program with the link you have been sent as a purchaser of the book. Doing so supports the continued work and ensures that the truths contained herein are shared in righteousness.

Thank you for your integrity and support.

Copyright © 2025 by Kelly Smith
ISBN: 979-8-9924216-3-7

All rights reserved. No part of this book may be copied, reproduced, stored in a retrieval system, or transmitted in any form or by any means—electronic, mechanical, photocopying, recording, or otherwise—without prior written permission from the publisher, except for brief quotations used in reviews, articles, or scholarly discussion.

Disclaimer:
This book is based on the author's personal revelations, scriptural interpretations, and spiritual insights. It is intended to inspire faith, encourage study, and provoke thought about prophetic events in the last days. The views expressed herein do not represent official doctrine of any religious organization but are shared with the hope of strengthening faith in Jesus Christ and His divine plan.

Author, Editor and Publisher: Kelly Smith
(All words are my own and were not generated by AI, except for three small sections. I used Grammarly for spelling and grammar.)

Cover Design, Illustrations and Tyesetting by Kelly Smith
(Dall-E, Photoshop, Ideogram, Leonardo, Canva, InDesign)

Printed in the United States of America (Worldwide)

For permissions or inquiries, contact:
Kelly@First-Horseman.com
https://First-Horseman.com
https://www.facebook.com/groups/thefirsthorseman
https://www.youtube.com/@TheFirstHorseman

Financial Contributor: Jacqueline Hunter
Revision 10.1 Updated 7/31/2025

Kelly Smith is married to his wonderful wife, Betsy, and they are proud parents of five children and four grandchildren. He was born in Reno, Nevada, and served a mission for the Church of Jesus Christ of Latter-Day Saints in the Seattle/Spokane area from 1977 to 1979. He attended BYU and earned a Bachelor of Fine Arts degree in Graphic Design, ranking among the top 10 illustrators in his senior class nationwide.

In 1992, he founded a digital printing company and became a pioneer in that field. He worked for various large companies across the country, including Apple, IBM, General Motors, Disney, Macy's, Calvin Klein, The Gap, the National Gallery of Art, National Semiconductor, Universal Studios, Warner Bros. Studios, Lollapalooza, Elton John, Kid Rock, and many renowned rock groups. Additionally, he printed graphics for two Super Bowls, two Olympics, and numerous other companies. His work has reached audiences around the world and has been featured in movies.

He was a Toastmaster for 15 years and loves speaking. He began website design in 2004 and continues this work to this day.

He has served as a Seminary teacher, Gospel Doctrine teacher, Elders Quorum instructor, Scoutmaster three times, High Councilor, a member of the Bishopric twice, Elders Quorum President, and Young Men's President; he is currently the Stake Emergency Preparedness Specialist and the Ward Technology Specialist in charge of Zoom for each meeting. He has cherished every role he's ever held. He worked with young men for 24 years, which he considers one of the greatest experiences of his life. Now, he enjoys spending time with his grandchildren and watching them grow up. This is true joy.

This book is dedicated to my wife Betsy, without whom my life would be incomplete. She is the love of my life, and I want to spend eternity with her.

Table of Contents

Foreword 7
The Structure of the Book of Revelation 13
Section 1 - The Seven Seals 23
Section 2 - Revelation 6 37
Section 3 - Revelation 12 48
Section 4 - Revelation 13 60
Section 5 - Revelation Chapters 7 & 14 72
Section 6 - Revelation 8 & 11, 15 & 16 82
Section 7 - The Seven Sevens of God 108
Section 8 - The Four Aspects of the Kingdom of God . 115
Section 9 - One Mighty and Strong 133
Section 10 - Christ's Prophecy in 3 Nephi 20-23 143
Section 11 - The Suffering Servant 155
Section 12 - Moses 169
Section 13 - Cyrus 187
Section 14 - Nephi, Mormon and Moroni's Warning .. 198
Section 15 - Kings and Queens of the Gentiles 212
Section 16 - Vision of the Tree of Life 232
Section 17 - Why people leave the Church 254
Section 18 - Conclusion 274
Endnotes 291
Index 294

THANK YOU for purchasing this book!
To help you get started, please watch the Video
Introduction. Just scan the code below. It's free!

Please Do Not Skip This Foreword

Thank you for purchasing this book. I appreciate that! As you probably know my name is Kelly Smith, and I am a member of The Church of Jesus Christ of Latter-day Saints. Although the name "Kelly" is often associated with females, it has origins in old Irish, meaning "warrior" or "bright-headed." So take that, Wonder Woman—it's a man's name!

Before diving into what this book is about, let me clarify: I am not a Prophet, Apostle, or anyone with official authority. I am an ordinary member who feels compelled to share the insights I have discovered. I take full responsibility for these words, and I will repent if I am in error. I never intend to lead anyone away from the Church I love or the Savior I worship. If you are not a member of my faith, I invite you to read this book with an open mind.

So, why am I writing this book? It all began on December 28, 2021, at 3:30 a.m., when the Spirit asked me to read the Book of Revelation. Though I was confused by such a request at such an early hour, I obeyed, and for the next three years, I studied it like never before. My heart suffered from a condition called Bigeminy, where its left and right sides failed to beat in sync. Doctors could offer no relief. I had great difficulty breathing, preventing me from carrying out even the simplest tasks. In my suffering, I pleaded with God for healing, only to receive something more significant—the gift of His Spirit.

In November 2022, I had learned so much about the Book of Revelation that I created a video and posted it on YouTube. I decided to make another one a few weeks later on Revelation Chapter 12. I outlined the entire chapter in PowerPoint and, at 10:30 pm, decided to sleep on it and film it the next day. That night, November 28, 2022, at 4 a.m., I experienced a severe Bigeminy episode. My heart was pounding, my chest was tight, and I could not breathe. I fell out of bed and pleaded with God for help. Strangely, my mind was drawn to the PowerPoint, and I wondered why, then these two words suddenly came to me in stunning clarity: "**Donald Trump**." I didn't hear or see them; I just knew them, and they would not be more apparent if there were a neon sign of his name in front of me!

I jumped up off my knees and said out loud, "What? What does Donald Trump have anything to do with Revelation Chapter 12?" No answer came, but I noticed my symptoms had disappeared! My heart was no longer pounding, my chest was not tight, and I was breathing perfectly normally. I was as calm as could be. "What just happened?" I thought.

(Note: A few months later, I underwent an ablation that cured the Bigeminy I experienced, as this was a temporary reprieve from the condition. Two years later I discovered that my 5G WiFi and Router caused all of these problems as I had been sitting too close to them for many years. I've gotten a lot of flack making this claim, but I stand by it.)

I wanted to share this revelation, but a close friend warned, "You can't tell anyone—no one will believe you!" I wanted to make a YouTube video like before, but God said no. I asked again, and He said no. I asked five times, and He said no five times, so for a long time, I remained silent, only talking to a few people.

I studied, prayed, and gained additional understanding. Two years later, I realized that I wanted my future great-grandchildren to know what I had experienced, so I decided to create a few books using self-publishing so they could have a record. A month later, in December 2024, God asked me to publish it to the world, and I was overwhelmed. It's one thing to create for your descendants but quite another to publish to the world.

Then, in January 2025, two years and two months after the November 2022 revelation, I finally understood what that two-word revelation meant, and I said out loud, "I can't publish this! People are not going to like this! They are going to hate me and demand my excommunication!" I made an appointment with my Stake President, who listened with interest, advising me to present my findings as personal insights rather than doctrine. I heeded his counsel and finished writing this book—not to claim authority, but to bear witness to what I have discovered.

This book delves into the unfolding of prophecy, Donald Trump's role, and our world's imminent transformation. He does not replace the ecclesiastical role of the Church of Jesus Christ of Latter-Day Saints in the Kingdom of God; however, his presidency and future actions align with the fulfillment of divine prophecy.

Some may scoff at these words, dismissing them as mere speculation.

Some have called me a kook and an apostate. Some hate him so badly they won't listen to anything. To them, I say: examine your heart and seek your own revelation. God has not ceased to speak. The question is—will you listen?

Shortly after President Russell M. Nelson was named the 17th president of the church, he provided this brief statement in an interview with the newsroom during his visit to Chile in October 2018:

"We're witnesses to a process of restoration. . . If you think the Church has been fully restored, you're just seeing the beginning. There is much more to come. … Wait till next year. And then the next year. Eat your vitamin pills. Get your rest. It's going to be exciting."[1]

The world stands on the brink of change. A significant division approaches, separating the righteous from the wicked. The Book of Mormon warns us about secret combinations, corrupt leaders, and the necessity of preparing for what lies ahead. Those with spiritual insight will recognize the signs.

I do not share these things lightly. You are about to read information you have never encountered before. Some of it will be very different from what you think or have been taught. I invite you to read with an open heart and ponder the scriptures yourself. What I have written is not meant to replace scripture or divert from the guidance of our Church leaders, as I have no authority. It is simply my testimony of what I have learnd during a very difficult time. I will thank Him forever for this experience.

There are several great authors, composers, sculptors, and painters who experienced intense bursts of spiritual inspiration over a relatively short period of time. I don't consider myself as one of them, I am just showing a similar pattern.

I experienced a four-month period when God poured out a fire hose of information that brought me to tears many times. Some of the principles you read in this book led me to go to my Father in Heaven many times in deep and humble prayer, filled with gratitude and emotion, marveling at what I had learned. This is the only time I will mention this in this book.

The Lord's return is imminent, and He invites His people to gather as there are many things that have to happen before He comes in judgement over the world. Things are changing. Will you be prepared? Will you accept those changes? I hope so because I want anyone and everyone who seeks the things of God to be able to find Him in the turmoil ahead. May this book help you on that path.

Thank You,
Kelly Smith

A couple of notes about this book: I'm a graphic designer and illustrator, and you will instantly notice that this is not just a book of text. I like to illustrate some of my ideas through images.I hope this will help engage you, the reader, and keep you involved. Because of the incredible new technologies of artificial intelligence, creating images like this has become quite simple, as long as you know how to give the right prompts. Illustrations in this book that would have taken me days or weeks to produce using traditional methods, were done in minutes with this new technology. Almost all had to be modified in Photoshop to get the right message, or at least as close to what I wanted to represent.

Additionally, because there are so many references to the word "chapter" related to the various chapters in the Book of Revelation, I have chosen to label each chapter of my book as a "Section" to avoid the numerous repetitions of the word "chapter."

If you are not a member of the Church of Jesus Christ of Latter-day Saints, there may be a few terms I use in this book that may be unfamiliar to you. Let me provide a short list of some that have very specific meanings and are important to understand. All of these terms come from the Book of Mormon, the Doctrine and Covenants (D&C), and the Pearl of Great Price, which are additional scriptures that complement the Bible. The Lord also commanded Joseph Smith to go through and fix many errors that had crept into the Bible, which is now known as the **Joseph Smith Translation (JST).**

Zion: This is the New Jerusalem prophesied to come forth in the latter days. There are actually two, one in America, centered in Jackson County, Missouri, and another in Jerusalem. Almost all of our discussion focuses on the one in America. This is not a Zionist movement or anything else that is considered extreme by many. Zion is the pure heart where there are no poor among them, and everyone is One with God.

I also want to be perfectly clear here because there are many references to Zion and its connections to the members of the Church of Jesus Christ of Latter-day Saints. Some people may think that only members of the church are allowed in Zion. **This is not the case.** The only ones allowed inside are those who keep the commandments of God and the higher level of righteousness contained within its walls. No wicked people will be allowed in Zion. God's Prophets and Apostles from the Church are the leaders in Zion, and all who come must recognize their position, but they don't have to be members. There are scattered groups connected to Zion throughout the world, and they will be the only places not at war. They will be the only places of peace in the world. Many will want to come within its walls, but they will not be allowed if they are not worthy, as this is the Kingdom of God, where only the righteous will dwell.

Anti-Nephi-Lehis: This is a group of people who were so converted that they refused to defend themselves. They are the ultimate pacifists. They were once very wicked, but through the conversion of Jesus Christ, they had no desire whatsoever to injure one another and would rather suffer death than defend themselves. Many of the people mentioned in Zion will be like this.

Gadianton Robbers: The Book of Mormon warns of secret societies in the last days, as two great nations lived in the Americas long before Columbus. Both nations were destroyed because of these secret societies, so the Book of Mormon gives us an example of what to watch out for. I use this term to mean everything you've heard before about the "Deep State," the "Illuminati," and several other secret groups. They are real. They are satanic. They have great power and secret oaths, signs, and rituals. We have been warned never to let them gain such power, but as we all know, it's too late.

At the end of the book, I've left a lengthy plea for everyone to read the Book of Mormon. It doesn't matter if they are members of the church or not; the importance of this book cannot be overstated. You will see what I mean when you get there.

The Structure of the Book of Revelation

Let's establish a basic understanding of the Book of Revelation as we prepare for the rapid and dramatic forces that escalate along the way. Please don't overlook this step, as it's crucial for what lies ahead. Things will pick up very quickly afterward, but understanding this structure will help everything make sense.

I believe the Revelation that John received was given in symbols, as shown. I don't think he's just interpreting what he's seeing; he's telling us exactly what he saw. He saw beasts with eyes and wings, Dragons with horns, a seven-headed beast with a prostitute sitting on its back, and so on. The Lord gave him this vision in this form so that its message would be preserved through the centuries without change, because God knew that dishonest scribes would alter the future Bible and remove many things.

I want to start by providing you with a basic foundation of this book as we prepare for the rapid and dramatic forces that are about to affect the earth. For some, discussing the structure of a book may seem extremely boring. For others, it is quite fascinating. However, there is something very important about the organization of the book of Revelation:

The Structure of the Book of Revelation helps reveal the messages in the Book of Revelation!

I encourage you not to overlook this information, as it is crucial for what is to come. As this book progresses, it will continue to intensify, revealing many ideas through its structure, as it is how God communicates. His words are not random or accidental; they are intentional and prophetic. Trust me when I say we can delve deeply into this subject, but I will refrain from doing so. I have a specific message I want to share, and that is where my focus will remain.

The Book of Revelation follows a chiastic organization, meaning that different sections mirror each other and provide multiple layers of understanding. Chiasmus appears as a series of mirrored sections, almost like a staircase where each step reflects its opposite on the other side. It is a visually striking and intricate arrangement, with layers of meaning and symbolism revealed upon closer examination.

THE STRUCTURE OF THE BOOK OF REVELATION

Chiasmus has become a well-known term among the Church of Jesus Christ of Latter-Day Saints members. This is thanks to the profound work done by John Welch, who first discovered chiasmus in the Book of Mormon while serving as a missionary in Germany in 1967. Finding evidence of an ancient Hebrew writing style in a book published 137 years before was truly remarkable. Even more astounding is that its revelator, Joseph Smith, never mentioned it. But now, chiasmus can be found all throughout the Scriptures, and hundreds of examples can be found in the Book of Mormon alone. It is just one of many powerful principles that testify to the truthfulness of this sacred text.

Chiasmus is from the Greek letter chi (which resembles the letter X), because lines connecting the parallelisms form an X. For example, note the diagram of the parallels in Psalm 124:7:

Our soul is escaped as a bird out of the snare of the fowlers:

The snare is broken, and we are escaped.

In other words, chiasmus is inverted parallelism.[2]

On the next page is an example of Alma 36 in the Book of Mormon diagrammed in Chiastic form that John Welch discovered and is shown on the website of the Church of Jesus Christ of Latter-day Saints. Here is a quote from the Church website discussing this wonderful feature:

> "In Hebrew texts, chiasmus is a poetic structure in which words or ideas are presented and then repeated in reverse order, with the center being the focal and most crucial point. The repetition intensifies in the latter half, emphasizing the main message.
>
> "Notice that the Savior is at the center of this example of chiasmus. Elder Richard G. Scott (1928–2015) of the Quorum of the Twelve Apostles taught about the blessings of centering our lives on Jesus Christ: "Enduring happiness, with the accompanying strength, courage, and capacity to overcome the greatest difficulties, will come as you center your life in Jesus Christ."

We know that having faith in the Savior will bless us eternally. But

THE STRUCTURE OF THE BOOK OF REVELATION

sometimes we forget how having faith can bless us right now. Through its display of chiasmus, Alma 36 shows us the power of faith and how it all points to Jesus Christ." [3]

Alma 36:1-30

A. Give ear to my words (verse 1)
  B. Keep the commandments of God, and ye shall prosper in the land (verse 1)
    C. Do as I have done (verse 2)
      D. Remember the captivity of our fathers (verse 2)
        E. They were in bondage (verse 2)
          F. He surely did deliver them (verse 2)
            G. Trust in God (verse 3)
              H. Supported in their trials, and their troubles, and their afflictions (verse 3)
                I. I would not that ye think that I know of myself-but of God (verse 4)
                J. Born of God (verse 5)
                  K. I went about seeking to destroy the church of God (verses 6-9)
                    L Neither had I the use of my limbs (verse 10)
                    M. I thought that I might not be brought to the presence of my God (verses 14-15)
                      N. The pains of a damned soul (verse 16)
                        O. Harrowed up by the memory of my marry sins (verse 17)
                          P. I remembered one Jesus Christ, a Son of God (verse 17)
                          P. I cried within my heart: O Jesus, thou Son of God (verse 18)
                        O. Harrowed up by the memory of my sins no more (verse 19)
                      N. Joy as exceeding as was my pain (verse 20)
                    M. My soul did long to be there (in the presence of God) (verse 22)
                  L. My limbs received strength again (verse 23)
                K. I labored to bring souls to repentance (verse 24)
              J. Born of God (verse 26)
            I. My knowledge is of God (verse 26)
          H. Supported under trials, troubles, and afflictions (verse 27)
        G. Trust in him (verse 27)
      F. He will deliver me and raise me up (verses 27-28)
    E. He has delivered our fathers from bondage and captivity (verses 28-29)
      D. Retain a remembrance of their captivity (verse 29)
    C. Know as I do know (verse 30)
  B. Keep the commandments of God, and ye shall prosper (verse 30)
A. This according to his word (verse 30) [4]

There are multiple possible Chiasms in the Book of Revelation as noted by various authors. This is an extremely well structured book. I will show just one option for Chapter 12 of the KJV to give you an idea. You can spend a lot of time researching this subject.

Ea: The Bride reflecting the glory of her husband 12:1
  Eb: The Child of the woman 12:2
    Ec: The Dragon tries to devour the Child 12:3-12:5
    Ed: The woman flees to the wilderness 12:6
      Ee: Dragon war in heaven 12:7-12:9
        Ef: Victory of Christ & His people over the Dragon 12:10-12:11
      Ee': Dragon war on earth 12:12-12:13
    Ed': The woman flees to the wilderness 12:14
    Ec': The Dragon's mouth & the earth swallows the serpents flood 12:15-12:16
  Eb': The rest of the offspring of the woman 12:17a
Ea': The church reflecting the word of Christ 12:17b [5]

I believe chiasmus represents The Language of God (thanks to H. Clay Gorton for his excellent book on that subject of the same name [6]), for only God could know the future and the past at once. When something is arranged so precisely and revealed in such a manner, it serves as a testament to His divine hand at work. The book of Revelation also adheres to this pattern, with chapter 12 as its central point.

While I will not exhaustively analyze the entire Book of Revelation, others have already provided great insight into understanding this marvelous book. My focus here will be on certain parts of it and its main message and what I have discovered. I will give an overall outline and connect it with chiasmus showing how it all fits together.

Revelation Chapters 1-3 contain letters addressed to each of the seven churches. Many people may overlook these letters and assume they were intended only for those living during John's time. However, these letters hold great relevance for us today, and it would be wise to take the time to understand their words and apply them to our lives. Every promise contained within these letters is meant for our day, and they offer valuable instruction and warnings for us to heed and repent from. As previously mentioned, we need to gather every ounce of faith we can to survive what is coming. These letters contain significant promises and warnings that apply to all of God's saints throughout history, particularly in our day. They address nearly every major issue that God has with His saints and what they need to do to overcome it. For each one, He offers a profound blessing, employing an almost carrot-and-stick approach to encourage us to leave the world behind and seek what He is offering.

Chapter 4 is a breathtaking portrayal of God the Father seated upon his throne. Every attempt to capture this divine moment in an illustration or painting falls short, unable to fully depict the overwhelming glory and majesty of the scene. It is important to remember that much of this is highly symbolic as the creatures described did not physically possess six wings or multiple eyes. This is further clarified by the prophet Joseph Smith in D&C 77, which provides insight into the true meaning behind these symbolic descriptions. (See the chapter on The Seven Seals).

Chapter 5 shifts focus to find someone who can open the book in God's hands on the throne. There is only one individual who can accomplish this task. It's made abundantly clear that it's God's own Son, Jesus Christ. No one else possesses the capability, power, or love needed to carry out this work to its fullest extent. He deserves all the power and wisdom that can be given to him. Every single creature praises him with the glory and honor he is due.

Chapter 6 deals with the opening of the first six seals and with which much of the rest of this book deals with.

Chapter 7 of Revelation showcases the marvelous work of the 144,000 in gathering people to Zion. Remember, this occurs after all these terrible destructions and wars have taken place, but it is also during the 6,000-year period. These individuals have endured tremendous tribulations, and they are led to a place where they will never hunger, where all their tears shall be wiped away. They are in Zion, with Christ, and it is then that the Sealed Book is finally opened.

Chapter 8 is when the seventh seal is open, and God's judgments are poured out upon the wicked. These calamities devastate the world and occur after most of the righteous have been gathered. A tremendous earthquake followed by what I presume is a horrific volcano described as a mountain on fire, causing immense devastation. Then, a giant meteor hits the ocean. It is called Wormwood because it poisons the water in the oceans, rivers, and lakes. A horrific number of people die from this. Then, all of a sudden, the sun is smitten, and I believe this is a supernova or giant solar flare that has devastating effects on the Earth. I will show you why in that chapter.

Chapter 9 brings up an astonishing war occurring all over the Earth. What I say differs from anybody I've ever read. It talks about an angel from heaven with a Key to open the bottomless pit.

Chapter 10 discusses John's mission, and I suggest that it does not fit into the Chiastic structure. However, it does show his place in the future and the work he is now assigned. He may be shown as the angel from the east who brings the sealing keys of God, but I'm not sure.

Chapter 11 presents a profound winding-up scene from one perspective in the battle of Armageddon. The two witnesses protect Jerusalem from the massive encroaching army. For three and a half years, they defend the city through the power and miracles of God. Eventually, they are allowed to be killed, and the world throws a huge party. However, it's short-lived as they are called up to heaven right in front of everyone, bringing tremendous fear upon the people. I am certain that this entire event will be broadcast on TV worldwide. This is not just a local occurrence; everyone will witness it.

Immediately after their resurrection, there is a tremendous earthquake, possibly the largest earthquake ever felt on Earth. As a side note, the Book of Revelation mentions multiple earthquakes, but some of them are identical due to this chiastic structure.

Chapter 11 ends with the righteous being taken to God and the temple of God opened in heaven, with the ark of the Testament. It also mentions another great earthquake and hail.

Chapters 6-11 extends from the First Horseman to the coming of Christ, and chapters 12-16 reaffirm this. It's possible that chapter 11 contains all that is presented in the second half of the Book of Revelation, starting from the battle of Armageddon onward. It offers a brief overview that is elaborated on in great detail in chapters 19 through 22. Once more, this is my personal opinion. I could be mistaken.

THE STRUCTURE OF THE BOOK OF REVELATION

Chapter 12 is very important to read the JST (Joseph Smith Translation) version because of the rearrangement of verses. This is a symbolic vision of major events; they don't actually occur in physical form as shown. It describes a woman about to give birth. A Dragon seeks to kill the manchild as soon as it's born, but remarkably, immediately after the birth, the woman and the child are whisked away to heaven and spared from death.

The Dragon exerts considerable effort to try to kill the child, but Michael and his angels protect both the child and the woman, so the Dragon fails. Since this chapter is presented in a chiastic format, the second half mirrors the first half, only in reverse order. The pivotal verse in this context is found in verse nine of the JST or verse ten in the King James version, as follows:

> JST Rev 12:9 And I heard a loud voice saying in heaven, Now is come salvation, and strength, and the kingdom of our God, and the power of his Christ:

The woman represents the church, and the man-child symbolizes the Kingdom of God. This verse is the most crucial in the Book of Revelation, serving as the center of everything—not just this chapter but the whole book. Establishing the Kingdom of God is fundamental to everything that follows. I will elaborate on this later.

Chapter 13 describes the Dragon's operations on Earth in extensive detail. A bizarre beast rises out of the sea, representing the kingdoms of this earth. This seven-headed beast is symbolic; it is not literal. Seven means "complete" in Hebrew, and because it has seven heads, it means it has complete control over all the governments of the Earth. Every government is under his direction. None of them were established by God, and therefore, they cannot be accepted.

This beast persecutes the Saints and exerts extensive and ruthless tyranny over everyone who does not comply with his demands. More on this later.

Chapter 14 discusses the 144,000 again (a repeat of Chapter 7), the preaching of the gospel throughout the Earth, and the gathering of the House of Israel. It also shows that Babylon has fallen and describes the extremely difficult time the Saints have while trying to keep their covenants. It takes great faith and patience to endure such persecution. Numerous individuals

and angels harvest the wicked all over the world, which becomes a terrible bloodbath.

Chapter 15 begins the seven plagues again, and I want you to notice that the Angels sing praises to God about how great and marvelous His works are in 15:3-4.

Chapter 16 covers each of the seven vials poured out onto the Earth, and they are in the same sequence as those in chapters 8 and 9.

Chapter 17 describes Babylon, the Mother of Harlots and Abominations, in great detail. This is not in sequence. It is a Spotlight that shows how terrible her sins were and the reasons for her utter destruction. Again, this is a symbol—it's not an actual woman sitting on a beast that eventually gets eaten by those who once supported her. This is all symbolic.

Chapter 18 depicts an angel announcing the destruction of Babylon to the world. It is not in sequence and highlights the contrast between those who followed God and those who did not. Those who heeded the command to flee Babylon are spared, while those who ignored it were not. It once again enumerates the horrific crimes and sins committed by the whore of Babylon and her supporters.

Rather than mourning her wickedness, the merchants of the Earth grieve that they can no longer profit from this dreadful system that depends solely on items as precious as silver and as despicable as selling human souls. Their only concern is making money, yet in a single hour, everything is erased. No more music or concerts. No more sports arenas. No more emphasis on gold and silver, sex, evil, and violence. It is the complete collapse of the great and spacious building that was not built on the foundation of God but upon pride and the world's vanities.

In **Chapter 19**, Jesus himself appears wearing multiple crowns on his head and a red robe, seated on a white horse. Multitudes of angels accompany him and destroy all those who have not fled Babylon and who have not repented of their sins even after everything that has been done. All of these wicked people are killed and given to the birds for food. It is a horrific scene.

The Beast, the Kings of the Earth, and the armies gather against him who sits on the horse, but they are all taken along with the false prophet,

THE STRUCTURE OF THE BOOK OF REVELATION

who performed miracles, deceived everyone, and was cast alive into the lake of fire, burning with brimstone. Every wicked soul is slain with them. Although symbolic, it is very graphic and accurate.

Chapter 20 describes an angel descending with the key to the bottomless pit (the same one named Abaddon or Apollyon), capturing the Dragon and imprisoning him for a thousand years. This brings immense joy throughout the world. He is now prevented from carrying out his evil deeds while everyone, both small and great among the dead, stands before God and our judge, evaluated according to what is recorded about their lives. This judgment occurs shortly after Christ arrives on Earth and defeats the wicked.

Chapters 21 and 22 describe the incredible beauty, peace, and harmony the world will experience over the next thousand years. We all long for this, but we have much to go through to get there.

Have you ever experienced insights from the Scriptures or had something revealed to you that helped in your daily life or while solving a problem? Elder Robert D. Hales said, "When we want to speak to God, we pray. And when we want Him to speak to us, we search the scriptures." [7]

I want to clarify that I did not have any visions or see any angels in what you are about to read. God opened the scriptures to me like never before, but what I am saying has no bearing on you or the church because I have no authority. The creation of this book has been one of the most challenging yet rewarding things I've ever done.

Please do not take what you are about to read as personal revelation for you. I am not instructing the church to do anything or go anywhere. Just consider it my opinion on what the scriptures mean. Whenever I mention seeing something in the Scriptures, it is all in my mind. I have pondered them and felt their meanings in my heart.

Some of this will be very different from what you are used to, what you have been taught or what you have read. Some of it will be completely new. Please don't stop reading just because you haven't heard of this before.

Section 1 - The Seven Seals

The Six Seals of Revelation Chapter 6 and the Seventh in Chapter 8

1. The First Seal – The White Horse (vs 1-2)
   - Symbol: White horse, crown, bow.
   - Interpretation: Represents God's chosen servant—the First Horseman. He begins the end-time events and helps establish the Kingdom of God.
   - Key Role: Sets the world stage for the fall of Babylon, the destruction of the beast system, and the preparation for Zion.

2. The Second Seal – The Red Horse (vs 3-4)
   - Symbol: Red horse, power to take peace from the earth, a great sword.
   - Interpretation: Symbolizes World War III and widespread civil unrest.
   - Key Event: Division and destruction across nations, including within the United States; a time of bloodshed and chaos.

3. The Third Seal – The Black Horse (vs 5-6)
   - Symbol: Black horse, a pair of balances (scales).
   - Interpretation: Signifies economic collapse and famine.
   - Key Themes: Scarcity, financial ruin, inflation. This is when the corrupt global economic system begins to crumble.

4. The Fourth Seal – The Pale Horse (vs 7-8)
   - Symbol: Pale (greenish-gray) horse, Death and Hell follow.
   - Interpretation: Represents plagues, mass death, and destruction.
   - Result: One-fourth of the Earth affected by sword, hunger, death, and beasts. These four horsemen symbolize the four directions of the Earth meaning they cover the whole earth

5. The Fifth Seal – The Martyrs Under the Altar (vs 9-11)
   - Symbol: Souls of martyrs crying for justice.
   - Interpretation: Represents those who are slain for their testimony and belief in Christ and Zion.
   - Connection: These are Saints persecuted and martyred during

SECTION 1 - THE SEVEN SEALS

    the tribulations

6. The Sixth Seal – Cosmic Disturbances (vs 12-17)
   - Symbol: Earthquake, blackened sun, blood-red moon, falling stars, heavens rolled back.
   - Interpretation: Global celestial and terrestrial upheaval. Symbolic of the beginning of divine judgment.
   - Event: All humanity—rich and poor—hide and fear the face of the Lamb. Marks a dramatic divine intervention in world affairs.

7. The Seventh Seal – God's Judgments Revelation 8-11
   - Symbols: This starts with Silence in heaven for about half an hour and goes through four chapters with multiple events that are discussed at length in this book.
   - Interpretation: Global celestial and terrestrial upheaval.
   - Opening Event: Marks the final thousand-year period (7th 1000-year day) in Earth's history.
   - Theme: Full outpouring of God's judgments on the wicked. The final cleansing before Christ's return and the Millennium.

Revelation Chapter 6 depicts a vision of events that will take place in the last days: the opening of the six seals. Most of the Christian world believes that these first Four Horsemen all represent evil figures and claims that the first one is the Antichrist. Some members of our church suggest that it could either be Enoch or Adam or maybe Joseph Smith or even Jesus Christ. The reason they do this is because of the revelation contained in D&C 77:

7 Q. What are we to understand by the seven seals with which it was sealed?

A. We are to understand that the first seal contains the things of the first thousand years, and the second also of the second thousand years, and so on until the seventh.

The concept of us being in the sixth or seventh seal has sparked much discussion and speculation. Some argue that if Adam existed 4,000 years before Christ, and another 2,000 years have passed since then, we are now after the year 2000, making it a total of 6,000 years since the beginning.

SECTION 1 - THE SEVEN SEALS

They refer to Revelation 8:1, which mentions a half-hour of silence, and calculate that this would roughly equate to 21 years. Many have concluded that this silence will end around the year 2021. However, as we are now in the year 2025 and no such events have taken place, it becomes clear that this theory may have flaws.

I posted a video I made about what I had learned in the first 11 months of 2022, claiming that none of the 7 Seals had been opened yet. This is where I received the biggest push back from members who disagreed with my analysis because they misinterpret D&C Section 77, which states that each seal represents 1,000 years. They examine the history of the earth and attempt to associate each seal with a specific leader, but this is impossible. Furthermore, the events don't align without significant interpretive gymnastics.

In D&C 77:10, it says,

10 Q. What time are the things spoken of in this chapter (Chapter 7) to be accomplished?

A. They are to be accomplished in the sixth thousand years, or the opening of the sixth seal.

If we are in the 7th Seal, when did these events take place? When were the 144,000 gathered and assigned their missions? Much speculation has surmised that there was probably a secret meeting and only those who were invited knew about it. According to the Answer in D&C 77:10, they are specifically associated with the opening of the sixth seal. If we adhere to the belief that each seal represents 1,000 years, then this event would have taken place in 1,000 AD. However, upon closer examination, none of the events described in Revelation 6:12-17 have actually occurred yet, let alone over a thousand years ago. These are all prophesied events that are still to come in the near future.

Most people do not like the interpretation because it goes against what they think it means. I propose that the half hour of silence lasts only 30 minutes. It's like taking a breather before the justice of God descends in all its fury upon the world. Everything that has happened so far has been child's play compared to what's coming next. Here are verses 12-17:

SECTION 1 - THE SEVEN SEALS

Rev 6:12 And I beheld when he had opened the sixth seal, and, lo, there was a great earthquake; and the sun became black as sackcloth of hair, and the moon became as blood;

13 And the stars of heaven fell unto the earth, even as a fig tree casteth her untimely figs, when she is shaken of a mighty wind.

14 And the heaven departed as a scroll when it is rolled together; and every mountain and island were moved out of their places.

15 And the kings of the earth, and the great men, and the rich men, and the chief captains, and the mighty men, and every bondman, and every free man, hid themselves in the dens and in the rocks of the mountains;

16 And said to the mountains and rocks, Fall on us, and hide us from the face of him that sitteth on the throne, and from the wrath of the Lamb:

17 For the great day of his wrath is come; and who shall be able to stand?

If we are in the 7th Seal, when have we witnessed the sun blacken like a sackcloth and the moon turn crimson-like blood? This must be an extraordinary occurrence, unlike the regular eclipses that come with expected frequency. These events will not be fleeting moments but rather extended periods of days, weeks, or even months. They may even coincide.

And when did the stars fall from heaven? Some believe it happened during Joseph Smith's time in the fall of 1833 when they witnessed a spectacular meteor shower. But that cannot fulfill this prophecy; it was too brief. No, this must be a sign of the very last days that may last for several days or weeks.

Perhaps verses 12 and 13 have already come to pass with the eclipses and meteor shower during Joseph's day. But when did verse 14 occur? When have we seen the heavens recede like a rolled-up scroll and every mountain and island shift from their place? Has there been such a cataclysmic earthquake that caused all the mountains and islands to move? Some suggest that a great earthquake in Syria in 1260 A.D. resulted in 30,000 deaths and could be the fulfillment of this prophecy, but it was not a worldwide event. The fact is we haven't seen any of these events.

SECTION 1 - THE SEVEN SEALS

Verse 15 tells us that people of every rank, from the wealthiest to the most destitute, will seek refuge in caves and crevices as they witness the heavens being rolled up. Why? Because they see something in the sky and state that it's the face of God sitting on His throne, they are filled with terror at the wrath of the Lamb, as described in verse 16.

None of these events have occurred yet, but when they do, it will mark the beginning of God's judgments.

How can there be an unfathomable 1000-year period of unrelenting war, where endless bloodshed and destruction reign supreme? How can there be a relentless 1000-year stretch of famine, with crops withered and food scarce? And how can there be a never-ending 1000-year plague of disease and death, where no one is left unscathed? The mere thought of such devastation is inconceivable. It defies all logic and reason.

The Book of Mormon serves as irrefutable evidence that such a scenario never occurred. None of those time frames are mentioned in the record at all. Yes, war, death, disease, plagues, etc. all took place, but they are significantly shorter than the 1,000 years people believe it implies, usually around 5-7 years. Not only does it include numerous accounts of wars and famines lasting just a few years, but it also chronicles the miraculous events that have shaped the history of our world—from the great flood to the parting of the Red Sea, from the establishment of Zion to the scattering of Israel, and from the life, sacrifice, and atonement of Christ to the restoration of His gospel through Joseph Smith. These are far more significant in the grand scheme of things than any war, famine, or plague. Why are these events not included in these thousand-year segments of history? How can there be no mention of Christ's atonement? It doesn't make sense.

I understand why people want these things to fit into their perceived time frame. We don't want to endure the tribulations they describe. The idea of a fifth seal filled with martyrs ahead is unsettling. That's why I mentioned we will need every ounce of faith we can muster, because once the first seal is opened, everything else falls into place. Everything is sequential, and we know precisely where we fit in the Book of Revelation.

One day, while studying the book, I knelt beside my bed, feverishly writing in a notebook the thoughts that came to mind and the insights I observed and I realized this:

SECTION 1 - THE SEVEN SEALS

"The seven seals are events which occur before the opening of the book containing the 7000-year history of the earth."

Now that made perfect sense and I looked at everything again and asked myself, "What sealed book is there that covers the 7000-year history of the earth?" There is only one complete book that does this: The Vision of the Brother of Jared. He had received a marvelous vision of the entire history of our world and was instructed to write it down. We now know this as the sealed portion of the gold plates that were given to Joseph Smith, though he was not allowed to open or look at them. One day, in a magnificent display of power and divinity, Christ himself will reveal this precious book. It is symbolically bound by seven seals, each symbolizing a profound truth. In this case, it signifies Christ unlocking the secrets within the sealed portion of the gold plates. And what a vision it embodies—an astonishing account of our Earth's journey from its creation to its ultimate destiny. (Ether 4:4)

It will show how it was conceptualized in a "seven-day" series in the presence of God in a spiritual way during its premortal life, much like an architect drafting plans. It then went through a "seven-day" period of physical creation in a realm where time does not exist, made from eternal materials. It's futile to attempt to determine how many years this took in our time since there is no correlation. The materials may be billions of years old, but the Earth itself is not. How old is it? We don't know. But this book will tell us something about it. (See my chapter on the Seven Sevens of God).

It was formed within a Terrestrial existence, and various kinds of plant and animal life were placed upon it. The continents, atmosphere, diverse materials, river systems, the arrangement of oceans and lakes, and the systems that would eventually be established, such as glaciers, were all included. These systems will cause ice to form at the poles. The moon was given to it to help regulate ocean tides and serve as a symbol for mankind. However, all of this was created in a place where nothing could die because it was made by God, who cannot create anything that dies. Everything He creates is meant to be everlasting. He is an eternal being, and He creates eternal creations. All this was done by the power of his word and under his direction. Nothing was left to chance.

On it, our Heavenly Parents partook of the fruit from trees planted there,

SECTION 1 - THE SEVEN SEALS

transforming the dust of the Earth into physical man. Through them, Adam and Eve were born into this same Terrestrial existence with physical bodies that could not die, yet they were destined to die. They had to fall so that we could be born. They were given the agency to choose between conflicting commandments: to bear children or to live forever. They needed to make a choice. This required opposition to the glorious beauty that He had created for them. God allowed Lucifer to descend and tempt them, deceiving them about the outcomes of their choices.

Before partaking of the fruit, their eyes were not opened; they could not see the consequences of their decisions. (Gen 3:5) After partaking of the forbidden fruit, they now found themselves in a dangerous situation. (Gen 3:7) If they partook of the fruit from the tree of life, they would live forever in their sins. They could never be redeemed. That fruit granted them eternal life, but they could not dwell with God because they had fallen. Therefore, God placed cherubim with a flaming sword to prevent their partaking of that fruit. (Gen 3:22-24) God then clothed them (Moses 4:27), established a covenant with them (Moses 5:5-12) and showed them how to return to Him through repentance and faith in His only begotten Son, Jesus Christ.

God then caused the Earth and everything on it to fall into this Solar System and enter a state of Telestial existence where sin, birth, and death could occur over a "seven-day" period of 1,000 years each. We should thank them for this choice because we would not be here without it. The Fall of Adam (and Eve) were all part of the plan!

This was all planned from the start. It wasn't a mistake. God could not bring about death, because then it would be his fault. The only thing that could bring about death was sin, and in this case, this transgression introduced death—a condition whereby a redeemer was needed to restore them to his presence. God planned all of this as part of his plan of salvation. Many of these powerful principles were removed from the Bible to confuse people about what happened (1 Ne 13:26-29). If Satan could confuse people regarding who they are, where they came from and the purpose of this plan, he could have greater control over them.

The Earth and everything on it were cast down to this solar system, which, according to an interpretation of a letter to William W Phelps from Joseph Smith, has been in use for over 2.555 billion years (we have no direct revelation on that number from the prophet[8]). It was placed in a precise orbit and tilted at 23.5° to provide us with seasons. It has now remained in this orbit for at least 6,000 years, as that marks its mortal existence. More than likely, God has been using this exact solar system all this time, and when it speaks of a new heaven and a new earth, it conveys a far different meaning than most people realize. There may have been many earths that have dwelt here and there may be more in the future.

The Earth is mortal. It has a spirit within it. It is alive (Moses 7:48). Someday it will die and be resurrected. It had to be baptized, just like everything else, in order to live with God again. In the future, it will become the sea of glass and fire, a habitation for those who achieve the Celestial Kingdom of glory (D&C 77:1, 88:26-29, 130:6-8). But right now, it is in pain because of the wickedness present on its surface. For the most part, weather patterns occur due to a variety of reasons, but there are times when she helps the righteous saints and punishes the wicked. She also follows the commandments and will achieve Celestial glory, as mentioned earlier.

In the meridian of Time, the Savior of all mankind and all life, will dwell upon this world and perform majestic miracles. The greatest event in history will be the atonement of Jesus Christ, performed in Gethsemane and on the cross. He will then be resurrected and appear to his children all over the world, giving them instructions and commanding them to write them down. In the future, we will have all those writings.

The Earth suffered great pain witnessing her Creator treated with such abject disrespect (Moses 7:55-56). Light and glory shone over the entire Earth at the time of Jesus's birth (3 Ne 1:15-19). Darkness, earthquakes, and calamities occurred during his crucifixion. The best record we have of all this is found in the Book of Mormon (3 Ne 8).

In the future, all the things written in the Sealed portion of the Gold Plates, along with other scriptures, will come to pass. The Earth will be

SECTION 1 - THE SEVEN SEALS

involved in these dramatic events.

As a side note, Adam is also Michael (D&C 27:11), one of God's great angels in this premortal life. He likely assisted Christ during His incredible trial of the atonement to help strengthen Him (Luke 22:43). All of these events stemmed from his transgression, and he probably felt a responsibility to do what he could to help our Lord and Savior endure such an ordeal. He will defend and protect God's kingdom during the onslaught from the dragon and his minions to ensure that the Earth, which he caused to fall, reaches its glorious promised state (Rev 12:7, Dan 12:1). He will defend it again at the end of the Millennium.

> D&C 88:111 And then he shall be loosed for a little season, that he may gather together his armies.
>
> 112 And Michael, the seventh angel, even the archangel, shall gather together his armies, even the hosts of heaven.
>
> 113 And the devil shall gather together his armies; even the hosts of hell, and shall come up to battle against Michael and his armies.
>
> 114 And then cometh the battle of the great God; and the devil and his armies shall be cast away into their own place, that they shall not have power over the saints any more at all.
>
> 115 For Michael shall fight their battles, and shall overcome him who seeketh the throne of him who sitteth upon the throne, even the Lamb.

Now back to our analysis of the book. The Brother of Jared witnessed the fall of Adam and the rise of the city of Enoch. He observed that the Earth was baptized during the flood of Noah and endured the consequences of mankind's sin. He noted everything related to the Tower of Babel, the parting of the Red Sea, the establishment of King David, the scattering of the House of Israel across the Earth, the birth, ministry, and atonement of Jesus Christ through the Garden of Gethsemane, His time on the cross, and His glorious resurrection.

He witnessed the apostles' demise, the Nephite people's destruction, and the gospel's glorious restoration. He observed all the astonishing technological advancements of our era, including everything described in the Book of Revelation, which culminates in establishing the Kingdom of God

SECTION 1 - THE SEVEN SEALS

and the return of Jesus Christ to reign for a thousand years on Earth. He foresaw the fall once more after that thousand years, leading to the death and resurrection of this earth to its Celestial state. (2 Ne 27:7)

This book holds everything. He sees you and me. This is the most glorious book ever written, and Christ will open it and reveal it to the world.

I can't wait for this book. It will answer every single question that science has about the Earth and the Universe. But it's more than that, as it demonstrates God's hand in everything. It showcases His power, wisdom, ability, and love for each of His children, revealing the love He has for you. The Brother of Jared saw everyone who would ever live on this planet. It will display God's foreknowledge of all things and unveil the history of the world from God's perspective, rather than from a biased historian's viewpoint. We will see what really happened and why. It's impossible to overstate how profound this revelation will be!

Since we know the proper timeline, we now understand exactly when and where this will be revealed. It will be revealed through Jesus Christ from the New Jerusalem established in Independence, Missouri (D&C 57:1-5). It will be disclosed to those who have partaken of the fruit of the tree and remained faithful. It promises to be an incredibly glorious experience. Moroni's words are profound:

> Ether 4: 4 Behold, I have written upon these plates the very things which the brother of Jared saw; and there never were greater things made manifest than those which were made manifest unto the brother of Jared.
>
> 5 Wherefore the Lord hath commanded me to write them; and I have written them. And he commanded me that I should seal them up; and he also hath commanded that I should seal up the interpretation thereof; wherefore I have sealed up the interpreters, according to the commandment of the Lord.
>
> 6 For the Lord said unto me: They shall not go forth unto the Gentiles until the day that they shall repent of their iniquity, and become clean before the Lord.
>
> 7 And in that day that they shall exercise faith in me, saith the Lord, even as the brother of Jared did, that they may become sanctified in me, then will I manifest unto them the things which the brother of

Jared saw, even to the unfolding unto them all my revelations, saith Jesus Christ, the Son of God, the Father of the heavens and of the earth, and all things that in them are.

There is no greater revelation anywhere on earth, and it will not be revealed to the members of the Church of Jesus Christ of Latter-day Saints or other righteous Gentiles until the day they repent of their sins and become clean before the Lord in the New Jerusalem. When we exercise our faith and become part of Zion, Jesus Christ himself will show us all these things! (Rev 8:1) As I mentioned, I truly look forward to that day!

The answer to the question of whether we are in the sixth or seventh seal is that ***none of the seals have yet been opened***. We are awaiting the first one to commence, which likely started with Trump's election and inauguration, as he confronts the unconstitutional Beast System. However, there is more to this, and in the remainder of this book, we will explore the profound establishment of the Kingdom of God that will ultimately dismantle all the kingdoms of the world and bring them under the rule of Jesus Christ. I hope this will clarify the discussion about which seal we are currently in, but I recognize human nature, so it may be unlikely. Many individuals resist believing this because it challenges their familiar perspectives. I encourage you to consider this possibility.

What this does for us is gives us the exact time frame of where we are in the book of Revelation. Once we see that the seals are starting to open, we will know that the Kingdom of God is finally coming to Earth! We can look forward to the day when we can raise our kids in righteousness, free from sin, death, disease, or the evil that so permeates our world. We will live in the day that the prophets have seen for millennia and wished they could be a part of. We need to do everything possible to prepare for this glorious day! We need to purify ourselves through the atonement of our Savior, Jesus Christ. We can flee from Babylon and not be so entrenched in its tentacles. We don't have to accept everything thrown at us in advertising, television, or on the Internet. We can make better decisions. We can choose to follow God today. We can eliminate bad habits, clean up our lives and thoughts, and become more like our Savior.

This is a glorious time! We have been called and placed here for a reason. Although we know that terrible things are coming, we can have faith that God will be with us. We need not look forward with fear but with faith that He will guide and protect us. We can put aside every argument against the church. We can ignore those who speak derisively about our beloved prophets, those who drive wedges of doubt into our trees of faith. We can act with confidence, knowing what is going to happen and which side we are on.

President Nelson gave this profound statement on October 2022 General Conference:

"My dear brothers and sisters, so many wonderful things are ahead. In coming days, we will see the greatest manifestations of the Savior's power that the world has ever seen. Between now and the time He returns "with power and great glory," He will bestow countless privileges, blessings, and miracles upon the faithful."[9]

The seven seals are about to open, and you have been chosen to be part of it. In the pre-mortal councils, you were chosen to come at this time in world history. God knows you, your heart, and what you can do. He sent his most valiant and faithful at this time so that you can help save as many of God's children as possible. This was not a chance appointment; this was God's foreknowledge, the one who knows all things. Our challenge is to recognize who we are and what we have been tasked to do. Our adversary will do everything possible to distract, defeat, tempt, and prevent us from achieving that mission.

There are countless fake things that bombard us every day. With the latest advancements in artificial intelligence, it's nearly impossible to look at something and determine whether it's real or not. This astonishing technology wields tremendous power, both positively and negatively, but it isn't genuine. We can be easily deceived. President Nelson said in April 2018 general conference, "In coming days, it will not be possible to survive spiritually without the guiding, directing, comforting, and constant influence of the Holy Ghost."

So how do we know that something is true? Alma 32 gives us a profound answer to that question, and I go into great detail about this in a later chapter. The feelings you get from God, the burning of the bosom, are real. Many people denounce those feelings, claiming they're nothing more than indigestion. I'm here to tell you that they have not experienced them in real life. Once you've had that experience, it is unlike anything else. You know

SECTION 1 - THE SEVEN SEALS

it's from God. I have felt it many times, and is part of the great desire I have to share the gospel with everyone I meet, I want them to feel it also. When the fire of the Holy Ghost fills your soul from head to foot, you know it's from God.

That feeling is real. There is nothing more real than the power of the Holy Ghost. It comes only through prayer, effort, desire, and waiting upon the Lord. Sometimes it arrives in a crisis, and other times it manifests through extended effort; but when it comes, you will know it.

It also comes in varying degrees to people of all religions. We denounce no religion because God has had a hand in all of them. The feeling people experience when reading the Bible comes from the Holy Ghost. All of these are intended to lead someone closer to Jesus Christ. We rejoice in witnessing people turn to God, but it's discouraging to see others believe they have reached the end when there is still so much more to do.

I pray that we each turn to our Lord and Savior, Jesus Christ, and receive the personal revelation necessary to become a savior on Mount Zion.

Section 2 - Revelation 6

Rev 6:1 And I saw when the Lamb opened one of the seals, and I heard, as it were the noise of thunder, one of the four beasts saying, Come and see.

2 And I saw, and behold a white horse: and he that sat on him had a bow; and a crown was given unto him: and he went forth conquering, and to conquer.

3 And when he had opened the second seal, I heard the second beast say, Come and see.

4 And there went out another horse that was red: and power was given to him that sat thereon to take peace from the earth, and that they should kill one another: and there was given unto him a great sword.

5 And when he had opened the third seal, I heard the third beast say, Come and see. And I beheld, and lo a black horse; and he that sat on him had a pair of balances in his hand.

6 And I heard a voice in the midst of the four beasts say, A measure of wheat for a penny, and three measures of barley for a penny; and see thou hurt not the oil and the wine.

7 And when he had opened the fourth seal, I heard the voice of the fourth beast say, Come and see.

8 And I looked, and behold a pale horse: and his name that sat on him was Death, and Hell followed with him. And power was given unto them over the fourth part of the earth, to kill with sword, and with hunger, and with death, and with the beasts of the earth.

9 And when he had opened the fifth seal, I saw under the altar the souls of them that were slain for the word of God, and for the testimony which they held:

10 And they cried with a loud voice, saying, How long, O Lord, holy and true, dost thou not judge and avenge our blood on them that dwell on the earth?

11 And white robes were given unto every one of them; and it was said unto them, that they should rest yet for a little season, until their fellowservants also and their brethren, that should be killed as they were, should be fulfilled.

SECTION 2 - REVELATION CHAPTER 6

12 And I beheld when he had opened the sixth seal, and, lo, there was a great earthquake; and the sun became black as sackcloth of hair, and the moon became as blood;

13 And the stars of heaven fell unto the earth, even as a fig tree casteth her untimely figs, when she is shaken of a mighty wind.

14 And the heavens opened as a scroll is opened when it is rolled together; and every mountain, and island, was moved out of its place the heaven departed as a scroll when it is rolled together; and every mountain and island were moved out of their places.

15 And the kings of the earth, and the great men, and the rich men, and the chief captains, and the mighty men, and every bondman, and every free man, hid themselves in the dens and in the rocks of the mountains;

16 And said to the mountains and rocks, Fall on us, and hide us from the face of him that sitteth on the throne, and from the wrath of the Lamb:

17 For the great day of his wrath is come; and who shall be able to stand?

Since we've already established that none of the seven seals have been opened (I hope you trust my assertion), let's examine Revelation chapter 6, noting its chiastic connection with chapters 12-13. Jesus Christ is the one who opens the seven seals, as no one else has the ability to do so. As previously mentioned, these words clearly describe what is happening here:

"The seven seals are events that occur before the opening of the book containing the 7,000-year history of the Earth."

The first four seals essentially represent the points of a compass: North, South, East, and West. This situation reflects what occurs in world wars, which in this case is initiated because Donald Trump comes forth to establish the Political Kingdom of God and to begin dismantling Satan's kingdoms who rises in significant opposition. This corresponds to the Second Horseman, who takes peace from the Earth using a great sword, one of the weapons of that era. In our time, those swords are far more lethal than anything that could have caused such destruction in John's time.

SECTION 2 - REVELATION CHAPTER 6

With laser-guided cruise missiles, hypersonic nuclear weapons, railguns, space-based kinetic rods, EMP bombs, cyber warfare tools, stealth drones, and AI-controlled missile defense systems, the instruments of war in our time are unimaginably advanced. B-2 stealth bombers, nuclear submarines, aircraft carriers, and orbital satellite arrays capable of tracking every movement on Earth—all form part of the "great sword" John spoke of. This isn't just symbolic language; it is the grim reality of tools designed to destroy nations and, potentially, billions of lives.

When wielded by Satan's minions, these weapons cause immense famine. It's incredibly difficult to plant and harvest crops amidst such death and destruction. This is why the fourth beast—death, disease, and hunger—devastates so many of God's children.

Since we are connecting this with chapters 12 and 13, it must be recognized that those who are part of the Beast System will blame all of this on those who supported and followed Donald Trump. They will claim that it's their fault that these things have come to pass. They will twist the truth in any way, shape, or form with the ultimate goal of destroying anyone who opposes their power and status. This is the day of the martyrs. This is the worst day in the history of the Earth. This is hard to talk about. No one wants to look forward to this. I will mention this multiple times, but our only safety is in Zion, the problem is not everyone is going to be worthy of being there and under God's promised protection.

But justice must prevail. God's Kingdom is being established, and those who oppose it are not on God's side. This is the day when the sword of the Lord goes forth into the world to separate the wicked from the righteous. Those who are martyred cry out to God for vengeance for their blood. They all receive tremendous blessings and white robes that signify celestial glory. They are, in essence, a sacrifice on the altar for the word of God and because of the testimony they upheld. They are slain for the word of God just as the Anti-Nephi-Lehites were in the Book of Mormon (more on this later). Soon will come the day of total Justice and Judgement.

Because of their faithfulness and the actions of evil ones against them, the sixth seal is opened, and a tremendous earthquake occurs across the entire earth, moving mountains and islands across continents. This quake is felt in every country. The sun turns black like sackcloth, and the moon

SECTION 2 - REVELATION CHAPTER 6

becomes red like blood. Massive meteor showers rain down, and heaven opens like a scroll. From the kings of the earth to ordinary people, they hide in their dens, bunkers, and fortifications, begging the rocks and mountains to conceal them from the impending justice.

What do they see? When the heavens open in the sky, it indicates they see the face of God sitting on the throne and wish to hide from the wrath of the Lamb for what they have done. They perceive something in the heavens that fills them with fear and dread. They realize they have done wrong and that they are on the wrong side. They understand it is deserved justice and would rather be crushed by the rocks than stand in His presence. The last verse in this chapter shows that almost no one will be able to withstand this day except those in Zion.

Rev 6:17 For the great day of his wrath is come; and who shall be able to stand?

How does all this occur? Numerous theories have emerged regarding the causes of these events. We know that God uses His natural creations to bring about the miraculous events we witness. Most likely, it relates to either a giant solar flare or possibly even a nova of the sun, although that may be reserved for a seventh seal event. Something causes the sun to turn black. We also know about the dramatic changes in the locations of the North and South Poles over the past few years. Currently, the North Pole is moving about 37 miles a year toward Siberia. There's a chance of a significant polar flip that has occurred in Earth's past history. This polar flip happens every 11 years on the sun, but according to geologists, it occurs approximately every 12,000 years on Earth (I can't get into the age of the Earth debate here. I need to stick to the subject). Additionally, the strength of Earth's magnetic field is greatly weakening and allowing the current dramatic changes in our weather as more cosmic rays penetrate the atmosphere. The stars falling from the sky are a precursor of what is to come during the seventh seal, and almost certainly, many of them impact the Earth and cause great destruction.

But this is not the end. This is not the final destruction. Most likely, it is the destruction of the world economies, which is highlighted in chapters 17-18. John is shown the wickedness of the mother of harlots and the great and abominable church. He is shown how the Gadianton Robbers bring the destruction of God upon the Earth because of their wickedness.

SECTION 2 - REVELATION CHAPTER 6

Rev 17:1 And there came one of the seven angels which had the seven vials, and talked with me, saying unto me, Come hither; I will shew unto thee the judgment of the great whore that sitteth upon many waters:

2 With whom the kings of the earth have committed fornication, and the inhabitants of the earth have been made drunk with the wine of her fornication.

3 So he carried me away in the spirit into the wilderness: and I saw a woman sit upon a scarlet coloured beast, full of names of blasphemy, having seven heads and ten horns.

4 And the woman was arrayed in purple and scarlet colour, and decked with gold and precious stones and pearls, having a golden cup in her hand full of abominations and filthiness of her fornication:

5 And upon her forehead was a name written, Mystery, Babylon the Great, the Mother of Harlots and Abominations of the Earth.

6 And I saw the woman drunken with the blood of the saints, and with the blood of the martyrs of Jesus: and when I saw her, I wondered with great admiration.

(Notice it says that they are drunken with!)

This is a perfect description of everything the world promotes and seeks today. Things that are precious in their eyes are obtained through secret combinations. (Notice the footnote to 5a: Secret Combinations!). This encapsulates what Mystery Babylon is all about. This is the great and abominable church. This is what people will sell their souls for—to acquire gold, precious stones, fancy cars, elaborate homes, private planes, yachts, and anything that makes them look better than their neighbors.

Don't get me wrong; there's nothing inherently wrong with any of that. What's problematic is the heart and how it views those things and what people do to obtain them. In this case, it's clearly shown that they are intoxicated with the blood of saints and martyrs. They don't want anyone speaking out against their heart's desires and they will also do anything to obtain them. They want the prosperity gospel. The money donated by faithful, loving people to wealthy pastors is used to purchase private jets and multi-million-dollar homes, only to claim that they are blessed by Jesus for teaching His gospel. These same preachers speak out against the true

SECTION 2 - REVELATION CHAPTER 6

and living God and the prophets and apostles of the Church of Jesus Christ of Latter-day Saints.

The woman is symbolized as a great city that reigns over the kings of the Earth. Our world is filled with "great cities" that do not seek the things of God. They build high towers as a symbol of Babylon, aiming to rise above the world and become gods themselves. However, God's justice will be poured out upon them, and in chapter 18, He reveals the destruction they will endure.

> Rev 18:5 For her sins have reached unto heaven, and God hath remembered her iniquities.
>
> 6 Reward her even as she rewarded you, and double unto her double according to her works: in the cup which she hath filled fill to her double.
>
> 7 How much she hath glorified herself, and lived deliciously, so much torment and sorrow give her: for she saith in her heart, I sit a queen, and am no widow, and shall see no sorrow.
>
> 8 Therefore shall her plagues come in one day, death, and mourning, and famine; and she shall be utterly burned with fire: for strong is the Lord God who judgeth her.

Everything they have ever done against those who followed God will be returned to them double. They invested in evil, and they shall receive a double punishment in return for their evil. While they once lived in glory and indulgence, now they will suffer from plagues, death, famine, and will be burned by fire. Most likely, this refers to nuclear war as pillars of smoke rise into the sky. It can also mean the sun going nova or solar flares.

What is the reaction of those who have participated in this mighty combination? This destruction is just like Sodom and Gomorrah. Do they lament it? Do they recognize the filthiness, sins, and evil ways of such a city? No.

> Rev 18: 9 And the kings of the earth, who have committed fornication and lived deliciously with her, shall bewail her, and lament for her, when they shall see the smoke of her burning,
>
> 10 Standing afar off for the fear of her torment, saying, Alas, alas, that great city Babylon, that mighty city! for in one hour is thy judgment come.

SECTION 2 - REVELATION CHAPTER 6

11 And the merchants of the earth shall weep and mourn over her; for no man buyeth their merchandise any more:

12 The merchandise of gold, and silver, and precious stones, and of pearls, and fine linen, and purple, and silk, and scarlet, and all thyine wood, and all manner vessels of ivory, and all manner vessels of most precious wood, and of brass, and iron, and marble,

13 And cinnamon, and odours, and ointments, and frankincense, and wine, and oil, and fine flour, and wheat, and beasts, and sheep, and horses, and chariots, and slaves, and souls of men.

14 And the fruits that thy soul lusted after are departed from thee, and all things which were dainty and goodly are departed from thee, and thou shalt find them no more at all.

15 The merchants of these things, which were made rich by her, shall stand afar off for the fear of her torment, weeping and wailing,

16 And saying, Alas, alas, that great city, that was clothed in fine linen, and purple, and scarlet, and decked with gold, and precious stones, and pearls!

17 For in one hour so great riches is come to nought. And every ship-master, and all the company in ships, and sailors, and as many as trade by sea, stood afar off,

18 And cried when they saw the smoke of her burning, saying, What city is like unto this great city!

19 And they cast dust on their heads, and cried, weeping and wailing, saying, Alas, alas, that great city, wherein were made rich all that had ships in the sea by reason of her costliness! for in one hour is she made desolate.

Sudden destruction now descends upon the city, obliterating everything in just one hour. This is the great and spacious building that Lehi and Nephi envisioned. This is where everyone lived in extravagant luxury but lacked a foundation. This highlights the reality of what we are witnessing and its implications for our time. Something constructed on such wealth, without a foundation, signifies it's built on debt and pride. Credit cards, loans, and interest rates all contribute to this false sense of luxury and indulgence. It's all an illusion.

SECTION 2 - REVELATION CHAPTER 6

All the gold, silver, aromas, ointments, beasts, horses, war machines, child sexual trafficking, and every form of slavery, as well as the souls of men, women, and children, are part of what this was built upon. They only cared about the fine and desirable things that could arise from it. It didn't matter what they did to anyone, including children, as long as they could get what they desired. All they wanted was money. They wanted to appear better than their neighbors. They sought to possess more than their neighbors. The ultra-exotic cars became symbols of their power and wealth.

The award ceremonies, the talk shows, the praise of the world were everything to them. And now it's all gone. In just one hour. And what do they have now? Nothing. They have spent their lives seeking worldly things rather than the things of God. All they can think about is what they have supposedly lost, not realizing the eternal cost of their choices. They have no place in the Kingdom of God that remains on Earth now that this great city has been destroyed. They have no relationship with God because He does not know them. They have not listened to the Spirit of God throughout their lives, which has tried to guide them in another direction, closer to Him.

One day, we will realize just how much God has done for each of us in His effort to bring us back to Him, and we will be astonished. He never gave up on us, but ultimately, He had to impose the justice of being trampled upon.

God tells His people to rejoice, for He has avenged them against her. He has repaid those who rejected the prophets and apostles and persecuted the Saints. He has sentenced them to eternal damnation, where they will never receive the gifts that were offered to them. They chose the things of the world over divine blessings. God tells His people to rejoice and be glad.

> Rev 18:20 Rejoice over her, thou heaven, and ye holy apostles and prophets; for God hath avenged you on her.

But this mighty city that was once the envy of the world that is now destroyed and laying in ruins because of its intense wickedness is now taken by...

> 18:21 ...a mighty angel took up a stone like a great millstone, and cast it into the sea, saying, Thus with violence shall that great city Babylon be thrown down, and shall be found no more at all.

SECTION 2 - REVELATION CHAPTER 6

22 And the voice of harpers, and musicians, and of pipers, and trumpeters, shall be heard no more at all in thee; and no craftsman, of whatsoever craft he be, shall be found any more in thee; and the sound of a millstone shall be heard no more at all in thee;

23 And the light of a candle shall shine no more at all in thee; and the voice of the bridegroom and of the bride shall be heard no more at all in thee: for thy merchants were the great men of the earth; for by thy sorceries were all nations deceived.

24 And in her was found the blood of prophets, and of saints, and of all that were slain upon the earth.

Why a Millstone? What is its significance? Who else taught that if someone offended one of his little ones, one of his children, a great millstone should be fastened around their neck and thrown into the sea? Jesus himself taught these things. Yet, the people in the great city ignored these teachings and became involved in pedophilia and child sex trafficking. God warned what would happen to those who offend one of his little ones.

Donald Trump will reveal the list of individuals involved in these despicable crimes. True justice will finally take hold of those who have so shamelessly exploited children—God's precious little souls who have been abused, trafficked, and killed for money and pleasure. While Satan is not permitted to tempt little children, he has certainly tempted adults to commit abuse against them.

Those involved in the various islands, parties, events, companies, and agencies will all face a fate they undeniably deserve as the records of their doings is unveiled. They will wish for mountains to collapse upon them, hiding them from the presence of God and the wrath of the Lamb. They would prefer to be buried under a trillion tons of rock rather than stand in guilt and shame before their Creator! They would rather evade the very people of the world who once awarded them great acclaim and even worship. Now, they will endure the most profound guilt imaginable, and the atonement of Jesus Christ will have no effect on them; they will be forced to confront their own sins and bear the punishments of God for as long as He sees fit.

As Isaiah warns:

2:18 And the idols he shall utterly abolish.

SECTION 2 - REVELATION CHAPTER 6

19 And they shall go into the holes of the rocks, and into the caves of the earth, for fear of the Lord, and for the glory of his majesty, when he ariseth to shake terribly the earth.

20 In that day a man shall cast his idols of silver, and his idols of gold, which they made each one for himself to worship, to the moles and to the bats;

21 To go into the clefts of the rocks, and into the tops of the ragged rocks, for fear of the Lord, and for the glory of his majesty, when he ariseth to shake terribly the earth.

Those awards and idols and medals of honor that they once craved and lived for, will be thrown into the very rocks and caves that they want to hide under and attempt to escape the wrath of God. But they can never escape it.

Since the election of Donald Trump, he has emerged "conquering and to conquer" (Rev 6:1-2). He is the First Horseman entrusted with a monumental mission to bring all nations under his rule and deliver them to Christ upon his return. Everything these wealthy, elite, powerful politicians, business tycoons and world leaders have done will be uncovered. True justice will finally be achieved. They cannot hide. Those who once controlled the media and believed they could evade accountability for their vile crimes in pursuit of power, control, wealth, and glory will face condemnation as that same media broadcasts their sins and crimes from the rooftops. This phrase stems from ancient Israel, where it was used to convey messages of warning or joy. People would stand on rooftops and announce to everyone nearby.

Now, we can read it in the palm of our hands anywhere in the world. It's the same concept. Everything will be exposed. Everything will be proven. That's why they've been fighting him so hard all these years. He told them what he would do, and the last thing they want is for the world to know just how evil and wicked they truly are. That's why there are four horsemen who bring about World War III. Trump's actions of going forth, conquering and to conquer, initiate that process. His crowning achievement will be the reestablishment of the Political Kingdom of God that will never be overthrown.

Section 3 - REVELATION 12

Revelation Chapters 6 and 12-13 are the same events. However, they show things from a different perspective, which concerns the book's chiastic structure. So now, let's examine chapters 12 and 13 and see what additional details we can glean from comparing what we have read in chapter 6.

The center verse of chapter 12 is 12:10 in the King James Version and 12:9 in the JST. It is actually the central verse of the entire book of Revelation. This climactic point is what everything leads to and emerges from. It's the most significant event upon which everything hinges. Here is the complete JST version of that chapter for reference. It's essential to use this version due to the changes in the order of the verses that alter the meaning and some specific wording that clarifies.

> Rev 12:1 And there appeared a great sign in heaven, in the likeness of things on the earth; a woman clothed with the sun, and the moon under her feet, and upon her head a crown of twelve stars.
>
> 2 And the woman being with child, cried, travailing in birth, and pained to be delivered.
>
> 3 And she brought forth a man child, who was to rule all nations with a rod of iron; and her child was caught up unto God and his throne.
>
> 4 And there appeared another sign in heaven; and behold, a great red dragon, having seven heads and ten horns, and seven crowns upon his heads. And his tail drew the third part of the stars of heaven, and did cast them to the earth. And the dragon stood before the woman which was delivered, ready to devour her child after it was born.
>
> 5 And the woman fled into the wilderness, where she had a place prepared of God, that they should feed her there a thousand two hundred and threescore years.
>
> 6 And there was war in heaven; Michael and his angels fought against the dragon; and the dragon and his angels fought against Michael;
>
> 7 And the dragon prevailed not against Michael, neither the child, nor the woman which was the church of God, who had been delivered of her pains, and brought forth the kingdom of our God and his Christ.
>
> 8 Neither was there place found in heaven for the great dragon, who

SECTION 3 - REVELATION CHAPTER 12

was cast out; that old serpent called the devil, and also called Satan, which deceiveth the whole world; he was cast out into the earth; and his angels were cast out with him.

9 And I heard a loud voice saying in heaven, Now is come salvation, and strength, and the kingdom of our God, and the power of his Christ;

10 For the accuser of our brethren is cast down, which accused them before our God day and night.

11 For they have overcome him by the blood of the Lamb, and by the word of their testimony; for they loved not their own lives, but kept the testimony even unto death. Therefore, rejoice O heavens, and ye that dwell in them.

12 And after these things I heard another voice saying, Woe to the inhabiters of the earth, yea, and they who dwell upon the islands of the sea! for the devil is come down unto you, having great wrath, because he knoweth that he hath but a short time.

13 For when the dragon saw that he was cast unto the earth, he persecuted the woman which brought forth the man-child.

14 Therefore, to the woman were given two wings of a great eagle, that she might flee into the wilderness, into her place, where she is nourished for a time, and times, and half a time, from the face of the serpent.

15 And the serpent casteth out of his mouth water as a flood after the woman, that he might cause her to be carried away of the flood.

16 And the earth helpeth the woman, and the earth openeth her mouth, and swalloweth up the flood which the dragon casteth out of his mouth.

17 Therefore, the dragon was wroth with the woman, and went to make war with the remnant of her seed, which keep the commandments of God, and have the testimony of Jesus Christ.

Since this text is organized chiastically, it's important to read from the center and in both directions. Events aren't repeated; instead, they are presented from different perspectives to reveal insights that may be hidden from those who don't grasp the structure.

SECTION 3 - REVELATION CHAPTER 12

Numerous videos, books, podcasts, and talks have been made about this chapter because even casual reading reveals that something significant is being shown here. Remember, these are all symbols and aren't actual people. It also isn't a celestial organization of the stars that can only be understood by the most complicated of modern computer technology showing Jupiter in retrograde in the constellation of Virgo. A lot of energy was expended on the study of that event. Thousands of Facebook posts and YouTube videos[10] were created to show how this is the fulfillment of these verses. I don't want to get too critical here, because people could do the same thing against me, but that sign in the heavens that John saw was not that event. It is a symbol of events that will happen in the last days.

The Woman is the Church of Jesus Christ of Latter-day Saints, and the manchild is the Kingdom of God. We must thank Joseph Smith for this insight because it is not clear in the King James version. The Dragon (and according to Joseph Smith, it should be the Devil) is there, ready to eat the child as soon as it's born, but it is not a person; the Dragon is those who are working under Satan's influence and are running his kingdom on earth. But I will still refer to the Dragon as an individual. He wants to kill God's Kingdom before it has any chance to grow. He wants no opposition whatsoever.

The man-child born through her is the Kingdom of God, which is divided into four sections: ecclesiastical, political, economic, and social. However, we currently possess only the ecclesiastical portion of His Kingdom on earth. Joseph Smith had the keys of all four areas and attempted to establish all the other sections but failed because the people were unwilling to follow God's commands. I have a chapter dedicated to understanding these four aspects.

SECTION 3 - REVELATION CHAPTER 12

The Woman undergoes great pains of deliverance, much like a woman giving birth. Once the child is born, they are both whisked off to heaven, and I suggest that heaven is heaven on earth: Zion. It is not in the sky. This marks the establishment of the New Jerusalem and modern-day Zion. This is the event that prophets have envisioned for millennia. They have longed for this day and have prophesied wondrous things about it. They have yearned to experience it and wished they could raise their families in such a state and environment. This remarkable event transforms the world and initiates the final downfall of Satan's kingdom.

Since all these symbols represent earthly things, the Dragon must symbolize those running Satan's kingdom in this country and the world. It likely refers to the current government that is unlawfully and unconstitutionally exercising its authority in a tyrannical manner. It includes those who are affiliated with the Gadianton Robbers, wielding power and control but failing to enact true justice. They are all part of a system that only benefits themselves and does not bring each other to justice. They profit from insider trading and engage in highly illegal activities, such as trafficking, drugs, weapons, and the military-industrial complex.

God's Kingdom on earth will threaten their power and income. It will systematically deliver true justice for the crimes they have committed. Those who lived under the false notion that they would never face justice due to their control of the media will find themselves languishing in both telestial and spiritual prisons. No wonder they want to fight against it! No wonder they oppose Trump! They cannot control him as they have every other president over the past 120 years.

The First Horseman rides out, conquering and to conquer (Rev 6:1-2). He cuts down everything in his path that won't lead to the establishment of God's Kingdom. He organizes the construction of the New Jerusalem in Independence, Missouri, a location designated as the "center place" of Zion (see D&C 57:1-3) The Saints during the early days of the church attempted to establish Zion, but the Dragon also fought against them. It's hard for most of us today to comprehend the challenges that our early pioneers faced. Most of us have not experienced the kind of opposition they endured. We haven't had our homes looted, people beaten or killed, or been driven out of town in the dead of winter with nothing but pajamas and in the snow with no shoes to escape the persecution!

SECTION 3 - REVELATION CHAPTER 12

It's been said that the main mistake of the early Saints was not focusing enough on building the temple. Maybe they simply didn't have it in their hearts. While I can't fully support that claim, it carries some validity when considering the reactions of those who sought freedom from their enemies. God wanted to create a Zion's Camp with 500 men to show up and rescue them, but they barely exceeded 200. The early church members likely did not fully grasp the significance of establishing Zion. God wanted them to accomplish it and even commanded them; however, they fell short.

What might have happened if they had continued to work on the temple amidst all the trials they faced? I don't know. It's easy for us to suggest that if they had been more converted and engaged in establishing Zion, it could have been founded 180 years ago. But God knows all things. The church has experienced numerous events since that time. It is emerging from the wilderness and has millions of deeply converted members, along with the financial resources to achieve this ambitious goal. My hope is that when the time comes, hopefully soon, we will be ready to build it as it was intended.

Will there still be opposition? Oh yes! There will be more opposition against it in the near future than there was in the past. It's even been said that the entire world will fight against Zion (2 Ne 27:3). This will take time to build, but build it we must. The House of Israel is going to assist us and the establishment of a safe zone like the one created in the Book of Mormon under Lachoneus and Gidgiddoni may be a type and shadow of the future. They were allowed to gather as the opposition hoped it would be a way for them to focus all of their efforts and wipe them out quickly. For the Gadianton Robbers, they hoped it would be a way to save money and energy. "Go ahead, let them gather! We will then go in and wipe them out!"

But because the people of Lachoneus' Zion kept the Commandments, built the fortifications, and gathered enough food and supplies to last seven years (3 Ne 4:4), they beat the Gadianton Robbers that thought it would be an easy victory. Those robbers swooped in with red paint on their heads. They marked themselves so there would be no mistake. They dressed in wild clothing to try and frighten the early Zion people. But those people turned to God and dealt decisive victories until all the Robbers were wiped out. (3 Ne 4)

This may be a type and shadow of our day:

SECTION 3 - REVELATION CHAPTER 12

> 3 Ne 21:29 And they shall go out from all nations; and they shall not go out in haste, nor go by flight, for I will go before them, saith the Father, and I will be their rearward.

Whether the Dragon pursues the woman and the child before, during, or after the creation of Zion, he will go after them, but he will not prevail against either of them or against Michael and his angels, who are there to help protect them.

> Rev 12:6 And the woman fled into the wilderness, where she hath a place prepared of God, that they should feed her there a thousand two hundred and threescore years.

> 7 And there was war in heaven: Michael and his angels fought against the dragon; and the dragon fought and his angels,

> 8 And prevailed not; neither was their place found any more in heaven.

Many people have used this verse to discuss our premortal war in heaven, an event in which everyone was given a choice to select between the Father's plan of salvation, in which Jesus Christ as the Son of God serves as the sacrifice needed to save all mankind, and Lucifer's plan, which removes our agency and compels everyone to act according to his control. I propose there is another option here that relates to the future and is a repeat of the same event, but now here on earth. Satan opposes the establishment of the kingdom of God, facing opposition for the first time since the fall of Adam. This evolves into a literal war as the nations of the Earth try to annihilate the birth and growth of Zion. Michael arrives with his angels to assist the Saints in overcoming this tremendous opposition. Since the Dragon does not prevail, he then targets all other righteous people and members of the church, dispersed throughout the world. This leads to the significant persecution prophesied in chapter 13 and the martyrs of the 5th Seal.

But the persecution starts right here in chapter 12. It was also seen by Daniel in Daniel chapter 7:

> Dan 7:21 I beheld, and the same horn made war with the saints, and prevailed against them; (for a time)

> 22 Until the Ancient of days came, and judgment was given to the saints of the most High; and the time came that the saints possessed

SECTION 3 - REVELATION CHAPTER 12

the kingdom.

23 Thus he said, The fourth beast shall be the fourth kingdom upon earth, which shall be diverse from all kingdoms, and shall devour the whole earth, and shall tread it down, and break it in pieces.

How do we reconcile the apparent contradiction between Daniel's view of how the Stout horn waged war against the Saints and prevailed, and what we read in Revelation 12, which states that he did not prevail against them? Michael is the key figure here. Michael is Adam, the man whose fall brought all of this into existence. He was present as the angel supporting Christ during his infinite atonement and He will be there in Zion to help us endure and overcome the assault from the Dragon and the Beast System. Michael and his Angels, the fellow resurrected sons of God, will be essential in the fight against a being who will try anything to prevent the establishment of God's kingdom.

Trump's calling, ordination, and anointing (something that will soon happen) along with his leadership and influence make it all possible. His instigation of the Kingdom of God initiates the division of the world into two parts. As the verses above indicate, the Saints will be at war with the Beast System led by someone described as a "stout horn." Jackson County, Missouri, is the site of the city of Zion. This is the location near the Garden of Eden, and Adam, the Archangel Michael, will return there with his angels to help protect the Saints from the great opposition thrust upon them.

Just as a child is born and water pours forth during the birthing process, the Dragon also issues a flood of water against the Saints to try to overcome them and stop them (Rev 12:15). We know from Revelation 17:15 that "The waters which thou sawest, where the whore sitteth, are peoples, and multitudes, and nations, and tongues."

The flood that Satan uses against the Saints is most likely a massive influx of people from all over the world, reminiscent of the prophecy of the Assyrian flooding the nation because of their refusal to accept the Gospel of Jesus Christ (smooth waters of Shiloah), as shown in Isaiah 8:6-8. It isn't merely propaganda, persecution, or opposition; it's actual people coming in by the millions, possibly over a billion! Some of them aim to destroy Zion, while others wish to join it. However, the earth itself comes

SECTION 3 - REVELATION CHAPTER 12

to the aid of the woman, swallowing up the flood of people. While it could be some kind of great earthquake, as shown in Rev 6:12, we need to look at a time when this has happened before, which will provide further clues as to what is going on here.

In Number 16, certain leaders of the people spoke against Moses, accusing him of taking things upon himself, not delivering them to the promised land, and leaving them out of holding the Priesthood. The Lord was angry! The reason they didn't achieve those things was their own wickedness! They had rejected everything He tried to give them, and in frustration, He caused the earth to open and swallow them up! (Num 16:31-35) They accused the brethren, the leadership of the Church, and were cast down! They followed the same pattern as in the premortal councils by listening to Lucifer and accusing God of the situation they found themselves in due to their own choices!

Those who accuse Trump of taking on too many things, changing the status quo, seeking glory for himself, and failing to fulfill his promises not out of lack of effort but due to opposition will be cast down. He will help establish Zion, and they will be barred from entry because they refused to accept the Gospel of Jesus Christ and repent; they will be swallowed up. He will deliver the political kingdom of God, and they will be thrown into the bottomless pit of Civil War, as shown in Section 6.

Trump won his election partly due to his stance on the southern border of our country to prevent tens of millions of illegal immigrants from pouring in. Once the Kingdom of God is established, however, once Zion is established it seems that America outside of Zion will decline, as that's the only way I can see these scriptures aligning. Outside of Zion, there are tremendous wars occurring across the land. It's happening all over the world, and people come here knowing it's the promised land. Even though it's in conflict, it's better than where they live, and it's the only place with a known city of peace!

We know Zion will eventually encompass all of North, Central, and South America.[11] However, for now, it seems that Zion will exist only as a part of that, located in Independence, Missouri. Meanwhile, the manchild—the fullness of God's Kingdom—grows in strength beyond the grasp of earthly powers. The woman, representing the Church, seeks refuge in the

SECTION 3 - REVELATION CHAPTER 12

wilderness of Zion, meaning away from Babylon. Here, nourished by revelation and shielded from the serpent's influence, she prepares for the final confrontation. As prophesied, the saints initially struggle for 3 ½ years, but they prevail and fulfill their tremendous mission for which they were sent to Earth. With Michael the Archangel, who is Adam, and all their forces, they descend to protect the righteous from further destruction.

Rev 12:5 of the JST states that the woman fled into the wilderness for 1,260 years. This has caused significant confusion among many people because it doesn't align with the 1,260 days or 3 ½ years timeline mentioned elsewhere in the book and in other prophetic texts, which many consider to represent "time, times, and half a time." This was not a casual alteration by Joseph Smith; rather, it reveals something intriguing and supports our argument that this signifies the beginning of the millennium here on Earth. Although the entire Earth has not yet been translated into a Terrestrial state, it starts for the righteous people on Earth—those worthy of living that existence. For 1,000 years, we will live in great harmony, and we are informed elsewhere that there is a short season mentioned in,

> Revelation 20:2 And he laid hold on the dragon, that old serpent, which is the Devil, and Satan, and bound him a thousand years,
>
> 3 And cast him into the bottomless pit, and shut him up, and set a seal upon him, that he should deceive the nations no more, till the thousand years should be fulfilled: and after that he must be loosed a little season.

This is when Satan is released from the bottomless pit to carry out his final destructive acts. If my interpretation is correct, that short season will last about 260 years after the 1000-year millennium. I could be mistaken, but that is the only logical sequence I can find for placing the 1260 years. Since this is a First Seal event and I've demonstrated that none of the seals have been opened before this, there isn't another time frame that fits. I presume I'll receive a lot of opposition to this, but I can't make any other numbers work.

Since this is chiastically organized, the Scriptures compare the 1260 YEARS in verse five with the 1260 DAYS as shown in verse 14. It appears we can surmise that the persecution against Zion will last for 3 1/2 years. The permanent placement of Zion will endure for 1000 years, followed by a short season of 260 years during which Satan is loose again before the final

SECTION 3 - REVELATION CHAPTER 12

death and resurrection of the Earth into its Celestial state.

It is assumed that the Second Horseman (Rev 6:3-4) is the Antichrist, the Stout Horn, and the Dragon, because we can learn several new things by comparing chapters 6 with chapters 12-13. Most likely, all four horsemen appear very close together in time. Throughout history, war, death, disease, and famine are all interconnected. Sadly, the fifth seal of the martyrs will coincide with this as well.

So far, we have primarily focused our efforts on Revelation chapter 12, but we need to ask if there are other places in the scriptures that discuss the same event. The answer is yes. Many passages provide more information about God's chosen servant in the last days before the coming of Jesus Christ. I will attempt to outline them by titles, though there are many overlaps between them.

As the Kingdom of God emerges, the lines between good and evil become increasingly stark. Enraged at his inability to destroy the woman and her child, the Dragon turns his fury upon the remnant of her seed—those who keep God's commandments and hold fast to their testimony of Jesus Christ. The world is rapidly polarizing. Those who align themselves with the Kingdom face mounting persecution from corrupt systems of power. Yet their faith in God's protection strengthens them.

Trump's role as the First Horseman becomes clearer as he works to dismantle the corrupt entity posing as the United States government. His actions, driven by a divine purpose, shake the very foundations of the Beast System that has dominated for so long.

Since Trump's election and inauguration in January 2025, he has begun to make his move. He has taken a firm stand against anything that the deep state, the United States Secret Combination, the Beast System, the Gadianton Robbers, the Church of the Devil, the Great and Abominable Church, and any other name you can think of, have imposed on the world. He has issued hundreds of executive orders that reverse previous ones and establish new directives with a tremendous impact on the future of America. The goal of all these systems has been to bring down America because they cannot impose their globalist Satanic agenda if there is a strong America. The abhorrent methods employed by these wealthy, power-hungry individuals to undermine America are nothing short of abominable.

SECTION 3 - REVELATION CHAPTER 12

Every means possible has been employed to bring it down, including the worst: establishing the Groves, which promote sexual immorality and idolatry, causing people to lose the spirit of God, just as the House of Israel did when Balaam instructed Balac on how to bring them down.

> Rev 2:14 But I have a few things against thee, because thou hast there them that hold the doctrine of Balaam, who taught Balac to cast a stumblingblock before the children of Israel, to eat things sacrificed unto idols, and to commit fornication.
>
> 15 So hast thou also them that hold the doctrine of the Nicolaitans (secret combinations), which thing I hate.

Flagrant immorality and even Satanism are promoted at every opportunity. Super Bowl halftime shows, concerts, the promotion of drag queen exhibits in libraries in front of children, and the countless R-rated movies—they're all centered on sex, evil, violence or horror. Porn sites are abundant on the Internet, with easy access to them, along with constant references to activities reminiscent of Sodom and Gomorrah that oppose God's plan. It's the same tactic.

We now understand our place in the Book of Revelation, as he is making his move right now. The first seal has been opened (or will be very shortly with a Moses-like event). We have only begun to see the effects of his leadership and changes in the world. And make no mistake: This will impact the entire world. This isn't just a normal or even an unusual election. It might even be the last election, as it represents a complete and utter transformation of America, bringing it back to what it was originally envisioned to be: the Kingdom of God ruled by the word of God, with laws inspired by the constitution, for a people willing to live by God's commandments. This kingdom will spread across the earth, and anyone who stands in its way will lose. People can either accept the direction of God's chosen servant and grow closer to Him through his leadership or choose the Beast System and take his Mark upon themselves.

The Second Horseman—the Antichrist—rises in opposition, wielding the full power of Satan's earthly kingdom. War erupts on a global scale, and we are thrust into Chapter 13. (And look for one more secret of Chapter 12 to be revealed later!)

Section 4 - REVELATION 13

Chapters 12 and 13 revisit the events of Chapter 6, providing greater detail and a different perspective. Few sections of scripture have been analyzed and speculated upon as much as Revelation Chapter 13. Its bizarre images and strange symbols have sparked curiosity for thousands of years. From Nostradamus to Newton to Edgar Cayce, many individuals have found it intriguing or too strange to delve into. Determining the number of books, films, and videos inspired by this material is impossible. The vivid imagery is unforgettable and, to most observers, remarkably odd. Multi-headed beasts, Dragons, and fire descending from heaven are peculiar in any culture, yet they resonate with our present time.

But understanding this concept is simpler than we might think. Everything becomes clear once you absorb the insights revealed in chapter 12. Now, I present to you the complete 13th chapter, seamlessly incorporating Joseph Smith's translations. These words carry significant meaning. Take a moment to read through the following, and my personal commentary will follow afterward.

> Rev 13:1 And I stood upon the sand of the sea, and saw a beast rise up out of the sea, having seven heads and ten horns, and upon his horns ten crowns, and upon his heads the name of blasphemy.
>
> 2 And the beast which I saw was like unto a leopard, and his feet were as the feet of a bear, and his mouth as the mouth of a lion: and the dragon gave him his power, and his seat, and great authority.
>
> 3 And I saw one of his heads as it were wounded to death; and his deadly wound was healed: and all the world wondered after the beast.
>
> 4 And they worshipped the dragon which gave power unto the beast: and they worshipped the beast, saying, Who is like unto the beast? who is able to make war with him?
>
> 5 And there was given unto him a mouth speaking great things and blasphemies; and power was given unto him to continue forty and two months.
>
> 6 And he opened his mouth in blasphemy against God, to blaspheme his name, and his tabernacle, and them that dwell in heaven.

SECTION 4 - REVELATION CHAPTER 13

7 And it was given unto him to make war with the saints, and to overcome them: and power was given him over all kindreds, and tongues, and nations.

8 And all that dwell upon the earth shall worship him, whose names are not written in the book of life of the Lamb slain from the foundation of the world.

9 If any man have an ear, let him hear.

10 He that leadeth into captivity shall go into captivity: he that killeth with the sword must be killed with the sword. Here is the patience and the faith of the saints.

11 And I beheld another beast coming up out of the earth; and he had two horns like a lamb, and he spake as a dragon.

12 And he exerciseth all the power of the first beast before him, and causeth the earth and them which dwell therein to worship the first beast, whose deadly wound was healed.

13 And he doeth great wonders, so that he maketh fire come down from heaven on the earth in the sight of men,

14 And deceiveth them that dwell on the earth by the means of those miracles which he had power to do in the sight of the beast; saying to them that dwell on the earth, that they should make an image to the beast, which had the wound by a sword, and did live.

15 And he had power to give life unto the image of the beast, that the image of the beast should both speak, and cause that as many as would not worship the image of the beast should be killed.

16 And he causeth all, both small and great, rich and poor, free and bond, to receive a mark in their right hand, or in their foreheads:

17 And that no man might buy or sell, save he that had the mark, or the name of the beast, or the number of his name.

18 Here is wisdom. Let him that hath understanding count the number of the beast: for it is the number of a man; and his number is Six hundred threescore and six.

We have already established that the beast encompasses the entire earth. The number seven signifies completeness and thus exists everywhere. When the kingdom of God is established through the influence of Donald Trump, he will inflict a deadly wound on one of the heads of the beast. Here's a suggestion as we consider a bit of history.

After the Civil War, when the country was in ruins, European nations offered financial assistance to help rebuild, but they wanted their own people in charge to ensure they would get their money back. This undermined the original inspired Constitution, and we have been under severe and extreme bondage to the Gadianton Robbers ever since. (See Endnotes[12] for short list of tactics)

Since Woodrow Wilson, every president chosen by this cabal of leaders was selected until Donald Trump's first election in 2016[13]. He was the first president elected by the people, which greatly alarmed the beast system because they could not control him. They have done everything possible to try to destroy him and prevent him from running again. They had to cheat immensely in 2020 to stop him from taking a second term, but that turned out to be a great blessing.

Like all of God's Servants, Donald Trump learns things through the things he suffered. Many have criticized his first term in office for making many mistakes, but he came in there, not knowing hardly anyone in Washington, because all of his contacts were in New York. He put his trust in people he thought would help him achieve his goals, only to discover that the Deep State, the Gadianton Robbers, had appointed almost all of them. Now in his second term, he has been far more picky and discerning in whom he appoints to offices. This action will dismantle the Gadianton Robbers, established after the Civil War.

How will he accomplish this? He's already begun addressing the bureaucratic nightmare that our country has become. The opposition he encounters proves that he's on the right path. Not only do they want to protect their source of wealth, but they also wish to evade responsibility for their crimes. I assert that everyone who opposed Donald Trump in any election benefited in some way from these unconstitutional fiefdoms. They did ev-

SECTION 4 - REVELATION CHAPTER 13

erything possible to incite public opposition against him, using the media to disseminate their propaganda.

Since we know that the current government in the United States is almost entirely corrupt, it reflects a one-party system. There is no genuine opposition; it's all a facade. They are all in it together and support each other in their illegal activities and wealth acquisition schemes. Here's a description of their operations from over 2000 years ago:

> Helaman 6:21 But behold, Satan did stir up the hearts of the more part of the Nephites, insomuch that they did unite with those bands of robbers, and did enter into their covenants and their oaths, that they would protect and preserve one another in whatsoever difficult circumstances they should be placed, that they should not suffer for their murders, and their plunderings, and their stealings.
>
> 22 And it came to pass that they did have their signs, yea, their secret signs, and their secret words; and this that they might distinguish a brother who had entered into the covenant, that whatsoever wickedness his brother should do he should not be injured by his brother, nor by those who did belong to his band, who had taken this covenant.
>
> 23 And thus they might murder, and plunder, and steal, and commit whoredoms and all manner of wickedness, contrary to the laws of their country and also the laws of their God.
>
> 24 And whosoever of those who belonged to their band should reveal unto the world of their wickedness and their abominations, should be tried, not according to the laws of their country, but according to the laws of their wickedness, which had been given by Gadianton and Kishkumen.

This is exactly how things are today. And when Donald Trump comes in and destroys it, they are going to go into absolute chaos. They're going to jump up and down and scream and yell that Trump has committed treason and anyone who has voted for him has also committed treason. They will commit blasphemy because they don't want justice upon themselves.

The chaos and upheaval will be unprecedented. As the corrupt system crumbles, its adherents will lash out in desperation, their true nature revealed. The media, long complicit in the deception, will amplify their cries of outrage and accusations of treason. But their words will ring hollow to

SECTION 4 - REVELATION CHAPTER 13

those who have awakened to the truth.

In the midst of this turmoil, a great awakening will spread across the land. People will begin to see through the lies and manipulation that have kept them in bondage for so long. The veil will be lifted, and the machinations of the secret combinations will be exposed to the light of day. And this was all prophesied by Isaiah himself:

> Isa 51:9 ¶ Awake, awake, put on strength, O arm of the Lord; awake, as in the ancient days, in the generations of old. Art thou not (he) that hath cut Rahab, and wounded the dragon?

According to Isaiah, Rahab is a Hebrew name emblematic of Egypt, which is seen as a symbol of the United States. Almost every reference to Egypt in Isaiah regarding the latter days points to the United States. The Dragon represents the Beast System we are discussing. It has been wounded. The wound inflicted by Donald Trump, the "arm of the Lord," on the Dragon in the United States signifies the destruction of the United States Secret Combination, which is the same wounded Dragon in Isaiah!

By restoring these eternal principles, society will experience a profound renewal, emerging from the darkness of the past. The family, as God's central institution, will act as the driving force behind this transformation, fostering a world where love, justice, and unity prevail. This all begins with the First Horseman establishing the kingdom of God, Zion, here in America. All of these profoundly beautiful principles will form the foundation upon which the kingdom of God will begin to grow and spread across the Earth[14]. The Constitution will become its founding law, and all forms of illegal, immoral, unethical, or incorrect additions to that Constitution will be eliminated.

"Our Constitution was made only for a moral and religious people. It is wholly inadequate to the government of any other."-John Adams[15]. It will become the rule of the land. It will become the rule of the world. In a future day, there will be two capitals on Earth, both named Jerusalem. From the New Jerusalem in America (AofF 10) will go forth the law (Micah 4:2), the Constitution. From the Jerusalem in the east in Israel, we will receive the Word of the Lord.

One will be the Political portion of the Kingdom of God and the other the Ecclesiastical, just like David and Samuel, or Mosiah and Alma. But

SECTION 4 - REVELATION CHAPTER 13

for now, we are discussing the beginning of the establishment of the one in America. And the Beast System will do everything it can to destroy it.

Comparing Revelation 6 with chapters 12-13 provides a clearer understanding of what is truly occurring here. Chapter 12 shows us that the kingdom of God has now been established on Earth under the leadership of Donald Trump. This is when the Constitution is saved from hanging by a thread. "Joseph Smith the Prophet said the time would come when the Constitution and government of the United States would hang by a thread, and the Latter-day Saints would step forward and save it from destruction.[16]" This is when the elders of Zion stand forth and save the country. Satan's kingdom now faces destruction and opposition, and he cannot have this!

These elements combine to illustrate a scene of war, death, disease, famine, and horrific martyrdom. As in the Book of Mormon in 3 Nephi 6-7, tribalism dominates the land beyond Zion. The opening of the first five seals occurs as World War III engulfs the Earth before the final appearance of our Lord and Savior to the entire world, which destroys the many.

Millions of government workers and unelected government contractors will lose their jobs. Thousands of unconstitutional laws, edicts, and fiefdoms will be eliminated. Hundreds of bureaucracies will be swept off the Earth. The leaders of these groups will writhe in pain and agony. They will accuse anyone who voted for Trump of committing treason. They will persecute anyone who is not contained in the New Jerusalem. Massive civil wars will take place. This will be a very dark time in our country.

The head of the Beast will eventually be healed as they establish a new fifth beast system in Revelation 13:11, which is an extension of the fourth beast, described in Daniel as horrific in every way. Its vicious claws, iron teeth, horns, and terrible heads will cause tremendous damage. This is how Daniel sees it in Chapter 7:

> Dan 7:19 Then I would know the truth of the fourth beast (which has been revived again because of the fifth beast), which was diverse from all the others, exceeding dreadful, whose teeth were of iron, and his nails of brass; which devoured, brake in pieces, and stamped the residue with his feet; *(Note: in Volume 2, I will spend more time on the Book of Daniel as this one is mostly focused on Revelation).*

These visions greatly troubled Daniel, and I feel that too many are un-

SECTION 4 - REVELATION CHAPTER 13

aware of what is about to happen in the world. Amid incredible tribalism and chaos outside of Zion, people will be seeking any form of stability. A great leader arises who speaks blasphemy against God and those who dwell in Zion. He makes war with the Saints and overcomes some of them. All the nations of the world come under this dynamic leader's power. Anyone whose name is not written in the book of Life turns to him for food and protection.

The fifth Beast is introduced in Revelation 13:11. He comes out of the earth, as opposed to the first one arising from the sea. This one resembles a lamb but speaks like a Dragon. Coming forth like a lamb is deception because Christ is the true lamb; therefore, this is the Antichrist. He has all the power of the fourth beast, whose wound was healed. He also possesses additional powers we have not seen with any other beast. He can perform tremendous miracles and do great wonders. It states that he brings fire down from heaven. He deceives them through the miracles he performs. He demands that people make an image of the beast that was healed. He holds up the globalist agenda as something we all need to work for. It's the idol he demands we all worship. He has the power to give life to that image through the miracle of Television and cell phones, causing it to speak, and those who do not worship it, he kills. Everyone in the world, of every status and age, must pledge allegiance to this lamb-like beast by receiving a Mark on their hand or forehead. They are not allowed to buy or sell anything without that Mark. He controls everything!

This Beast is controlled by the same one who opens his mouth in blasphemy against God and those in Zion. He is the "stout horn" (Dan 7:19-25). This fifth beast indicates a change in tactics. He proclaims himself the savior of mankind, performs tremendous miracles, and compels people to worship him. Instead of merely being a government that guides all humanity and solves all of their problems, he claims to be the only way they can be saved, even promising immortality through the technology he controls and demonstrates by helping people to see and walk.

Isaiah states that he will seek to have his throne set above the stars and above God, but in the process, he will weaken the nations (Isa 14:12-14).

This fifth beast is not known on Earth yet. We have not seen it. We are only familiar with the fourth beast with seven heads that currently rules the Earth. The fifth beast arises after the establishment of Zion and acts in great retaliation against the rest of the world. It exerts tremendous power against those who dwell in the new Jerusalem but does not conquer them, doubling its efforts against everyone else and demanding total allegiance and worship. The fifth beast is the system, and the Antichrist is its leader. He proclaims that the seven-headed beast that was wounded, the Socialist, Communist, Marxist, and Globalist systems that it exposed, were good.

He claims that it simply wasn't finished, so we must ensure that it works this time and eliminate every aspect of individual freedom along with the Constitution of the United States of America. He will point out how unfair it was! There were rich and poor people, and we aim to make sure that everyone is equal. You will own nothing and be happy! He demands that everyone worship this image or plan, yet in Revelation 14:7, we are commanded to worship God. That's the choice; those who refuse to worship this image will be killed. If you are not with us, then you are against us. Our system will ensure everyone is safe, equal, and happy. If you oppose that, we have no use for you. It's the Church of the Lamb or the Church of the Devil (the fake lamb, the Antichrist).

It will utilize absolutely anything available in the world of technology to achieve its goals. Certainly, artificial intelligence will serve as its central core, as it surpasses the ability and speed at which humans can think. It will know everything that everyone does at any time of day. It will say, *"See what happens when we allow people to do as they wish! They destroyed what we know works. They went off and formed their own group, and this must not be allowed. Look what we can do for you. Unless you take this Mark, you are on your own. We will provide you with safety, security, and food; otherwise, you will have nothing, no ability to defend yourself, and be of no use to me. Therefore, you will be imprisoned and killed."*

Since day one, we have been encouraged to be self-reliant, self-sufficient, and completely independent. Therefore, this will be a tremendous trial for many who fail to heed the warnings from our prophets and apostles. Without access to a banking system, suffering under debt and dependency will lead to despondency. This will truly be one of the most challenging times in Earth's history.

This is the AntiChrist, the Man of Sin, the Assyrian, etc.

SECTION 4 - REVELATION CHAPTER 13

This is Satan incarnate, and many will be killed. Isaiah calls him "the Assyrian" because of his incredibly brutal nature. Even a brief review of the history of the violence and methods of the people of ancient Assyria, claimed to be the most violent kingdom in the history of the Earth, suggests that such events will repeat. They are so horrific that I will not recount them here, as they have shocked historians who have reviewed their history. This time, it will occur globally, and he will wield incredible technology to enforce his rule. He is the "lawless one" (2 Thes 2:8 shown as 'wicked' from the Greek) and cares nothing for the things of God or for human rights.

I need to note here that I've shown the fourth beast of Daniel has teeth of iron and nails of brass, and it stamps with its feet. It is described as being like a lion, a bear, and a leopard, and the prophet Ezra informs us that there are three eagle heads (2 Esdras 12:22-24). The one in Revelation 13:1-2 has seven heads and ten horns (as in Daniel 7) and the fifth beast like a lamb with two horns in Revelation 13:11. There are wings, horns, and heads that symbolize different aspects of this beast across the three prophets. The question is: Am I confusing the three heads in one vision with the seven heads in another and the one with two horns in yet another? The answer is No. ***They present different aspects of the same beast kingdom.*** As stated before, the seven heads represent the fact that it covers the entire earth. The three eagle heads of Ezra represent three powerful entities: government, military, and media, that exert tremendous control over the world. The one that resembles a Lamb shows that it is Antichrist and uses deception and force to achieve its goals while claiming to be the Savior of mankind.

As the new beast system rises from the ashes of the old, it will be more insidious and controlling than ever. The technology that once promised freedom will become the chains that bind humanity. Digital currencies will replace cash, enabling total surveillance of all transactions. Social credit scores will dictate access to basic necessities. Dissent will be stifled through algorithm manipulation and deplatforming.

Those who refuse the mark will find themselves outcasts, unable to buy food, seek employment, or participate in society. Many will flee to the wilderness, forming communities of resistance. These modern-day pioneers will relearn the forgotten skills of self-sufficiency and mutual aid. Their faith and resilience will be tested daily as they endure hardship and persecution.

Since they have rejected the gospel, a great woe has been pronounced upon them. All the verses that Jesus warned them about will come to pass as chaos reigns in the land. They will lose what they once had. Massive waves of illegal immigrants will flood the land and take everything with them. And why is that? Because of the sins and wickedness that Jesus outlined. He warned them that he would cut them off from among his people if they did not repent. (See Section 10 on Jesus Christ's prophecy).

They had the opportunity to accept the gospel, but they refused and, in many cases, fought against it.

Meanwhile, the Beast will strengthen its power on a global scale. National borders will blur as a global government emerges. Ancient prophecies will reveal themselves before our eyes. The false prophets and teachers will spread across the Earth. This is the time referred to in the Book of Mormon when there will be only two churches: the Church of the Lamb and the Church of the Devil. A tremendous division will exist between those in Zion and those who are not, and they will have no effect whatsoever on the people in Zion. They are protected and will actively seek those willing to join them.

We know this is how this works because of the scripture that Jesus quotes from Isaiah 54 and is contained in,

> 3 NE 22:15 Behold, they shall surely gather together against thee, not by me; whosoever shall gather together against thee shall fall for thy sake.
>
> 16 Behold, I have created the smith that bloweth the coals in the fire, and that bringeth forth an instrument for his work; and I have created the waster to destroy.
>
> 17 No weapon that is formed against thee shall prosper; and every tongue that shall revile against thee in judgment thou shalt condemn. This is the heritage of the servants of the Lord, and their righteousness is of me, saith the Lord.

Those in Zion's all over the world will be shielded from those who assemble against them. They employ any weaponry they can to attempt to destroy the beautiful city, but nothing succeeds. No matter what they do, it fails to make an impact or even a dent. Their righteousness is the reason they are protected and safe. Those who are righteous are also protected, as shown in,

Isa 4:5 And the Lord will create upon every dwelling place of mount Zion, and upon her assemblies, a cloud and smoke by day, and the shining of a flaming fire by night: for upon all the glory shall be a defence.

It's as if a "Dome of Protection" will be over each dwelling place as pockets of resistance endure all around the world. Hidden communities await the protection promised to the faithful. The 144,000 seek them out and bring them to Zion.

This message represents the pinnacle of prophetic insights found in scripture, each one echoing through time to resonate with our present day. We aren't merely referencing events from 20 years ago; we are speaking about the urgent realities of today. When the First Horseman makes his decisive move, every corner of the globe will feel the tremors, and nothing will ever be the same again. For centuries, humanity has yearned for the establishment of God's Kingdom. Now, amidst tremendous opposition, it is on the brink of emerging, fueled by unwavering faith, the miraculous wonders of God, and the most profound demonstrations of the power of Jesus Christ that our world has ever witnessed. And in a remarkable twist of fate, God has chosen YOU to be here, at this pivotal moment in history. Embrace this calling!

Section 5
Revelation 7 & 14

Section 5 - Revelation Chapters 7 & 14

I claim that these two chapters, Revelation 7 and 14, belong together and are connected chiastically, giving us additional valuable information. I'm going to quote both of them in their entirety and then make my comments below.

> Rev 7:1 And after these things I saw four angels standing on the four corners of the earth, holding the four winds of the earth, that the wind should not blow on the earth, nor on the sea, nor on any tree.
>
> 2 And I saw another angel ascending from the east, having the seal of the living God: and he cried with a loud voice to the four angels, to whom it was given to hurt the earth and the sea,
>
> 3 Saying, Hurt not the earth, neither the sea, nor the trees, till we have sealed the servants of our God in their foreheads.
>
> 4 And I heard the number of them which were sealed: and there were sealed an hundred and forty and four thousand of all the tribes of the children of Israel.
>
> 5 Of the tribe of Juda were sealed twelve thousand. Of the tribe of Reuben were sealed twelve thousand. Of the tribe of Gad were sealed twelve thousand.
>
> 6 Of the tribe of Aser were sealed twelve thousand. Of the tribe of Nepthalim were sealed twelve thousand. Of the tribe of Manasses were sealed twelve thousand.
>
> 7 Of the tribe of Simeon were sealed twelve thousand. Of the tribe of Levi were sealed twelve thousand. Of the tribe of Issachar were sealed twelve thousand.
>
> 8 Of the tribe of Zabulon were sealed twelve thousand. Of the tribe of Joseph were sealed twelve thousand. Of the tribe of Benjamin were sealed twelve thousand.
>
> 9 After this I beheld, and, lo, a great multitude, which no man could number, of all nations, and kindreds, and people, and tongues, stood before the throne, and before the Lamb, clothed with white robes, and palms in their hands;
>
> 10 And cried with a loud voice, saying, Salvation to our God which sitteth upon the throne, and unto the Lamb.

SECTION 5 - REVELATION CHAPTERS 7 & 14

11 And all the angels stood round about the throne, and about the elders and the four beasts, and fell before the throne on their faces, and worshipped God,

12 Saying, Amen: Blessing, and glory, and wisdom, and thanksgiving, and honour, and power, and might, be unto our God for ever and ever. Amen.

13 And one of the elders answered, saying unto me, What are these which are arrayed in white robes? and whence came they?

14 And I said unto him, Sir, thou knowest. And he said to me, These are they which came out of great tribulation, and have washed their robes, and made them white in the blood of the Lamb.

15 Therefore are they before the throne of God, and serve him day and night in his temple: and he that sitteth on the throne shall dwell among them.

16 They shall hunger no more, neither thirst any more; neither shall the sun light on them, nor any heat.

17 For the Lamb which is in the midst of the throne shall feed them, and shall lead them unto living fountains of waters: and God shall wipe away all tears from their eyes.

SECTION 5 - REVELATION CHAPTERS 7 & 14

Chapter 14

Rev 14:1 And I looked, and, lo, a Lamb stood on the mount Sion, and with him an hundred forty and four thousand, having his Father's name written in their foreheads.

2 And I heard a voice from heaven, as the voice of many waters, and as the voice of a great thunder: and I heard the voice of harpers harping with their harps:

3 And they sung as it were a new song before the throne, and before the four beasts, and the elders: and no man could learn that song but the hundred and forty and four thousand, which were redeemed from the earth.

4 These are they which were not defiled with women; for they are virgins. These are they which follow the Lamb whithersoever he goeth. These were redeemed from among men, being the firstfruits unto God and to the Lamb.

5 And in their mouth was found no guile: for they are without fault before the throne of God.

6 And I saw another angel fly in the midst of heaven, having the everlasting gospel to preach unto them that dwell on the earth, and to every nation, and kindred, and tongue, and people,

7 Saying with a loud voice, Fear God, and give glory to him; for the hour of his judgment is come: and worship him that made heaven, and earth, and the sea, and the fountains of waters.

8 And there followed another angel, saying, Babylon is fallen, is fallen, that great city, because she made all nations drink of the wine of the wrath of her fornication.

9 And the third angel followed them, saying with a loud voice, If any man worship the beast and his image, and receive his mark in his forehead, or in his hand,

10 The same shall drink of the wine of the wrath of God, which is poured out without mixture into the cup of his indignation; and he shall be tormented with fire and brimstone in the presence of the holy angels, and in the presence of the Lamb:

11 And the smoke of their torment ascendeth up for ever and ever: and they have no rest day nor night, who worship the beast and his

SECTION 5 - REVELATION CHAPTERS 7 & 14

image, and whosoever receiveth the mark of his name.

12 Here is the patience of the saints: here are they that keep the commandments of God, and the faith of Jesus.

13 And I heard a voice from heaven saying unto me, Write, Blessed are the dead which die in the Lord from henceforth: Yea, saith the Spirit, that they may rest from their labours; and their works do follow them.

14 And I looked, and behold a white cloud, and upon the cloud one sat like unto the Son of man, having on his head a golden crown, and in his hand a sharp sickle.

15 And another angel came out of the temple, crying with a loud voice to him that sat on the cloud, Thrust in thy sickle, and reap: for the time is come for thee to reap; for the harvest of the earth is ripe.

16 And he that sat on the cloud thrust in his sickle on the earth; and the earth was reaped.

17 And another angel came out of the temple which is in heaven, he also having a sharp sickle.

18 And another angel came out from the altar, which had power over fire; and cried with a loud cry to him that had the sharp sickle, saying, Thrust in thy sharp sickle, and gather the clusters of the vine of the earth; for her grapes are fully ripe.

19 And the angel thrust in his sickle into the earth, and gathered the vine of the earth, and cast it into the great winepress of the wrath of God.

20 And the winepress was trodden without the city, and blood came out of the winepress, even unto the horse bridles, by the space of a thousand and six hundred furlongs.

As noted in Revelation chapter 6, after all the cataclysms that occurred during the first part of the sixth seal, a tremendous sign has been shown across the world. This sign has caused men of every category, race, wealth status, and power stance on Earth to hide in dens, rocks, bunkers, and caves. They seek to hide from the presence of God and the wrath of the Lamb.

This may be a celestial cataclysmic event similar to those witnessed by our ancestors and recorded in petroglyphs worldwide. Known as the "stick man," it is an enormous plasma display that somewhat resembles a human form. Please don't misunderstand; I'm not making this claim categorically, but it could explain the numerous attributes of the description in Revelation 6:14-17. It describes the heavens opening like a scroll and being visible to

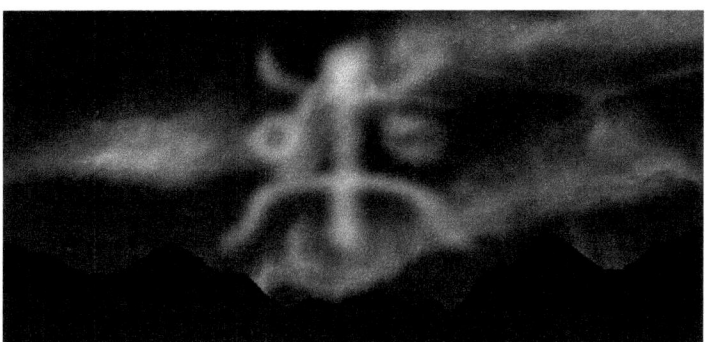

the entire world.[17] These plasmic events that have occurred in the past are immense in size and easily seen from all over the Earth. Any human form, even that of God himself, would not have his face visible from such a distance. The people of the Earth recognize this as an extraordinarily traumatic event, filling their souls with the fear of God as they hide in whatever ways they can.

Here is an image of what it might look like and comparing it to the Petroglyphs we have seen.

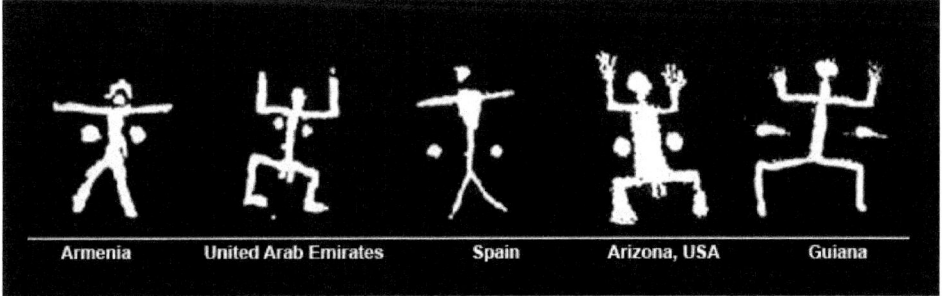

Of course, I may be wrong here, and again, I'm not stating this as fact. I just want to open your eyes to the possibility of what is happening. This is a natural phenomenon that has happened before.

This sets the stage for chapter 7, which occurs during the sixth thousand-year period. Tremendous destruction has taken place over the last several years of World War III. Hundreds of millions of people have died, been

SECTION 5 - REVELATION CHAPTERS 7 & 14

killed, or murdered. From Zion, the New Jerusalem, a host of God's chosen servants now go out to seek those still living who have remained faithful amid all this terrible destruction. They seek anyone connected in any way to the 12 tribes of Israel.

They have a covenant with God that they don't even know about. They are connected to the early prophets such as Abraham, Isaac, and Jacob; through blood, they are blessed to be sought after and invited into the House of Israel. God knew the House of Israel would fail in their attempt to live up to their being chosen of God. God's foreknowledge used that failure to spread the covenant throughout the Earth through blood. Now these people, who don't even know they are connected, are sought for by the 144,000.

Once the mission is complete, the invitation is open to everyone in the world, regardless of their status, condition, or covenant relationship. Jesus shares a marvelous parable about this event in:

> Luke 14:15 ¶ And when one of them that sat at meat with him heard these things, he said unto him, Blessed is he that shall eat bread in the Kingdom of God.
>
> 16 Then said he unto him, A certain man made a great supper, and bade many:
>
> 17 And sent his servant at supper time to say to them that were bidden, Come; for all things are now ready.
>
> 18 And they all with one consent began to make excuse. The first said unto him, I have bought a piece of ground, and I must needs go and see it: I pray thee have me excused.
>
> 19 And another said, I have bought five yoke of oxen, and I go to prove them: I pray thee have me excused.
>
> 20 And another said, I have married a wife, and therefore I cannot come.
>
> 21 So that servant came, and shewed his lord these things. Then the master of the house being angry said to his servant, Go out quickly into the streets and lanes of the city, and bring in hither the poor, and the maimed, and the halt, and the blind.
>
> 22 And the servant said, Lord, it is done as thou hast commanded, and yet there is room.

SECTION 5 - REVELATION CHAPTERS 7 & 14

23 And the lord said unto the servant, Go out into the highways and hedges, and compel them to come in, that my house may be filled.

24 For I say unto you, That none of those men which were bidden shall taste of my supper.

Everyone is invited! The gospel has been presented to many throughout the centuries, but each group has ultimately lost that chance. Now, it is accessible to all, regardless of whether they are in covenant with God or not. Those who keep the commandments are the covenant people of the Lord!

1 Ne 14:14 And it came to pass that I, Nephi, beheld the power of the Lamb of God, that it descended upon the saints of the church of the Lamb, and upon the covenant people of the Lord, who were scattered upon all the face of the earth; and they were armed with righteousness and with the power of God in great glory.

They hear the voice of the angel flying in the midst of heaven, declaring the everlasting gospel, for the hour of His judgment has come. They have not taken upon themselves the Mark of the Beast. This is a significant key for those who will now be brought back into Zion. They are now arrayed in white robes, having been baptized, washed, and anointed, and they stand before the throne of God. They no longer hunger. They sing a new song before the throne of God and the four beasts in Heaven.

Following that angel is another, proclaiming to the world that Babylon has fallen. What they once served and engaged in is now completely destroyed. They have shown tremendous faith and patience during this difficult time.

And that judgment is now upon the Earth as multiple angels wield their sickles to gather the wicked into the winepress. This is when the wicked of the Earth, those who have been drunken with iniquity and slain the Saints, are now fed with their own flesh. They kill each other in a horrific scene of cannibalism and slaughter. It says the blood is so high that it comes unto the horse's bridles. This is another reference to World War III, the Four Horsemen. This is the pit they had dug to kill the Saints, and now it turns into a Civil War where they kill each other. They fill this pit with their own bodies.

Perhaps this is the time prophesied when,

SECTION 5 - REVELATION CHAPTERS 7 & 14

D&C 133:25 ... the Lord, even the Savior, shall stand in the midst of his people, and shall reign over all flesh.

26 And they who are in the north countries shall come in remembrance before the Lord; and their prophets shall hear his voice, and shall no longer stay themselves; and they shall smite the rocks, and the ice shall flow down at their presence.

27 And an highway shall be cast up in the midst of the great deep.

28 Their enemies shall become a prey unto them,

29 And in the barren deserts there shall come forth pools of living water; and the parched ground shall no longer be a thirsty land.

30 And they shall bring forth their rich treasures unto the children of Ephraim, my servants.

31 And the boundaries of the everlasting hills shall tremble at their presence.

32 And there shall they fall down and be crowned with glory, even in Zion, by the hands of the servants of the Lord, even the children of Ephraim.

33 And they shall be filled with songs of everlasting joy.

34 Behold, this is the blessing of the everlasting God upon the tribes of Israel, and the richer blessing upon the head of Ephraim and his fellows.

The cataclysms that occur all over the Earth, including shaking, the seas heaving themselves beyond their bounds, and the ice flowing down at their presence, are all events that take place during the gathering of all the house of Israel into Zion. If the magnetic poles of the Earth shift, causing the world to reel to and fro like a drunken man, this will cause the ice to flow down at His presence. Those who have listened to the Spirit and taught those seeking the truth, even if they are not officially a part of the Church of Jesus Christ of Latter-day Saints, are still prophets in their own right and will heed God's chosen servant. These dramatic scenes of cataclysmic upheaval are akin to the parting of the Red Sea, saving each of the houses of Israel from all over the world. They all lead to Zion and are all under the direction of the First Horseman. The Kings and Queens of the Gentiles carry them as nursing fathers and mothers.

SECTION 5 - REVELATION CHAPTERS 7 & 14

They are crowned with glory through the authority of the church comprised mostly of the house of Ephraim. They receive the same blessings and covenants. They bring their rich treasures with them just like the house of Israel took the wealth of Egypt with them on their way to the promised land. If everyone has a double blessing which allowed them the ability to take the gospel throughout the world and the rest of the houses of Israel will pay them back because it all goes to Zion and the New Jerusalem. This is an astonishingly glorious time at the same time its such a disaster for everyone else.

Mormon, Moroni, and Ether (in Section 14) witnessed a terrible scene unfold in their own lands and among their people. They witnessed this horrific destruction and recorded it for us to learn from. They cried out in agony at the loss of their people because they would not heed the voice of God. They refused to turn from their sins and come unto their Savior, Jesus Christ. They were filled with satanic influence that controlled all their actions. These three great prophets have shared their message in the book that is accessible to anyone in the world. This warning has been conveyed to you.

And to those who heed the message, follow the spirit, repent, are baptized, and follow our modern-day Moses will receive those great blessings, while those who ignore it or fight against it will witness the destruction that the Book of Mormon prophets foresaw.

A baby nursed by its parent knows only hunger, tiredness, or discomfort. It doesn't know where it came from, who its parents are, or what its future holds. It is completely dependent on others for truth and guidance. The Kings and Queens of the Gentiles nurture and teach infants in the gospel. They reveal their identity, origins, and possible divine destiny. With loving and tender care, they introduce these infants to the true God and His covenant, showing the blessings that await those who obey Him.

These Kings and Queens help bring them to Zion—a place filled with resurrected, translated, mortal, and angelic beings. Everyone is invited, but only those who covenant to keep God's commandments may enter. Zion isn't limited to one religion, although its leadership consists of Prophets and Apostles from the Church. Entrance requires obedience, not membership. It will be the only place of peace on Earth. Many desire peace but refuse to live according to the laws necessary to attain it.

Section 6
Revelation
8–11, 15–16

SECTION 6 - REVELATION CHAPTERS 8 - 11, 15 & 16

Section 6: REVELATION 8-11, 15-16

Just a note before reading this chapter: I've combined Chapters 8-9 and 15-16 to enable chronological reading, unifying the content and added notes on Chapters 10 and 11. Please note the indications of which chapter is being quoted. I hope this clarifies the consequences and events that were originally separated due to their chiastic organization.

In the next chapter, I will include a detailed list of how many times the number seven appears throughout scripture. I initially intended to include D&C 88:94-107 alongside these two chapters, but I discovered something remarkable. Since they all discuss the same events: silence in the heavens, trumpets, and destructions, etc. I assumed they were the same, but it didn't make sense. How can we have the trumpets announcing the redemption of every class of being concurrent with God's judgments being poured out upon the world? The wicked, those who refuse to change and accept the atonement of Jesus Christ, will not be resurrected until after the millennium. Why is this mentioned here? So I conducted some research and hope that I've found a satisfactory solution. But we need to cover these chapters first.

The Opening of the Seventh Seal.

Now, after all those years of establishing and growing Zion, after the destruction of nations and peoples from around the world who opposed Zion, the cataclysms of the sun, earthquakes, nuclear war, volcanoes, tsunamis, hurricanes, plagues, and diseases, followed by the gathering of those who have not taken on themselves the Mark of the Beast, God's judgments are now being poured out in an astonishingly dramatic way. If you thought everything that occurred during the sixth seal was enough or more than you could handle, everything is about to go into hyperdrive now.

A giant congregation of saved saints, rescued from the calamities of the first six seals, are now gathered together. Christ, the greatest being in the universe, is about to open the seventh seal and initiate the destructions sent from God upon those who have trampled Him underfoot. As mentioned earlier, a half-hour of silence takes place as the entire congregation of millions knows what is about to happen. The anticipation is immense. These people have endured so much, and it is through their faith in Jesus Christ that they have arrived at this place. Some have faced incredible suffering, and it's possible that many of them here have been killed and are the martyrs of the fifth seal, but they are now either resurrected or attending in spirit to witness God's judgments poured out upon those who have persecuted them.

Imagine, if you will, this congregation of millions of people in complete silence. Many have prayed and begged God to pour out His justice upon their adversaries. They wonder why those same adversaries have not received their judgment before. But God has a plan and will use their opposition to fulfill His purposes. That opposition filters out those who are willing to become Saints and receive celestial glory. It's a difficult test. How could we feel comfortable in the presence of such great prophets from the past if we were not willing to do the same?

This profoundly solemn event, where millions of people gaze in the same direction at the same being, is filled with gratitude, humility, and recognition of what he has done for them. He is now poised to fulfill his promise of retaliation and judgment, with vengeance and fury that he claimed as his own. For 30 minutes, everyone waits with high anticipation for these judgments to arrive. Once it begins, nothing can halt it, and these will be the final judgments before the Earth is burned and experiences Terrestrial glory for 1,000 years. These scenes will cleanse the world of all evil, wickedness, and abominations that have existed for 6,000 years. Ultimately, this immense destruction will rid the world of its abominations. Glorious peace rests upon their souls as they exclaim, "Great and marvelous are thy works, Lord God Almighty!" (Paraphrased from Rev 4:11).

SECTION 6 - REVELATION CHAPTERS 8 - 11, 15 & 16

I submit that chapters 8-9 are chiastically connected to chapters 15-16. These are the same events seen from different perspectives. They do not occur twice; they happen once. The trumpets and vials represent the same thing. However, what I'm about to show you will be very different from anything I've ever read. I have tried to present some of these ideas before but have been shut down. People do not want to hear this. They can't comprehend it. To them, it's bizarre thinking that makes no sense from their perspective. Let's take a look at these chapters as I try to connect the verses between them to clarify their messages.

Revelation 8:1 And when he had opened the seventh seal, there was silence in heaven about the space of half an hour.

2 And I saw the seven angels which stood before God; and to them were given seven trumpets.

3 And another angel came and stood at the altar, having a golden censer; and there was given unto him much incense, that he should offer it with the prayers of all saints upon the golden altar which was before the throne.

4 And the smoke of the incense, which came with the prayers of the saints, ascended up before God out of the angel's hand.

5 And the angel took the censer, and filled it with fire of the altar, and cast it into the earth: and there were voices, and thunderings, and lightnings, and an earthquake.

These first five verses of chapter 8 connect with chapter 15 in its entirety. Here is that chapter:

Rev 15:1 And I saw another sign in heaven, great and marvellous, seven angels having the seven last plagues; for in them is filled up the wrath of God.

2 And I saw as it were a sea of glass mingled with fire: and them that had gotten the victory over the beast, and over his image, and over his mark, and over the number of his name, stand on the sea of glass, having the harps of God.

3 And they sing the song of Moses the servant of God, and the song of the Lamb, saying, Great and marvellous are thy works, Lord God Almighty; just and true are thy ways, thou King of saints.

4 Who shall not fear thee, O Lord, and glorify thy name? for thou only art holy: for all nations shall come and worship before thee; for thy judgments are made manifest.

5 And after that I looked, and, behold, the temple of the tabernacle of the testimony in heaven was opened:

6 And the seven angels came out of the temple, having the seven plagues, clothed in pure and white linen, and having their breasts girded with golden girdles.

7 And one of the four beasts gave unto the seven angels seven golden vials full of the wrath of God, who liveth for ever and ever.

8 And the temple was filled with smoke from the glory of God, and from his power; and no man was able to enter into the temple, till the seven plagues of the seven angels were fulfilled.

An angel approaches the altar and fills the golden censer, which was given much incense. The smoke of this incense represents the prayers of all the saints who have cried out for justice. Many of them have attained celestial glory, as noted in 15:2, where they rest upon the sea of glass mingled with fire, symbolizing a celestialized earth. They have triumphed. They possess the harps of God and sing the song of Moses, the servant of God,

SECTION 6 - REVELATION CHAPTERS 8 - 11, 15 & 16

as well as the song of the Lamb. They give praise to God for His great and marvelous works.

The angel then casts his censer, filled with fire from the altar, to the Earth, causing tremendous thunder, lightning, and earthquakes. The rest of this chapter addresses numerous cosmic events that bring great destruction upon the Earth. This is God's wrath. These events are real; they are not symbolic. The seven angels are most likely real but with symbolic trumpets ready and vials poised to pour out. The temple is filled with the smoke of the prayers of all those who have sought this day, yearning for justice to come upon the Earth.

And so now his judgments begin. Let's combine them from the two chapters and read them in order.

> Rev 8:6 And the seven angels which had the seven trumpets prepared themselves to sound.

> 16:1 And I heard a great voice out of the temple saying to the seven angels, Go your ways, and pour out the vials of the wrath of God upon the earth.

The Angels with the trumpets and the vials are now commissioned to go forth and do what they have been commanded to do. They spread out over the Earth as the trumpets announced their arrival and judgments.

> Rev 8:7 The first angel sounded, and there followed hail and fire mingled with blood, and they were cast upon the earth: and the third part of trees was burnt up, and all green grass was burnt up.

--

> Rev 16:2 And the first went, and poured out his vial upon the earth; and there fell a noisome and grievous sore upon the men which had the Mark of the Beast, and upon them which worshipped his image.

The King James translators had never seen a meteor hit the Earth. The only thing they knew that came from heaven that was hard as a rock was hail. Somehow it is mixed with fire and blood in the translation which doesn't make sense if it is ice. But it does make sense if it is a massive wave of asteroids that hit the Earth. They are with fire as they are glowing in their descent through the atmosphere. The trees and grass cannot withstand these somewhat smaller meteors. The large ones are later. But something in the chemical makeup of these meteors causes a terrible sore upon the men (and women) who had the Mark of the Beast and worshiped his image. This concept of extraterrestrial chemical reactions happens several times in this chapter. Also remember that none of this affects those in Zion or who are the covenant people of the Lord.

Just like when Moses performed the multiple miracles in Egypt only the first three affected both the Egyptians and the Israelites. After that, it was only the Egyptians. This hail and fire concept did not affect those in Goshen. This is the same thing for our day. Since we are told that there are covenant people throughout the world who have not physically gathered to Zion, there must be, I will call it, "domes of protection" over those people. Maybe it's individual houses or gathered together in churches or communities, it doesn't matter, they are protected.

All of the plagues that occurred against the Egyptians occur again in the last days and this is significant as we are dealing with a modern day Exodus. They are not all referenced in Revelation, but are shown in other scriptures. But as damaging as those plagues were to pharaoh and his people, it is orders of magnitude larger in the last days under our modern Moses.

Rev 8:8 And the second angel sounded, and as it were a great mountain burning with fire was cast into the sea: and the third part of the sea became blood;

8:9 And the third part of the creatures which were in the sea, and had life, died; and the third part of the ships were destroyed.

SECTION 6 - REVELATION CHAPTERS 8 - 11, 15 & 16

Rev 16:3 And the second angel poured out his vial upon the sea; and it became as the blood of a dead man: and every living soul died in the sea.

The second angel causes a massive volcano to erupt, severely damaging the ocean. Significant tsunamis circle the Earth, and the tremendous destruction of sea creatures leads to the loss of life. This may be the largest volcano in world history, despite previous massive eruptions. The super volcanoes of Yellowstone and Krakatoa are likely less destructive than this one. Hundreds of millions of people die as a result of this event.

> Rev 8:10 And the third angel sounded, and there fell a great star from heaven, burning as it were a lamp, and it fell upon the third part of the rivers, and upon the fountains of waters;
>
> 11 And the name of the star is called Wormwood: and the third part of the waters became wormwood; and many men died of the waters, because they were made bitter.

--

Rev 16:4 And the third angel poured out his vial upon the rivers and fountains of waters; and they became blood.

5 And I heard the angel of the waters say, Thou art righteous, O Lord, which art, and wast, and shalt be, because thou hast judged thus.

6 For they have shed the blood of saints and prophets, and thou hast given them blood to drink; for they are worthy.

7 And I heard another out of the altar say, Even so, Lord God Almighty, true and righteous are thy judgments.

Now, a large asteroid or comet from heaven falls to Earth, glowing and bright like a lamp. It's called wormwood because it is poisonous to all sources of water on Earth. While the previous volcano caused great destruction to the ocean, this meteor affects freshwater, making it bitter like wormwood. Perhaps it explodes in the atmosphere, causing its chemical makeup to distribute all over the Earth.

Notice that the angel exclaimed that God is righteous and that they deserve such a terrible judgment. It's almost as if this angel doesn't really want to do this because of how many people are killed by it, but he does his job because God is righteous, and judgment must come upon the wicked.

Many people have proposed various alternate interpretations of these verses. This isn't science fiction; there are no aliens from another planet coming to ours. This is not a metaphor for terrible wars or a symbol of something else. The Antichrist has come long ago in the Second Seal. These are all Seventh Seal events. This is a literal asteroid that causes tremendous damage to Earth. However, no one in Zion is affected. Whether Zion is currently on Earth is debatable, and I see a few reasons for both recommendations:

According to Rev 8:1 it says:

Rev 8:1 And when he had opened the seventh seal, there was silence in heaven about the space of half an hour.

And this easily corresponds to D&C 88:95 which says this:

D&C 88:95 And there shall be silence in heaven for the space of half an hour; and immediately after shall the curtain of heaven be unfolded, as a scroll is unfolded after it is rolled up, and the face of the Lord shall be unveiled;

But then it gives this added detail:

D&C 88:96 And the saints that are upon the earth, who are alive, shall be quickened and be caught up to meet him.

This would clearly be a glorious solution, as none of the Saints would be present to endure the horrific judgments unleashed upon the Earth. Howev-

SECTION 6 - REVELATION CHAPTERS 8 - 11, 15 & 16

er, there are a couple of issues with this, as the next verse states:

> D&C 88:97 And they who have slept in their graves shall come forth, for their graves shall be opened; and they also shall be caught up to meet him in the midst of the pillar of heaven—
>
> 98 They are Christ's, the first fruits, they who shall descend with him first, and they who are on the earth and in their graves, who are first caught up to meet him; and all this by the voice of the sounding of the trump of the angel of God.

Every trumpet that follows corresponds to resurrecting or redeeming different types of people and culminates in significant world-ending events, such as announcing that everything is finished and that the Lamb of God has trodden in the wine press alone.

In an upcoming chapter, we will discuss the Kings and Queens of the Gentiles, the 144,000 who travel across the Earth seeking those who have not taken the Mark of the Beast. God's army also moves across the Earth against those who bear the Mark. All of these come from Zion and consist of Terrestrial and Celestial beings, with no power of Satan able to stop them.

But perhaps the Saints exist in both places simultaneously. Some are caught up to be with God, while others remain on Earth to continue the necessary work of redeeming as many people as possible, as explained in future verses. The Zion on Earth is protected from all these calamities because I'm going to show you what is about to happen.

> Rev 8:12 And the fourth angel sounded, and the third part of the sun was smitten, and the third part of the moon, and the third part of the stars; so as the third part of them was darkened, and the day shone not for a third part of it, and the night likewise.

--

> Rev 16: 8 And the fourth angel poured out his vial upon the sun; and power was given unto him to scorch men with fire.
>
> 9 And men were scorched with great heat, and blasphemed the name of God, which hath power over these plagues: and they repented not to give him glory.

Now the sun, our local star that provides us with light and heat and around which we rotate each year, joins in the action. We've already seen

SECTION 6 - REVELATION CHAPTERS 8 - 11, 15 & 16

in Chapter 6 that it had gone dark, but now it becomes super bright and hot. Is this a supernova of the sun?[18] It's possible. Is it a large solar flare? We're not quite sure, but we know that either could cause the effects described in these verses. Tremendous heat scorches those on Earth with fire. This fire is so intense that there is no protection. People blaspheme God's name because of how terrible it is, and they do not repent, which is the reason for these destructions.

> 8:13 And I beheld, and heard an angel flying through the midst of heaven, saying with a loud voice, Woe, woe, woe, to the inhabiters of the earth by reason of the other voices of the trumpet of the three angels, which are yet to sound!

And even after all of that, the angel warns the people of the earth that what is coming is worse. It's hard to imagine anything worse than what has happened so far, but God's judgment will come forth in all his fury. He has been patient and merciful all these years, and yet the vast majority of people have trampled upon these gifts. They refused to repent. He granted them life and created this earth so they would have the opportunity to become like him. All they needed to do was listen to his chosen leaders, call upon his name, read his words, and rely on their Savior, Jesus Christ, to be forgiven of their sins, but they refused. They killed his Son and scoffed at his chosen ones. God is a God of mercy, and he will still extend some of that in the next chapter, but justice must be served. There comes a point at which even God, the most merciful being in the universe, cannot continue with that profound gift. Let's continue with these vials and trumpets and witness God's desire to save as many as possible even after all of this rejection.

SECTION 6 - REVELATION CHAPTERS 8 - 11, 15 & 16

Chapters 9 and 16

Rev 16:10 And the fifth angel poured out his vial upon the seat of the beast; and his kingdom was full of darkness; and they gnawed their tongues for pain,

11 And blasphemed the God of heaven because of their pains and their sores, and repented not of their deeds.

Rev 9:1 And the fifth angel sounded, and I saw a star fall from heaven unto the earth: and to THE ANGEL was given the key of the bottomless pit.

I need to present the fifth angel from chapter 16 first because the remainder of chapter 9 is a chiastic comparison, and we may overlook the significance of its effects, as illustrated in the vial/trumpet of chapter 9. What I'm about to share is something I have never read or heard anyone mention. I perceive this very differently than anyone else.

The name of this angel is Abaddon or Apollyon, and most people presume that this is another name for Satan. I disagree. The only ones who hold priesthood keys to perform any kind of action are those ordained by God to do so.

This is God's Army, which goes forth throughout the world with tremendous power to pursue those who do not have the seal of God on their foreheads (verse four). This is not persecution against the church or the righteous; rather, it arises from the angelic power of God's political kingdom against those who have still not chosen to repent and follow God.

The bottomless pit possibly symbolizes yet another world war or an extension of the previous one, but this time, the battle is against God's Army. As depicted in the Book of Mormon, we confront the pit of the Civil War, which destroyed both nations entirely; likewise, this conflict will obliterate Satan's minions. This angel is the destroying angel, and like during the time of Moses, it passed through the entire company of Pharaoh, the Egyptians, and the Israelites. Anyone who did not have the blood on the doorpost or the lentils from the lamb lost their firstborn. This time, it targets those who have received the Mark of the Beast.

The Word of Wisdom actually has some significance here.

D&C 89:18 And all saints who remember to keep and do these sayings, walking in obedience to the commandments, shall receive health in their navel and marrow to their bones;

19 And shall find wisdom and great treasures of knowledge, even hidden treasures;

20 And shall run and not be weary, and shall walk and not faint.

21 And I, the Lord, give unto them a promise, that the destroying angel shall pass by them, as the children of Israel, and not slay them. Amen.

The destroying angel will pass by those who keep the Word of Wisdom. Is there a connection between keeping the Word of Wisdom and the Mark of the Beast? I don't know; I only know that those who uphold the Word of Wisdom will be spared, just as they were in ancient Egypt. Those who observe the Word of Wisdom are the ones allowed in the temple and receive the blessings it contains. The temple is our only place of safety. Those who attend the temple face Zion as they focus their lives on serving in the house of the Lord.

Rev 9:2 And he opened the bottomless pit; and there arose a smoke

SECTION 6 - REVELATION CHAPTERS 8 - 11, 15 & 16

out of the pit, as the smoke of a great furnace; and the sun and the air were darkened by reason of the smoke of the pit.

The key to the pit has now been unlocked. It doesn't refer to a cavernous crater in the Earth that spews forth smoke; rather, it is a pit from which the seven-headed beast, the Antichrist (Rev 13:11), has previously emerged as he sought to ensnare everyone. His time is now over, and the Angel unleashes God's Army in judgment against him and his followers. They will fill that pit with those who dug it (1 Ne 14:3). There is no law or order; everything is chaos. There is no government, only tribalism. Peace exists only in Zion..

The intense billowing smoke is not only the commotion of war and destruction, it's also the prayers from millions of saints pleading to God for justice and salvation, leading up to the final battle at Armageddon, where the Beast gathers his armies from across the Earth. However, the locusts here are not describing them. These are God's Army, a force of over 200 million men using God's power to perform one last act of mercy.

> REV 9:3 And there came out of the smoke locusts upon the earth: and unto them was given power, as the scorpions of the earth have power.
>
> 4 And it was commanded them that they should not hurt the grass of the earth, neither any green thing, neither any tree; but only those men which have not the seal of God in their foreheads.
>
> 5 And to them it was given that they should not kill them, but that they should be tormented five months: and their torment was as the torment of a scorpion, when he striketh a man.
>
> 6 And in those days shall men seek death, and shall not find it; and shall desire to die, and death shall flee from them.

God's Army comes from Zion, and consists of translated and resurrected beings who cannot be tempted by Satan nor suffer death. They now go out and inflict pain upon those who have not the seal of God on their foreheads. Just as the three Nephites could withstand anything the world threw at them without suffering pain or death, God's Army possesses a unique ability: ***they can inflict pain on people without allowing them to die.*** Nothing these individuals can do will remove this pain; they cannot die. This is a Terrestrial ability with one purpose: to hopefully prompt repentance.

Amidst all this terrible pain, following the devastation that has swept through the Earth and destroyed so much, it is hoped that someone will repent and finally realize they are on the wrong path. Their suffering results from a series of poor decisions and a refusal to humble themselves and turn to Jesus Christ. This is not forced repentance, it's justice and it aims to humiliate them in the hopes that they will turn to God.

As I mentioned, no one I know presents this material like this. I believe this chapter is the exact same vision shown to Isaiah in chapter 13.

> Isa 13:1 The burden of Babylon, which Isaiah the son of Amoz did see.
>
> 2 Lift ye up a banner upon the high mountain, exalt the voice unto them, shake the hand, that they may go into the gates of the nobles. *(The Nobles here refer to the Kings and Queens. They are God's chosen ones, distinguished not by worldly status but by their elevated position in God's kingdom. They shake hands, which means they wave their hands and invite people to join them.)*
>
> 3 I have commanded my sanctified ones, I have also called my mighty ones for mine anger, even them that rejoice in my highness. *(Under his command, the sanctified ones, the purified ones, and the mighty ones that rejoice in his glory are here and ready to do his work).*
>
> 4 The noise of a multitude in the mountains, like as of a great people; a tumultuous noise of the kingdoms of nations gathered together: the Lord of hosts mustereth the host of the battle. *(It is a great battle as the kingdoms of the surviving nations come together. The Lord assembles His host and prepares to swoop down on them.)*
>
> 5 They come from a far country, from the end of heaven, even the Lord, and the weapons of his indignation, to destroy the whole land. *(They have gathered from all over the world here to Zion so that they may praise and worship God and perform his work).*
>
> **Rev** 9:7 And the shapes of the locusts were like unto horses prepared unto battle; and on their heads were as it were crowns like gold, and their faces were as the faces of men.
>
> 8 And they had hair as the hair of women, and their teeth were as the teeth of lions.
>
> 9 And they had breastplates, as it were breastplates of iron; and the

sound of their wings was as the sound of chariots of many horses running to battle.

10 And they had tails like unto scorpions, and there were stings in their tails: and their power was to hurt men five months.

John is shown in vision what future warfare will look like through symbolic images. Everyone recognizes horses in battle, crowns, and lion's teeth. We all know the buzzing of locust swarms and the sound of many horses charging into combat. We are familiar with the sting of a scorpion's tail, but God didn't let us get distracted by the many advanced weapons of our time.

When Joshua became the leader of the House of Israel and replaced Moses, God encouraged him to be strong and faithful (Joshua 1:1-9), and He would show that he was the one now chosen by God. As they crossed the Jordan River, it parted in a miraculous way (Joshua 3). They then arrived at Jericho, and using the ark of the covenant, they surrounded the city each day for seven days, blowing the horns but speaking no words. On the seventh day, they surrounded the city seven times, blew the horns seven times, and then everyone shouted. A tremendous earthquake destroyed the city, and anyone left was killed (Joshua 6).

God's Army does not fight with traditional weapons. They wear crowns of gold that symbolize their authority and power from God. The woman-like hair shows the strength of the prophet Samson. Their lion's teeth indicate that they are speaking the words of Christ. The Iron Breastplate indicates that they are High Priests and are executing the Covenants made to the House of Israel against those who fought against them.

This is a shadow of a future day when all in the world who have refused the invitation to accept the atonement of Jesus Christ face justice. Since they have not chosen Him, they have chosen the Beast system and taken upon themselves the mark. They are now destroyed after being given one

SECTION 6 - REVELATION CHAPTERS 8 - 11, 15 & 16

last chance for repentance, feeling a pain they cannot escape. Once they reject that, they are eliminated. Justice must be served.

We've never seen a war like this in world history. The closest examples might be Enoch or Melchizedek and the strength of the priesthood and faith they possessed. It's not about land, gold, or power; it's about converting people who have sworn allegiance to the opposing side, the Beast system, and have taken a Mark to prove it. God is doing everything possible to save them! Remarkably, most still refuse to repent.

> 9:12 One woe is past; and, behold, there come two woes more hereafter.

It's astonishing how bad things become as this is technically a fourth world war and yet there are two more woes from God to punish the wicked!

> Rev 16:12 And the sixth angel poured out his vial upon the great river Euphrates; and the water thereof was dried up, that the way of the kings of the east might be prepared. *(Note: I think Joseph Smith may have overlooked this verse because he previously altered "Euphrates" in 9:14 to refer to the bottomless pit. To me, it makes no sense to involve the river Euphrates here. The bottomless pit makes perfect sense, as that's where all this originates.)*
>
> 13 And I saw three unclean spirits like frogs come out of the mouth of the dragon, and out of the mouth of the beast, and out of the mouth of the false prophet.

Do you remember the plagues in Egypt when frogs overran the land? Now we see three frogs, but I submit that these represent millions of satanic spirits, as indicated in the next verse. The reason it mentions three is that they come from the mouths of the Dragon (Government), the Beast (Military), and the False Prophet (Media). Every facet of what remains of Satan's kingdom will unite in an effort to defeat God's army in Armageddon.

I can picture a scene reminiscent of the end of the Jaredite nation when they all gathered around Cumorah for one last battle. Shiz assembled his forces over four years, and I envision them assuring one another that this would finally rid them of their enemies. They believed they would swoop down in the greatest military victory in history. They spread all sorts of lies to gather everyone together. In the end, all died except Coriantumr.

> Rev 16:14 For they are the spirits of devils, working miracles, which go forth unto the kings of the earth and of the whole world, to gather them to the battle of that great day of God Almighty.

These three aspects of the Dragon's kingdom possess power that allows them to perform miracles, promising those who follow him that they can succeed if they band together to defeat God's army. These miracles certainly include some of the technology we are familiar with today, and additional advancements that have yet to be revealed. However, the misuse of this technology will lead to their destruction, for "no weapon formed against thee shall prosper." They remain unaware that this is the final destructive battle and do not realize that Jesus Christ is about to arrive and eliminate them all. By the power of his word, he could annihilate this entire army. As he states in the next verse:

> Rev 16:15 Behold, I come as a thief. Blessed is he that watcheth, and keepeth his garments, lest he walk naked, and they see his shame. *(It's highly significant that those who have a covenant with God and have received their garments keep them. This illustrates how the destroying angel identifies those who lack the Mark of the Beast but possess the Mark of God. Upholding our covenant is the only way we will be saved. This also shows that there are Saints on the Earth during this difficult time.)*

> 16 And he gathered them together into a place called in the Hebrew tongue Armageddon.

> Rev 9:13 And the sixth angel sounded, and I heard a voice from the four horns of the golden altar which is before God,

> 14 Saying to the sixth angel which had the trumpet, Loose the four

angels which are bound in the bottomless pit.

15 And the four angels were loosed, which were prepared for an hour, and a day, and a month, and a year, for to slay the third part of men.

16 And the number of the army of the horsemen were two hundred thousand thousand: and I heard the number of them.

17 And thus I saw the horses in the vision, and them that sat on them, having breastplates of fire, and of jacinth, and brimstone: and the heads of the horses were as the heads of lions; and out of their mouths issued fire and smoke and brimstone.

18 By these three was the third part of men killed, by the fire, and by the smoke, and by the brimstone, which issued out of their mouths.

19 For their power is in their mouth, and in their tails: for their tails were like unto serpents, and had heads, and with them they do hurt.

God is doing everything he can to encourage their repentance. He aims to save as many as possible. For five months, they endured tremendous pain but could not die and now, for 13 months, many people are killed through the power of the Word of God coming from their mouths. The covenantal Breastplates destroy them as promised. But as noted in the next verses:

Rev 9:20 And the rest of the men which were not killed by these plagues yet repented not of the works of their hands, that they should not worship devils, and idols of gold, and silver, and brass, and stone, and of wood: which neither can see, nor hear, nor walk:

21 Neither repented they of their murders, nor of their sorceries, nor of their fornication, nor of their thefts.

They will not give up their sins, even in the face of death! This is clearly outlined in the Book of Mormon, which describes two civilizations that lost the spirit of God and sought only the destruction of their enemies. This will happen again, but on a much larger scale, as it will be worldwide.

Now the Angel announces three Woes.

WOE 1: Chapter 9:1-11 Opening the Bottomless Pit
WOE 2: Chapter 11: 3-13 Two Witnesses-Earthquake
WOE 3: Chapter 11:15-19 The Ark of the Covenant is revealed!

SECTION 6 - REVELATION CHAPTERS 8 - 11, 15 & 16

In chapter 8:13, the Angel announced that three woes would befall the inhabitants of the earth. The first woe was the opening of the bottomless pit and the great war led by Abaddon. We have already addressed the first one above.

Revelation Chapter 10 serves as an interlude that introduces an angel to John the Revelator, who provides him with his mission in life. John requested from Jesus the gift of translation so that he could bring more souls to Him.

D&C 7:1 And the Lord said unto me: John, my beloved, what desirest thou? For if you shall ask what you will, it shall be granted unto you.

2 And I said unto him: **Lord, give unto me power over death, that I may live and bring souls unto thee.**

3 And the Lord said unto me: Verily, verily, I say unto thee, because thou desirest this thou shalt tarry until I come in my glory, and shalt prophesy before nations, kindreds, tongues and people.

He wished to engage in more missionary work out of his love for the Savior. This visitation from the angel occurs after Christ's death, and the angel instructs him to take a book and eat it. This book is initially sweet, reflecting his desire to serve the Savior and lead souls to Him, much like taking the fruit from the tree of life. It was a marvelous aspiration.

As the book gets into his belly, it becomes sour and upsetting. We don't exactly know why, but I believe that John's mission will be filled with tremendous opposition and very few people accepting his message. This brings a sour taste to his soul. He wants everyone to feel the joy and love that he knows personally and wants to offer it to everyone, yet few will accept it. This will become a difficult mission as he watches so many people reject the profound gift he wants to give them.

In Chapter 11, he is then instructed to measure the temple, which means designating an area of protection for a time. The temple is protected by the two olive trees, the two candlesticks, and the two witnesses (all the same) with the power of God who defy the armies of the Beast. They have tremendous power, just like Melchizedek, whose priesthood they hold.

Many inside and outside the church have spoken of this well-known chapter. According to Bruce R. McConkie, these will be apostles or prophets of the Church of Jesus Christ of Latter-day Saints. I have no reason to think otherwise, as they stand there in sackcloth (humility), much like John the Baptist, and speaking with great power that can smite the armies and the Earth with plagues as often as they want.

These mortal Apostles are permitted to be killed by the Beast system. This is another example of why Zion must still exist on Earth. Apparently, they are not translated beings but mortals. Some suggest that Moses and Elijah are fighting here because they were translated millennia ago, but that cannot be true as they were resurrected at the time of Jesus Christ.

Their death brings tremendous excitement across the Earth as they probably yell out, "At last, these troublesome apostles are defeated, allowing us to move in and destroy the Jews residing in the city!" This is broadcast worldwide, and celebrations erupt everywhere. It has been many years since they have won any kind of battle, and now it seems they have finally achieved victory at the end.

But their joy is short-lived as they are resurrected right before them and taken up to heaven, hearing God's voice inviting them to come to Him. The world's joy then turns into utter panic, and the second Woe is thrust upon them: a massive worldwide earthquake.

> Rev 16:16 And he gathered them together into a place called in the Hebrew tongue Armageddon.
>
> 17 And the seventh angel poured out his vial into the air; and there came a great voice out of the temple of heaven, from the throne, saying, It is done.
>
> 18 And there were voices, and thunders, and lightnings; and there was a great earthquake, such as was not since men were upon the earth, so mighty an earthquake, and so great.
>
> 19 And the great city was divided into three parts, and the cities of the nations fell: and great Babylon came in remembrance before God, to give unto her the cup of the wine of the fierceness of his wrath.
>
> 20 And every island fled away, and the mountains were not found.

The Earth reacts to the rejection of these chosen leaders of God. It shakes like never before, causing entire continents to shift and islands to flee. This is the greatest earthquake that has ever occurred on the face

SECTION 6 - REVELATION CHAPTERS 8 - 11, 15 & 16

of the Earth. It isn't a localized one like Jericho, it's worldwide. Even though it speaks of the great city being divided into three parts, all the cities of all the nations are obliterated. Their desires to create Babylon wherever they live are crushed and the merchants of the Earth mourn her loss. Babylons all over the world constructed with towering skyscrapers, apartment complexes, office buildings, and transmission towers everywhere are all destroyed. Most likely, this is likely an 10.0+ earthquake that envelops the entire world and lasts for days, maybe even weeks. No buildings survive except those in Zion and those protected by God.

Since 2019, the Salt Lake City Temple has been undergoing reconstruction to ensure it can withstand an 8.0 magnitude earthquake. This remarkable engineering project was directed under the leadership of President Russell M. Nelson, who aimed to make sure that it fulfills its mission to serve as a temple of God throughout the millennium. This was also the goal of Brigham Young when he first envisioned it. They spent 40 years building it, and over the past 140 years, they have modified, strengthened, and updated it. However, this latest upgrade is unlike any other building in the world.

I need not rehearse for you all the things they did to make it capable of withstanding these great earthquakes that are coming. I bring this up from an entirely different perspective. If we view this as a symbol of the church and our personal relationship with God, how much time and energy have we invested to fortify our foundations against the coming trials upon the Earth? Some people have done nothing to change their lives for the better. They continue on as if nothing is going to change. Others have improved to varying degrees as they have listened to the spirit. And there are those who have devoted significant time and money, immersing themselves in service, food storage, financial reserves, education, Temple work, prayer, and scripture study to become the strong members they need to be, so they are ready for the coming of our Lord.

I'm confident that each of us can do more than we have in these areas, or at least in some of them. This preparation isn't just physical or even spiritual; it includes financial, emotional, familial, health, and mental aspects. Just as every part of the Salt Lake City Temple has been strengthened to endure what lies ahead, we must do the same in our lives, families, and Wards. It's not only about food storage, but those who neglect it will face challenges. It's not just spiritual preparation, because without a strong spiritual foundation, the amount of food you have will not be sufficient. I suggest we do everything we can to be ready and come to know him personally.

We know what's coming, but we've always thought it was years away. How many times have I heard people say, "My parents or grandparents once had a year's supply of food, and they never used it, so what's the point?" Other people say that it's been prophesied forever that Jesus Christ would return, but he never has, so why should I do anything more than what I'm doing? This is all part of those people who say that the Lord delays his coming.

The main purpose of this book is to clearly illustrate our current position in the Book of Revelation. Events are poised to unfold rapidly, much faster than we realize. Meanwhile, the church continues to plan for the distant future. We should adopt the same approach. It's a challenging mindset to maintain. We must prepare as if cataclysmic destruction could occur next month, while also planning for it to arrive 30 years later and planting cherry trees in the meantime. Even though we understand how imminent some of these events are, we cannot predict how long it will take to experience them. I've repeatedly tried to inform people that numerous events must occur, and many of the timelines I've observed over the past 50 years, which have never materialized, may still not hold true. Prepare for destruction both for tomorrow and in the long run.

One of the most important things we must do is get out of debt. I know that most people don't want to hear this because they want what they want right now. Our society has made it so easy to buy things on credit and avoid waiting. Most people will go for it if they can afford the payments for a bigger house. I recommend that we eliminate our debt before we try to move on to something fancier, larger, or more impressive. We are never truly free if we are in debt.

We finish off this section talking about the third Woe.

> Rev 11:15 And the seventh angel sounded; and there were great voices in heaven, saying, The kingdoms of this world are become the kingdoms of our Lord, and of his Christ; and he shall reign for ever and ever.
>
> 16 And the four and twenty elders, which sat before God on their

SECTION 6 - REVELATION CHAPTERS 8 - 11, 15 & 16

seats, fell upon their faces, and worshipped God,

17 Saying, We give thee thanks, O Lord God Almighty, which art, and wast, and art to come; because thou hast taken to thee thy great power, and hast reigned.

18 And the nations were angry, and thy wrath is come, and the time of the dead, that they should be judged, and that thou shouldest give reward unto thy servants the prophets, and to the saints, and them that fear thy name, small and great; and shouldest destroy them which destroy the earth.

19 And the temple of God was opened in heaven, and there was seen in his temple the ark of his testament: and there were lightnings, and voices, and thunderings, and an earthquake, and great hail.

16:21 And there fell upon men a great hail out of heaven, every stone about the weight of a talent: and men blasphemed God because of the plague of the hail; for the plague thereof was exceeding great.

The mission of the First Horseman, Donald Trump, is now complete. Just as Joshua was given the promised land, all the kingdoms of the world have come under Trump's rule. He presents them all to our Lord and Savior, Jesus Christ, so that He may reign forever and ever. All the elders, beasts, and countless hosts bow down before God and give Jesus Christ thanks for His power, knowledge, and wisdom. They express gratitude for making it possible for them to live with Him again. Everyone who feared His name and even died for Him will receive the blessings of the covenant given by God to the House of Israel.

The Ark of the Covenant opens in heaven just as it's presence showed God's power with Joshua. It symbolizes the mercy seat, and just as the two angels who sat in Jesus's tomb bore witness to the apostles that He was not there, the wings of two angels above the Ark testify that the atonement of Jesus Christ has accomplished all of this. The Ark contains the law as given by Jehovah Himself, the same one that paid the penalties for that law.

In the premortal councils, Lucifer tried to persuade the masses that God could use His power to save them all. He told us all something like this: *"God has tremendous power. Look at what He has created! He could use that power to save everyone. We don't have to go through this! There's a better way! We don't have to lose anyone. Now His plan calls for someone*

SECTION 6 - REVELATION CHAPTERS 8 - 11, 15 & 16

to die, but I propose that no one has to die. No one needs to be sacrificed. If He will just give me His power, I will go down and make sure that no one is lost. We can all see His power! He has the ability to do this! We need to convince Him that there is a better way and that no one will get lost!"

Some people have proposed some rather unusual theories about who tempted Lucifer to follow this path. I'm here to tell you that only one thing caused his downfall: pride. There was no external influence. We have witnessed this repeatedly in our society and even within the church. Pride has led many into the depths of despair and destruction. He ruined his own life and billions of others, all because of pride.

This war of words (war in Heaven) persisted for some time, yet God did everything possible to persuade them not to follow this plan. They were his children, and he exerted great effort to help them recognize what was wrong with their intentions. He cared deeply for each one of them. He warned them of the consequences of pursuing this path. Some people wavered between ideas, unsure of which direction to take. Others were very firm in their beliefs, but ultimately, the day of decision arrived. Those who refused to listen to God and follow his plan of salvation, which included the sacrifice of his eldest son, Jesus Christ, Jehovah, would be cast out. This was a terrible day.

Lucifer did not share the same love for God's children that Jehovah did. Furthermore, his plan would have been impossible since he attempted to fulfill it without sacrifice and prevent all sin. Instead, he aimed to rely on force, much like the worldly kingdoms have done since the fall of Adam. Moreover, Lucifer, who became Satan, was not doing it for God or His glory, it was all for his own. He wanted power and control.

For those of us who understand our eternal future, some individuals will refuse to become like our Heavenly Father because they fear facing such a tragedy of losing so many. Don't get me wrong, God resides in eternal bliss, but the Scriptures even state that He weeps for the loss of His children. Now, for all of those who have come to this earth and accepted His plan, they were tested to see if they would uphold it. This is the end; we don't know the percentage, but we know that a significant number of people did not accept that plan. Yet, the joy He has in those who do makes everything He has done worthwhile. He is so joyful for those of us who succeed!

These chapters discuss the destructions that befall those who refuse to repent. He tries everything possible to encourage them to change and accept the wonderful beauty and eternal life He desires for them. It's astonishing how many have rejected this offer.

We see this happening every day: the lies told about Joseph Smith and the Book of Mormon, the darkness that descends on the Internet as false stories are spread to demean the Church, its leaders, and its doctrine. Everything is twisted to make people uncomfortable with even looking at the Church or reading the Book of Mormon. These are all Satan's tactics to lead us to reject God's plan so that he can rule over them. Please see my chapter on the reasons why anyone who leaves the Church does so for the exact same reason as anyone else. We will all be tested to the max.

And with this Ark now visible in heaven, tremendous lightning, thundering, and earthquakes are observed and felt all over the Earth. But as bad as those are, possibly the greatest damage to date comes from a plague of 75-100 pound meteors that pummel the Earth and destroy everything that remains. It is stated that the plague was exceedingly great, and they would blaspheme God because there was nowhere to hide and nothing they could do to prevent it. It was long past time for repentance, and they failed to take advantage of it even after all the events that attempted to prompt them to repent.

These events are also recorded in Revelation chapter 19 as the King of kings and Lord of lords descends from heaven, clothed in red, accompanied by millions of others on white horses, to conquer the remaining kingdoms. In Revelation chapter 20, the angel who possesses the key to the bottomless pit, Abaddon/Apollyon, seizes Satan and the Beast, confining them within the bottomless pit and preventing their release for 1,000 years. Everything after chapter 20 in the book of Revelation represents what all of this creates: the most beautiful kingdom the world has ever known, free from death, sin, and disease, filled with righteous individuals who freely partake of the tree of life and the waters of life, and who commune with their Lord and Savior, Jesus Christ.

I long for this day. It isn't very far away. And that brings us to what I term the Seven Sevens of God.

Section 7 - The Seven Sevens of God: A Divine Pattern of Completion and Revelation

Throughout scripture, God uses the number seven as a symbol of completeness, perfection, and divine order. The number is repeated in the Bible, the Book of Mormon, the Doctrine and Covenants, and the Pearl of Great Price, underscoring its significance in God's work. This pattern is not arbitrary; rather, it is a divine signature woven into creation, prophecy, and covenant history to reveal His hand in all things. From the creation of the world to the final judgments of mankind, God's use of sevens is evident in His dealings with His children. Here, we explore seven key instances of this pattern and the overarching purpose behind it.

First Seven: The Creation of the Earth

"But the seventh day is the sabbath of the Lord thy God: in it thou shalt not do any work..." (Exodus 20:10)

The creation of the Earth was organized into seven distinct periods, often referred to as "days" in Genesis. While time as we know it may not have applied in the same way, the structure is significant:

1. Light was created, separating it from darkness.
2. The firmament divided the waters.
3. Dry land appeared, and plant life was introduced.
4. The sun, moon, and stars were set to govern times and seasons.
5. Life in the seas and air was created.
6. Land animals and mankind were brought forth.
7. God rested, sanctifying the seventh day as holy.

This pattern is echoed in modern revelation, where we learn that the earth itself was first created spiritually (Moses 3:5). The number seven represents a complete process: organization, preparation, and sanctification. The cycle of work and rest is a model for mankind, teaching us to recognize divine order in creation.

Second Seven: The 7,000-Year Temporal Existence of the Earth

"For a thousand years in thy sight are but as yesterday when it is past..." (Psalm 90:4)

SECTION 7 - THE SEVEN SEVENS OF GOD

The temporal history of the Earth is prophesied to last 7,000 years. This concept is reaffirmed in modern revelation:

"The first seal contains the things of the first thousand years... and so on until the seventh." (D&C 77:7)

The Brother of Jared saw a vision of all seven dispensations of time (Ether 3:25), and John the Revelator was given a similar record (Revelation 6:1-14). Each thousand-year period marks significant developments in God's plan:

1. Adam to Enoch – The first dispensation, ending with the translation of the City of Enoch.
2. Noah to Abraham – The flood and the establishment of the Abrahamic covenant.
3. Abraham to Moses – The Law of Moses given to Israel.
4. Moses to Christ – The meridian of time, culminating in Christ's Atonement.
5. Christ to the Restoration – Apostasy and the Restoration of the Gospel.
6. The last days – The building of Zion and the return of Jesus Christ.
7. The Millennium – A thousand years of peace before the final judgment.

This timeline shows that history is not chaotic but ordered according to divine design. The coming millennium will be the final period before the celestialization of the Earth.

Third Seven: The Seven Seals in the Book of Revelation

"And I saw in the right hand of him that sat on the throne a book written within and on the backside, sealed with seven seals." (Revelation 5:1)

The seven seals represent seven distinct periods of Earth's history, each marked by a phase of human progression and prophetic fulfillment. This concept is explained in D&C 77:6-7, indicating that each seal contains records of a thousand years of history. As Christ opens each seal, judgment and significant events unfold.

1. The First Horseman-White Horse-God's Servant
2. The Second Horseman-Red Horse-The Dragon

SECTION 7 - THE SEVEN SEVENS OF GOD

3   The Third Horseman-Black Horse-Famine
4   The Fourth Horseman-Pale Horse-Plagues
5   The Seal of Martyrs
6   The Beginning of cataclysmic events poured out on the earth, and the 144,000.
7   The Judgments of God poured out on the wicked in groups of Seven (the 4th group of Sevens below)

"The seven seals are events which occur before the opening of the book containing the 7000 year history of the earth."

These seals reveal God's long-term plan, ensuring that history follows a structured path leading to the Second Coming.

Now lets deal with the three sets of 7 in the Book of Revelation regarding the destructions and their relation to the prophecy in D&C 88.

TRUMPETS 1-7 OF REVELATION 8-11
VIALS 1-7 OF REVELATION 16
TRUMPETS OF D&C 88:94-107

1st Trumpet
Hail, fire, and blood burn a third of the earth (Rev 8:7)
Sores upon those with the Mark of the Beast (Rev 16:2)
Resurrection of Christ's first fruits (D&C 88:94-98)

2nd Trumpet
Great mountain burning with fire cast into the sea (Rev 8:8-9)
Sea becomes blood, all life in it dies (Rev 16:3)
Resurrection of those in Terrestrial glory (D&C 88:99-100)

3rd Trumpet
Great star (Wormwood) falls, poisoning rivers and waters (Rev 8:10-11)
Rivers and fountains become blood (Rev 16:4-7)
Resurrection of those in telestial glory (D&C 88:101)

4th Trumpet

SECTION 7 - THE SEVEN SEVENS OF GOD

Sun, moon, and stars darkened by a third (Rev 8:12)
Sun scorches men with fire (Rev 16:8-9)
Resurrection of those not redeemed (D&C 88:102)

5th Trumpet
Abyss opened, locusts torment humanity (Rev 9:1-11)
Darkness and pain upon the Beast kingdom (Rev 16:10-11)
Announcement of Satan's final battle (D&C 88:103)

6th Trumpet
Four angels released, a third of mankind killed (Rev 9:13-21)
Euphrates dries up, way prepared for kings of the East (Rev 16:12-16)
Final judgments poured out (D&C 88:104)

7th Trumpet
Kingdoms of the world become Christ's (Rev 11:15)
Great earthquake, Babylon falls, islands and mountains move
    (Rev 16:17-21 same as 11:13 and maybe 11:19)
Christ's return, final events completed (D&C 88:106-107)

Fourth Seven: The Seven Trumpets of Judgment

"And the seven angels which had the seven trumpets prepared themselves to sound." (Revelation 8:6)

The seven trumpets signal progressive judgments upon the world during the seventh seal. These plagues and events, described in Revelation 8-11, serve as a final warning before Christ's reign. Doctrine and Covenants 88:94-107 expands upon these judgments, explaining that each trumpet calls forth another phase of God's justice.

The trumpets serve as a sign of both destruction and deliverance, ensuring that those who will listen have a final opportunity to turn to God.

Fifth Seven: The Seven Vials of Wrath

"Go your ways, and pour out the vials of the wrath of God upon the earth." (Revelation 16:1)

In parallel to the seven trumpets, the seven vials (or bowls) of God's wrath represent the complete outpouring of justice upon the wicked before the Second Coming. These judgments serve as the final cleansing

SECTION 7 - THE SEVEN SEVENS OF GOD

before Christ establishes His millennial reign.

This cycle of judgment demonstrates the justice of God, showing that His mercy is extended as long as possible, but ultimately, wickedness will be eradicated.

Sixth Seven: The Seven Final Trumpets of Resurrection and Judgment

"And after this another angel shall sound, which is the second trump; and then cometh the redemption of those who are Christ's at his coming..." (D&C 88:99) In D&C 88:94-107, we learn of a second round of seven trumpet blasts. These do not bring destruction, but rather, resurrection and final judgment:

1. The righteous dead are resurrected.
2. Those in Terrestrial glory are judged.
3. Telestial souls are brought forth.
4. The final wicked are cast out.
5. Satan and his followers are bound.
6. The earth is prepared for celestialization.
7. Final judgment is pronounced.

This demonstrates the ultimate fulfillment of God's justice and mercy, ensuring that every soul is placed according to their choices and the atonement of Christ.

Seventh Seven: The Seven Angels Reveal the Secret Acts of Mankind

"And then shall the angels be crowned with the glory of his might, and the saints shall be filled with his glory, and receive their inheritance." (D&C 88:107)

In D&C 88:108-116, the angels who previously sounded their trumpets will sound again, this time revealing the secret acts of every person. Nothing will be hidden; all things will be made manifest. This final act ensures complete justice and transparency before the Lord.

The last seven brings all things into the light, reinforcing the truth that God sees and knows all things.

SECTION 7 - THE SEVEN SEVENS OF GOD

Why God Uses the Pattern of Seven

God's repeated use of sevens in scripture is not accidental—it serves to reveal His perfect order in all things. By structuring history, prophecy, and covenants in this manner, He teaches several divine truths:

1. God's Hand Is in All Things – Through the number seven, we see that history is carefully guided by divine intent.
2. Patterns Allow Us to Recognize His Work – Understanding these cycles helps us prepare for what is to come.
3. Mercy Before Judgment – The repeated cycles of seven show that God extends opportunities for repentance before executing final justice.
4. Completion and Fulfillment – God's work follows an established order, ensuring that His promises are fulfilled exactly as prophesied.

Through the "Seven Sevens," we see that God does not act arbitrarily—He operates according to eternal laws of justice, mercy, and order. Recognizing His patterns allows us to strengthen our faith, prepare for His return, and take part in the glorious work of establishing Zion.

The invitation remains: Will you be part of God's divine completion?

Section 8
The Four Aspects of the Kingdom of God

Section 8 - The Four Aspects of the Kingdom of God

Regarding the four different sections of the Kingdom of God, let's discuss each one for a moment. Here's how leaders and scholars within the Church of Jesus Christ of Latter-day Saints might define the four aspects of the Kingdom of God:

Political:

Definition: This aspect refers to the governance and administration of the Kingdom of God, which is expected to be established with Jesus Christ as the supreme ruler. It involves laws, order, and the political structure that will govern the earth during the Millennium, a thousand-year period following the Second Coming of Christ.

Role in the Kingdom: The political aspect anticipates a theocratic government where Christ will reign personally upon the earth. This governance would be characterized by perfect justice, peace, and righteousness, with no need for traditional human governments as we understand them today.

Ecclesiastical:

Definition: This involves the religious or church organization, including priesthood authority, ordinances, and church structure. It's the spiritual dimension where members are organized under priesthood leaders to worship, teach, and serve.

Role in the Kingdom: The ecclesiastical aspect is seen as preparatory for the full establishment of God's kingdom. It includes the restoration of the priesthood, temple work, and missionary work, all of which are steps towards the ultimate unification of all under one spiritual banner with Christ at the head.

Economic:

Definition: This aspect deals with the economic systems or stewardship principles that would govern resource distribution and labor in the Kingdom of God. Concepts like consecration and stewardship are central here, where individuals contribute to a collective good but manage their own affairs responsibly.

Role in the Kingdom: The economic system is envisioned as one of equality and stewardship, where there's no poverty due to the equitable sharing of resources. The United Order, practiced in early LDS history, is often cited as an example, although adapted for the future kingdom, emphasizing personal responsibility, collective welfare, and private ownership in the form of stewardship as outlined in scripture.

Social:

Definition: This pertains to the social structure, relationships, and community life within the Kingdom of God. It involves how individuals interact, form families, and create a society based on love, peace, and mutual respect.

Role in the Kingdom: Socially, the kingdom would be a place of perfect harmony, where all live in accordance with divine laws, promoting unity, love, and respect among all people. The eradication of social ills like crime, prejudice, and discord would be a hallmark of this aspect, with an emphasis on the family as the core unit of society.

"In LDS theology, these four aspects are interconnected, each playing a vital role in the full realization of the Kingdom of God on earth, particularly during the Millennium. They are seen as both preparation for and characteristics of the divine governance that will come with Christ's Second Coming, leading to a time of peace, justice, and righteousness under His direct rule. However, interpretations can vary, and these descriptions aim to capture the general teachings and expectations within the Church."[19]

While that's a solid overall observation, and I don't have many complaints, I want to highlight a couple of points here. Regarding the political aspect, we are discussing the preparation for the return of our Savior, Jesus Christ. He will be the one to rule over all the nations of the Earth throughout the millennium. The First Horseman must set all of this in motion, which involves subduing nations and the emergence of the New Jerusalem, along with everything else we've been discussing. This is Donald Trump's mission—his foreordained calling to achieve on the earth.

SECTION 8 - THE 4 ASPECTS OF THE KINGDOM OF GOD

While much of this book focuses on the Political Kingdom of God, I want to mention a few words about the Social aspect of the kingdom of God and then delve into the Economic side of it. The definition of the social side provided is accurate, as it centers around family. But what makes this family different from the ones we currently have? Why does it need to be restored? Why was it lost in the first place? Is there a way we can start this process right now? Is there something we need to change right now to get ready?

God's kingdom is structured under a patriarchal system. A man serves as the patriarch of his family. He collaborates with his wife but retains the presiding authority.

Now I can already hear some people cringing at this suggestion. Our society has diminished the power of patriarchs so much that many want nothing to do with it. All they focus on are the terrible things that men have done. I'm not denying that awful events have occurred, but please bear with me for a moment and allow me to show you where I think we should go.

Imagine for a moment that a husband and wife have two sons and two daughters. Each of them gets married and has two sons and two daughters, continuing this pattern until we reach four generations. How many people does that total? According to ChatGPT, it adds up to 341! (I have no idea why it's an odd number.)

I remember the birth of my first children as if it were yesterday. It was one of the greatest experiences of my life. The spirit of God came upon me, making me aware that He had entrusted me with one of His children (in this case, two because we had twins) to teach and raise to the best of my abilities, according to the commandments and teachings I believed to be true. It was a powerful spiritual experience, and I know that many others have had similar experiences. I had the same experience with all my children, but the first one holds a special place because it's the first.

However, a different feeling washes over you when you see the birth of your first grandchild. It is an incredible joy, likely linked to the knowledge that your legacy continues. It's an amazing sensation, and each of my grandchildren brings me immense joy. They look at me and listen to my words. They respect my opinions and love spending time with me. I can also relax a bit more, as being a grandparent is easier than being a parent; you have them for a few hours, and then you can send them home. You've

SECTION 8 - THE 4 ASPECTS OF THE KINGDOM OF GOD

already faced all the challenges of everyday parenting.

I'm far from being a great-grandparent, but I can't imagine it would be any less joyful than my first grandkids. It might even be better. However, there are families with four generations of living children, which can form quite a large group. I've used simple numbers above just to illustrate a point.

In the patriarchal social structure of the kingdom of God, this is a crucial aspect of life. A family raised in a system where men are respected and regarded as patriarchs can have a significant impact on everyone in the family.

This is God's system, and Satan has done everything possible to destroy it. I know that many people struggle with patriarchy because the media has worked hard to portray it negatively. Every negative example has been shoved in our faces to dismiss it. Any form of abuse, being overbearing, angry, or the buzzword of the day, "toxic masculinity," is all they focus on. Yes, it's true that these things have occurred, but that doesn't make the system bad; it indicates that these men were not fully embodying it.

As I watch almost anything today on movies or television, men and fathers receive little support or encouragement in their role as the head of the household. They are often the butt of jokes. Men were once portrayed as the providers, protectors, and defenders of their families. They were the ones who caught the bad guys, arrested criminals, and served justice. Now, they have been almost entirely replaced. Wonder Woman has emerged and shattered everything that used to represent men. Who needs a husband or a man when a beautiful, strong woman with incredible power can accomplish the task?

Men have little to look forward to at present. The media portrays them as needing to be either like Dwayne "The Rock" Johnson or Pee-wee Herman, leaving little room in between. When women are encouraged to embody roles beyond just the loving and nurturing figure of family, which includes the rightful bearing and raising of children, and are instead expected to be breadwinners, men often feel excluded. Our society has strayed significantly regarding finances, necessitating that most families have both parents working to earn a living. As a result, men frequently feel unnecessary. If they don't earn enough money in the eyes of women who see the extravagant lifestyles showcased on TV and social media—such as luxury cars and elaborate trips—they may feel inadequate and worthless. They struggle to

SECTION 8 - THE 4 ASPECTS OF THE KINGDOM OF GOD

keep up.

I know that many women think it's silly for a man to be upset when she earns more than he does. They often view it as a sign of jealousy or a lack of understanding. They belittle such men and move on to find someone else. I'm just here to tell you that if men cannot be the providers they are meant to be, they will never feel truly happy. If they are competing with their wives over who can earn the most, it's already a losing battle. You can resist it all you want, you can complain about reality, but it cannot be changed. I don't care how many men say it doesn't matter to them; deep down, it does, but they won't admit it. They desperately need something to prove that they have meaning, purpose, and a reason to be part of the family.

It's impossible to list everything that has gone wrong with the family over the last 50 years. However, this needs to be restored for the Kingdom of God to move forward properly. This will be very difficult because it will require a drastic change in attitude and understanding.

But why change it anyway? Because of the influence of a properly run patriarchal order on the family. Watching children grow up, they need good examples. They need a loving mother and a father who encourages them to try something different and difficult. Go ahead and skin your knee. Go ahead and fight for yourself and stand up against the bully. Mothers cringe at such things, but boys need to learn this.

We rely heavily on the criminal justice system to manage teenagers who have gone out of control. Such a situation is unlikely in a patriarchal system, as it would probably never escalate to that point. When a family is united and justice is administered within a patriarchal system, there is little need for our current family court system. When children understand that being part of the family brings benefits, they are much easier to guide toward doing the right thing. Who wants to be excluded from such blessings? Who wants to be ostracized from a tribe they belong to? From a group that loves, cares for, and provides them with focus and purpose.

Everyone enjoys exploring genealogy to learn about their relatives. Some might say, "My ancestors came on the Mayflower!" Others might claim, "I'm a descendant of Charlemagne." When a family operates within a patriarchal system and in a society that is economically balanced—where they contribute what they can at their respective ages—it's truly a beautiful thing. When the education system is structured under the patriarchal model, they learn in ways that could never be taught in our current schools.

Patriarchs, fathers, and grandfathers who hold authority in this system resemble kings, though not the kings of the world. These kings care deeply for their descendants and the decisions they make. They ensure that these descendants are educated in the right way and manner. None of these values prevail in our society because there is little motivation beyond a weekly paycheck. There is no incentive to impart morals, ethics, or practical skills like fixing a car. It is merely a job. Consequently, the leadership of organizations such as the Department of Education has sought to undermine family values. They are teaching content that directly contradicts God's teachings and the patriarchal order, as well as subjects that they should not be imparting.

The only true department of education that we need to be involved in is the patriarchal order. I'm not dismissing the possibility of having classes of the same age meet together from neighboring families taught by men and women of different backgrounds and specialties. That seems to make a lot of sense, as no one family will possess all the tools necessary to teach their children every subject. However, multiple families collaborating can yield astonishing results.

We need to establish this order if we want to be ready for Zion. We must begin today and bring back the roles of husbands, fathers, and patriarchs of our families and give them the respect they deserve. Oh, it will be difficult. I've already mentioned that society has done everything it can to destroy fathers, but it's the only way to move forward.

We often discuss the need for change in the economy and to live according to the law of consecration. We anticipate a political system led by a strong, just, and fair leader who fulfills the role as intended. However, we rarely address the necessity for a shift in our social structure and a return to what God ordained in pre-mortal life! The destruction of the family is one of Satan's most devastating actions. He will stop at nothing to dismantle that order because it holds such power.

I pray that we will seriously consider this because the alternative is what we currently have, and it isn't working. Men need to be treated as men. They need to be masculine, determined, and in charge. They need to be the defenders and protectors of their families. Anyone who does anything to their children should be met with justice by the father and supported by society. They need to be revered for their role instead of diminished, so they can't perform it.

I encourage women to become feminine, look up to their men, and give them applause and appreciation. Honor him. Thank him. Compliment him, and encourage him to be the man you want. He won't be perfect—no one is—but find the good in him, and it will grow.

Many men today fear that they lack value, using their natural attraction to women as an excuse to seek someone else who makes them feel manly. I'm not justifying his adultery or escapades; I'm merely presenting a reason. There is no justification for it. In their pursuit of another person, they feel more masculine. Instead of being judged and made to look foolish, someone else desires them.

Let's return the family to its intended design: a husband and wife working together to bring about the next generation in righteousness. The husband is the leader, provider, and protector; he is neither abusive nor overbearing. I hope you've had the chance to hear the powerful words shared by a temple sealer who joins a man and woman in celestial marriage. They each covenant to uphold very specific commitments that align with God's desires for His children. They covenant to love each other, and the husband promises to rule with unfeigned love.

One day, I was driving my pickup with my son. He was sitting in the seat next to me, and I was playing a game with him. I don't remember the game's details, but he was laughing. We were having a wonderful time at a stop sign, doing something silly.

SECTION 8 - THE 4 ASPECTS OF THE KINGDOM OF GOD

I noticed a school bus pull up next to us. I happened to glance at the windows and saw about a dozen boys around his age, their noses pressed against the glass as they looked down at us. I thought that was a bit odd, but I could tell they were very interested in what we were doing. I then looked at the name on the side of the bus; it was a boys' club for children without parents. My heart broke. These poor children longed for the attention of a loving father. They had no one to look up to. Every child needs to be raised by both a father and a mother—not just a father, not just a mother, not two fathers or two mothers, but a father and a mother who love each other and work together.

One day, I was walking through the park on a sunny afternoon when a group of boys on bicycles and skateboards started having fun together. But boys will be boys, and they began to fight in a somewhat playful manner, yet with real consequences. Mind you, no one had mouth guards or boxing gloves, and I watched as someone got hit on the chin and reeled back in pain. I'm not sure how long it went on as I walked past, but I was thinking of two things. First, I wondered how many of these boys had fathers in their homes. Did they have someone to teach them how to defend themselves and how to be boys? What kind of examples did they have to guide them in such situations?

The other thing I was thinking about is how sad I am that the boy scouting program has lost its moral compass. Instead of aligning with Lord Baden Powell's original goals of teaching young men to become men, they seem to prioritize increasing membership; in other words, it's about money. I've been to Scout camp dozens of times, and I have always regretted having any girls there in any position. Whether it was a lifeguard or someone behind the Cracker Barrel, once there was a girl at camp, the boys turned into idiots. They need to learn how to be boys. I'm hoping the Boy Scouts will return to their original foundation instead of the woke ideology that has destroyed such a wonderful program.

This is part of God's plan for the establishment of His kingdom that is approaching.

Many individuals have been quite critical of the Church of Jesus Christ of Latter-day Saints and the doctrine that we can become like God. How dare we! That is blasphemy and offensive! You're promoting the same idea

SECTION 8 - THE 4 ASPECTS OF THE KINGDOM OF GOD

that Satan tried to convey to Adam and Eve, leading them astray!

Let's examine these verses closely:

Gen 3:1 Now the serpent was more subtil than any beast of the field which the Lord God had made. And he said unto the woman, Yea, hath God said, Ye shall not eat of every tree of the garden?

2 And the woman said unto the serpent, We may eat of the fruit of the trees of the garden:

3 But of the fruit of the tree which is in the midst of the garden, God hath said, Ye shall not eat of it, neither shall ye touch it, lest ye die.

4 And the serpent said unto the woman, Ye shall not surely die:

5 For God doth know that in the day ye eat thereof, then your eyes shall be opened, and ye shall be as gods, knowing good and evil.

According to verse five, it states that they shall become gods, knowing good from evil. It's important to recognize that Satan always mixes truth with lies. If he only told lies, we would quickly realize that nothing he said was correct. Many people teach that he only speaks lies, but that can't be true, and this serves as a perfect example. He mixes truth with lies to deceive us. When we hear the truth, we recognize it, making it easier to accept a lie if it is tied to that truth. The lie here is that they would not die. He was suggesting that God was a liar. God said that if they took the fruit, they would die, while Satan claimed that wasn't true. He then stated that on the day you eat of it, your eyes will be opened, and you shall be like gods, knowing good and evil. And that's precisely what occurred. They became like God, knowing good and evil!

Gen 3: 22 ¶ And the Lord God said, Behold, the man is become as one of us, to know good and evil: and now, lest he put forth his hand, and take also of the tree of life, and eat, and live for ever:

23 Therefore the Lord God sent him forth from the garden of Eden, to till the ground from whence he was taken.

24 So he drove out the man; and he placed at the east of the garden of Eden Cherubims, and a flaming sword which turned every way, to keep the way of the tree of life.

SECTION 8 - THE 4 ASPECTS OF THE KINGDOM OF GOD

God clearly states that they have become like one of us, knowing good and evil. The purpose of this entire scenario was to lead them to introduce death into the world. Adam and Eve were unable to have children. They needed to replace the spiritual fluid in their bodies with blood, which could only occur through sin, or in this case, transgression.

This was all part of the plan. However, if Adam and Eve had rushed forward and eaten the fruit from the tree of life, they would have lived forever in their sins. They would never have been able to overcome that, and God could not save them in that condition. It would be impossible for Him to do anything to bring them back, so He placed a Cherubim there to protect them.

The main purpose of this analysis is that we are to become like God. That's what His entire plan of salvation is about. Satan told part of the truth; however, it isn't complete until after they are resurrected. That's another topic for another day, so let me return to this point now.

I mentioned earlier the glorious spirit I felt when I had my first children. Let me say again, it's a marvelous experience. And what joy I felt when my children had children! Was I jealous that they had children? Heavens no! I wanted them to have children. I wanted them to experience the same joy that I did. This brings me tremendous joy. No grandfather is jealous of his grandson achieving the status of father.

The same is true in the heavens. God wants us to become like Him. He's not jealous of us achieving His status. He has created this entire system so that we can become like Him. He desires for us to live forever with Him in eternal glory, engaging in the same activities He does. He's filled with joy when we reach that status. We will always honor and worship Him for granting us this astonishing opportunity. Our love and reverence toward Him and His Son, Jesus Christ, for making it all possible will never diminish. This is the eternal cycle of the Celestial Kingdom.

You'll notice that we don't hear about our Mother in Heaven. I know there has been much discussion on this topic, and people have gone to great lengths to demonstrate that this may have been the case in the past, but we must rely on what we know. We are aware that she exists because of the teachings of the prophet Joseph Smith and his marvelous revelations. We recognize that a few instances in the scriptures have been altered to remove her existence from our records, but I submit that there's another reason. Our Father and God wants to protect His wife. It's one thing to curse and demean Him, as is often done on a daily basis in our society, but I don't believe He'd be as patient if someone used those same terms against His love. In other words, it's for our protection that He has reserved detailed knowledge about her. I also believe there are several other reasons why she remains hidden, but that's for another day.

This is what patriarchy represents: becoming like our Father in Heaven, who rules over billions of children and protects his wife. That patriarchal order is what we should emulate here on Earth. When a father and husband is treated as someone deserving of respect, nothing can stop him from fulfilling his responsibilities within his family. Nothing. I don't want to use the word "worship" here; let's use "respect" instead. If he is respected for his position and his potential future, he can achieve anything.

Let's return to the patriarchal order of God, which represents the social aspect of the political kingdom of God. We should have started this 50 years ago.

Economic portion of the Kingdom of God.

Many books discuss how the law of consecration works in the church and society. The Doctrine & Covenants has 17 sections devoted to this subject. Living within the system makes it possible for us to follow God's commandment in D&C 49:20:

SECTION 8 - THE 4 ASPECTS OF THE KINGDOM OF GOD

"But it is not given that one man should possess that which is above another; wherefore the world lieth in sin."

This is very different from the Babylonian world we currently live in.

God's laws are based on the fact that He owns everything, and we are appointed as stewards over a particular portion of that property. It is not just land or a home; it's everything we have: our businesses, our responsibilities, and our duties. It is given to us as a steward for as long as we live and are responsible for maintaining it.

The world lives by one motto: have more than your neighbor. There is an insatiable urge to constantly acquire more, as additional property often brings additional power or influence. We respect those who own multimillion-dollar homes or fancy cars. If money is the only objective, without ethics attached, it's very easy to make. Too often, we associate the wealthy with being blessed by God, when in reality, several other factors usually contribute to the property they have acquired.

Much of what they have is not truly theirs. In this desire for recognition and superiority, people have taken on great debts to maintain a specific image. But problems arise when their expected income drops for any reason. Whether it's an economic depression, an accident, an illness, fraud or deception by employees, partners, competitors, or natural disasters like floods or tornadoes, once the stream of income they depended on stops coming, they are faced with difficult decisions.

My father told me a story about a farmer who faced an extremely difficult challenge that could result in the loss of his family farm, which had been in the family for over 150 years. Farming is a tough business, but he found himself in a position where the only way he could think of to get the money he needed to pay his bills was to fake an accident by shoving his hands into a wood chipper. When the insurance company conducted their investigation and uncovered the fraud, he found himself in really deep trouble. I don't know what happened in the end, but it doesn't matter. People have done far worse than that when they are financially destitute or worried about what to do next.

As I mentioned in Section 4 regarding Revelation 13, we have been commanded to become self-reliant, independent, and self-sufficient since the beginning of the Restoration of the Gospel. However, when we see someone who has more than we do, human nature, for a large percentage of the population, does not like that. They don't want to wait, save, build, or plan for the future. They want it right now, and the Babylonian system we live under makes it possible for you to appear as though you can have it right now if you'll just sign this form and turn over your life. Our life is actually what we are exchanging for the things we possess. Whatever time we spend on anything is the cost of that object.

God's law of consecration does not work that way. We are not to have more than another, and this is one of the reasons why it did not work in the early years of the restoration. This is something we must overcome in order to be allowed to live in Zion. I submit that, of all the things that are going to be required of us, even in the midst of the possibility of world war, this may be the most challenging because it requires humility, complete conversion to the gospel, and putting others above self.

One day, I was walking through the BYU bookstore after graduating. I saw a book on the shelf entitled, "Approaching Zion" by Hugh Nibley. Something drew me to it, and I immediately bought it. I devoured that book. I was so impressed with it that I walked up to Hugh Nibley's house, knocked on the door, and asked him to sign it. I thanked him personally for writing it and told him how much it meant to me.

When I started a business in 1992, this book proved to be a great source of guidance for me in building my company. I didn't take the usual dog-eat-dog world approach; I tried to view things as best I could from a Zion perspective. Sadly, in the competitive realm of international business, it's very difficult to maintain. Everything is so cutthroat, and everyone is so greedy. It caused me considerable stress to adhere to those teachings, as I was concerned about upholding correct values and gospel principles while simultaneously building a business and owing money on very expensive machinery.

Everything in the business world revolves around one word: profits. Although people claim other factors matter, if there's ever a conflict between profits and anything else, profits prevail.

There are countless business, marketing, management, strategic, and historical books on how to make money. I'm not going to delve into that

SECTION 8 - THE 4 ASPECTS OF THE KINGDOM OF GOD

here. None of them adhere to the scripture quoted above, which states that, according to God, the world lies in sin because it's not intended for one person to have more than another. None of those books teach that principle. They wouldn't sell if they promoted that idea. Everyone wants to know how to have more.

The opposite side of that is Satan's plan to make everybody equal, executed with force, not out of love and not from the heart. It exploits people's natural inhibitions regarding the vast gaps between the rich and the poor and asserts that by appointing a small group of people to oversee everything, they will ensure that everyone is equal. Socialism has never worked. It never will work. Hundreds of millions of people have died as testimony to that fact.

So that brings us to a significant dilemma: how can we achieve the equality required by God to participate in the law of consecration amid current conditions driven by self-interest?

Let's examine a few aspects of the current corporate world we inhabit.

We have all seen the deplorable conditions of massive chicken farms, where the birds never see the light of day and are injected with chemicals to plump them up to the point where they cannot even walk. Or consider the multiple high-rise pig farms, where the animals never touch the ground and are housed in concrete and metal, hosed off and cleaned daily, and butchered mechanically. How about the cows on immense dairy farms that never experience green pastures? These poor animals have no life whatsoever; they were not created to live this way.

Those who have created these mechanical profit-making devices are disobeying a very important principle from God. In D&C 59:16-20, he gives us the following marvelous words and answer to how we should treat the things of the Earth that provide food and clothing:

> 16 Verily I say, that inasmuch as ye do this, the fulness of the earth is yours, the beasts of the field and the fowls of the air, and that which climbeth upon the trees and walketh upon the earth;
>
> 17 Yea, and the herb, and the good things which come of the earth, whether for food or for raiment, or for houses, or for barns, or for orchards, or for gardens, or for vineyards;

SECTION 8 - THE 4 ASPECTS OF THE KINGDOM OF GOD

> 18 Yea, all things which come of the earth, in the season thereof, are made for the benefit and the use of man, both to please the eye and to gladden the heart;
>
> 19 Yea, for food and for raiment, for taste and for smell, to strengthen the body and to enliven the soul.
>
> 20 And it pleaseth God that he hath given all these things unto man; for unto this end were they made to be used, with judgment, not to excess, neither by extortion.

There is one word in this section that alters everything in the inhumane corporate money grab I outlined above. Do you see what it is?

The word is extortion. Does that not perfectly describe exactly what's happening to these poor animals? They are being extorted. In the race for profitability, every single corner has been cut, but the most important thing that has been eliminated is their ability to enjoy any life whatsoever. That's not the life God intended for them. What does it say in Genesis regarding the world God created for them?

> Genesis 1:20 And God said, Let the waters bring forth abundantly the moving creature that hath life, and fowl that may fly above the earth in the open firmament of heaven.
>
> 21 And God created great whales, and every living creature that moveth, which the waters brought forth abundantly, after their kind, and every winged fowl after his kind:
>
> 22 And God blessed them, saying, Be fruitful, and multiply, and fill the waters in the seas, and let fowl multiply in the earth.
>
> 24 And God said, Let the earth bring forth the living creature after his kind, cattle, and creeping thing, and beast of the earth after his kind: and it was so…and God saw that it was good.

He said to fill the Earth, the skies, and the seas, not 18-story high-rise complexes with no windows. Not gigantic metal behemoths that house 2 million birds all packed right next to each other. Not row after row of cattle that provide milk through machines and are penned up in a small stall barely bigger than the animals.

We are all caught in this trap because consumers demand the lowest prices. They will see something that's $.10 less than another item and buy it,

SECTION 8 - THE 4 ASPECTS OF THE KINGDOM OF GOD

claiming that the corporation is greedy. The entire world is driven by money, but it's all an illusion. And sadly, the extortion extends far beyond these examples. In Section 11 I will show another sin in how we misuse the land.

When Donald Trump establishes Zion, the kingdom of God, and within it lies the law of consecration, the prosperity, productivity, and livelihood of everyone in this city reveal tremendous growth and potential. The kings of the earth will desire this for themselves. What they've never heard, they will consider. This has never been taught to them. It was never even an option, as they could only perceive capitalism, communism, or socialism. Understand me; the law of consecration is a capitalist system, but it's not the same as the purely selfish version we currently live under.

When people adhere to the law, follow the commandments, and prioritize one another's well-being, everyone benefits, thrives, and has their needs met. People are much healthier when they produce most of their own food, and living a pure life greatly diminishes the incidence of diseases and ailments.

Children in Zion are educated in schools that impart righteous principles, allowing everyone to learn about the things of God. They are nurtured in a spirit of education, improvement, and becoming like God. Ultimately, when the entire world transforms into a terrestrial planet, there will be no disease, poison, pain, or death. *We won't even be eating animals, as the lion will eat straw like the ox!* (Isaiah 11:6-9)

This day is approaching quickly. We need to rethink how we operate our businesses, how we treat our bosses and employees, the kind of work we do, and our motivations for earning more money. If our only goal is to have more than our neighbors and appear superior to them, we will never be able to embrace the law of consecration. This is as crucial as preparing a year's supply of food, saving a year's supply of money or fuel, and attending the temple to become spiritually ready. Our attitudes toward employment and our efforts to uplift those around us are also evaluated. One of the best indicators of how well we are progressing in this area is through our tithing, fast offerings, service, and ministering assignments.

We stand on the brink of the most significant transformation in world history. Most of the prophecies we've received all point to this moment. This change calls for a profound shift within each of us. Consider the

SECTION 8 - THE 4 ASPECTS OF THE KINGDOM OF GOD

parable of the five wise and five foolish virgins—it is a reflection on the active members of our church today. Among those who are active, only half have adequately prepared themselves to enter the bridegroom's chamber. The other half, while making commendable efforts towards this goal, are still missing one essential element. Will you take a moment to discover what that is?

> Matt 25:1 Then shall the kingdom of heaven be likened unto ten virgins, which took their lamps, and went forth to meet the bridegroom.
>
> 2 And five of them were wise, and five were foolish.
>
> 3 They that were foolish took their lamps, and took no oil with them:
>
> 4 But the wise took oil in their vessels with their lamps.
>
> 5 While the bridegroom tarried, they all slumbered and slept.
>
> 6 And at midnight there was a cry made, Behold, the bridegroom cometh; go ye out to meet him.
>
> 7 Then all those virgins arose, and trimmed their lamps.
>
> 8 And the foolish said unto the wise, Give us of your oil; for our lamps are gone out.
>
> 9 But the wise answered, saying, Not so; lest there be not enough for us and you: but go ye rather to them that sell, and buy for yourselves.
>
> 10 And while they went to buy, the bridegroom came; and they that were ready went in with him to the marriage: and the door was shut.
>
> 11 Afterward came also the other virgins, saying, Lord, Lord, open to us.
>
> 12 But he answered and said, Verily I say unto you, **Ye know me not**.
>
> 13 Watch therefore, for ye know neither the day nor the hour wherein the Son of man cometh.

Joseph Smith, in his inspired translation of the New Testament, altered those four words in verse 12. There has been much discussion regarding what defines someone as a wise or foolish virgin. The key here is knowing Jesus Christ. This is the most worthwhile goal we can achieve in this life.

Section 9-One Mighty and Strong

In the Doctrine and Covenants, it has been prophesied that one mighty and strong will come forth with a scepter of power. Here is the verse that is most often quoted:

> D&C 85:7 And it shall come to pass that I, the Lord God, will send one mighty and strong, holding the scepter of power in his hand, clothed with light for a covering, whose mouth shall utter words, eternal words; while his bowels shall be a fountain of truth, to set in order the house of God, and to arrange by lot the inheritances of the saints whose names are found, and the names of their fathers, and of their children, enrolled in the book of the law of God;

What is sad is that most people have misquoted this verse and misused it as a weapon against the current church leadership over various issues. A casual reading suggests that something is prophesied to be wrong with the church, and therefore God is going to send someone mighty and strong to correct the problem. That is incorrect.

I'm only going to list one subject associated with this issue because it's still fresh in our minds and has led many people to leave the church. That subject is the COVID-19 vaccine. I don't think any of us will ever forget the chaotic world we entered in February 2020. I don't need to recount the bizarre scenario that was thrust upon us, forcing everyone to wear masks, maintain social distancing, stop attending church, believe that just two weeks would make everything better, refrain from going to work, work from home, avoid stores, yet find it acceptable to go to bars, along with a host of other arbitrary, capricious, and tyrannical mandates. One of the most egregious as-

SECTION 9 - ONE MIGHTY AND STRONG

pects of this whole situation was watching those videos of nurses dancing in the hospital, attempting to lighten the seriousness of what was happening. It's proof that we were all deceived.

I know many people lost their jobs for refusing the shot, but most did not stand up against it. The heavy-handed censorship of anyone who tried to speak out against this flagrant misuse of medical tyranny resulted in their firing, disbarment, removal of licenses, shadow banning on social media, and even suspension of their accounts. Anyone who "questioned the science" was deemed someone who didn't care about others and would not bow to an authority that knew what was right. This was a terrible time in the world, and someday we will know the full truth regarding this issue and the reasons for all of the deception, heavy-handedness, and tyrannical actions.

President Russell M. Nelson was the prophet of the church at that time and suggested that everyone get the vaccine, and to consult with their doctors and pray before receiving it. In August 2021, a letter was issued, signed by the First Presidency, conveying the same message. Many interpreted this as a commandment, but it was not. Yes, they were shown on television getting the shot and appeared to comply with everything the government mandated.

As was later revealed to the public, the shots distributed by the government were not what they were advertised to be and have caused numerous injuries and even deaths. The whole world was deceived regarding this terrible pandemic, including President Trump. President Nelson faced heavy criticism for his actions, and many people have used D&C 85:7 as a basis for either their departure from the church or for demands that he be replaced because they did not understand a couple of very important principles.

From the 1840s to the 1890s, the church practiced polygamy, which was consistently viewed unfavorably by outsiders. I don't have time to delve into all the details of this practice, so please forgive me for not including every nuance. What I will say is that neither Joseph Smith nor Brigham Young wished to partake in it. Ultimately, when Wilford Woodruff became president of the church, the government was determined to abolish this practice. At least, that's how it has been represented over the years. The true motive may actually differ, and this was promoted as the official justification. It's possible that there was opposition to the church establishing its own banking system, and they wanted everyone to conform to the current system we live under today.[20] This has happened to multiple countries over the years.

The point is that the government came in and arrested many of our church leaders. They confiscated church property, resources, and money. There was extreme pressure on the church that nearly destroyed it. Reading the story in the book series "The Saints" will help you understand just how difficult this was to endure. President Woodruff received the Manifesto ceasing the practice and informing all the members that we would no longer live by this law. From that moment on, the church continued to move forward, and this grew into what it is today, but it was a long process before it gained much traction. Many members denounced President Woodruff and claimed he was a false prophet. They argued that the command had come from the prophet Joseph Smith and that he had no right to discontinue it. We needed to stand up to the government and not allow this commandment to be ignored. Many people left the church because of its capitulation on this issue, and almost every offshoot of the church that exists today was born from this conflict.

When COVID-19 emerged and the Beast System did everything it could to force people under its rule, I'm positive they were looking for someone to be the poster child for what happens when orders are ignored. If the church had stood up and demanded our constitutional rights, claiming we had no reason to submit to such unjust acts, I believe they would have come in and shut down the church. Do I have proof of this suggestion? No, but it's the only explanation that makes sense regarding why our leadership encouraged us to go along with it.

Why do I mention this here? Because we are not the entirety of God's political kingdom. We lack the ability to engage politically, with military force and all it entails, against this profoundly unjust action. As we now understand, Covid and it's "prevention and cures" has claimed millions of lives around the world, but if the church had opposed it, we wouldn't be rebuilding and reinforcing the Salt Lake Temple today. We wouldn't be announcing new temples across the globe. We wouldn't be involved in missionary work, humanitarian efforts, and the genealogical and educational initiatives we are currently undertaking. We would have exemplified to the world what happens when anyone refuses to yield to tyranny.

SECTION 9 - ONE MIGHTY AND STRONG

I'm sure President Nelson did not want to issue that directive. It may have been the hardest thing he's ever done, considering his significant experience as a doctor. He recognized that these vaccines did not undergo the appropriate trials and testing. He understood that this was misleading medicine and sensed something else was afoot. I believe this was a significant challenge for President Nelson to confront, yet he complied with the instructions given.

In the future, things will be different when we are the complete Kingdom of God, with the ability to stand up and defend ourselves. We won't have to tolerate anything like this again.

Now, to those who have distanced themselves from the church because of this issue, I encourage you to return. I have friends and church members who lost their lives due to COVID-19, the vaccine, the treatments- everything. I have friends who have left because of the actions of church leadership and others who are still allowing it to fester against their testimonies. This was a difficult trial for everyone. I nearly died from COVID myself, and the only thing that saved me was the horse paste that the news media claimed wasn't for human consumption.

This has been a significant trial for many members of the church and continues to be. They discuss matters negatively and reference all sorts of evidence they believe point to an incorrect analysis of why President Nelson acted as he did. We will all be judged by how we respond to this and every other situation in the world and in the church. I encourage anyone who harbors hard feelings about this to recognize what is truly happening and to return. If you found it difficult to cope with, it was only a glimpse of what's ahead. Tremendous trials await us that will require every ounce of faith we possess. We will need faith, spirit, testimony, healing, power, and the priesthood like never before.

But you won't stand a chance outside the church. Please return.

Let's examine D&C 85 in more detail, which discusses a mighty and strong one who will come forth in the latter days. If you read the entire section, it pertains entirely to establishing Zion and the associated inheritances.

Let's look at the first five verses of the same section:

D&C 87:1 It is the duty of the Lord's clerk, whom he has appointed,

SECTION 9 - ONE MIGHTY AND STRONG

to keep a history, and a general church record of all things that transpire in Zion, and of all those who consecrate properties, and receive inheritances legally from the bishop;

2 And also their manner of life, their faith, and works; and also of the apostates who apostatize after receiving their inheritances.

3 It is contrary to the will and commandment of God that those who receive not their inheritance by consecration, agreeable to his law, which he has given, that he may tithe his people, to prepare them against the day of vengeance and burning, should have their names enrolled with the people of God.

4 Neither is their genealogy to be kept, or to be had where it may be found on any of the records or history of the church.

5 Their names shall not be found, neither the names of the fathers, nor the names of the children written in the book of the law of God, saith the Lord of Hosts.

This section focuses on maintaining records and establishing Zion through consecration under the bishop's guidance. The church must document everything that occurs within its community, including the statements made by individuals who have apostatized after receiving inheritances.

Clearly, some things have changed somewhat since this was first presented in 1832, as individuals were expected to transfer their property and then receive what they were to inherit in return. If they renounce their faith, the record of their life, faith, and works will not be documented.

But the purpose of all this is to prepare us for the day of vengeance and burning. If we do not receive our inheritance through consecration, our genealogy will not be maintained, and our name will not appear in the church records! Neither our fathers nor our children are written in the book of the law!

Most people fail to recognize the importance of this chapter. It does not address future leaders who will replace those God has appointed; the leader who arises in the last days will organize Zion similarly. Instead, it discusses those who wish to be part of Zion and offers a serious warning against those who believe they have a better idea and attempt to steady the ark: the shaft of death!

SECTION 9 - ONE MIGHTY AND STRONG

D&C 85:8 While that man, who was called of God and appointed, that putteth forth his hand to steady the ark of God, shall fall by the shaft of death, like as a tree that is smitten by the vivid shaft of lightning.

Notice the specific details here. Someone called of God and appointed to a position in the church has responsibility over something. Whether it is a Stake President, Bishop, Elders Quorum or Relief Society President, Deacon, Teacher, or Priest, etc. and this injunction is not limited to men. If they speak out, claiming a better way, they put themselves above those God has chosen to lead the church. They will fall like lightning, similar to how Lucifer fell from heaven. Have you ever seen a video of a tree being hit by lightning? It is astonishing. That same danger awaits those who think they have a better way or claim that God's appointed have fallen.

Just as Moses was a great builder, Donald Trump is also a great builder and understands real estate and building. He will organize Zion for the righteous. Those who speak out against him risk suffering this consequence.

This is where he becomes the prophesied King David, who sits on his throne and rules the world. Most people consider this to be Jesus Christ, but this is incorrect. It refers to God's Servant. It's been said that this servant will be named David, but that is a title. His name is Donald Trump, and he will rule the world. His name actually means "world ruler who triumphs." There are numerous references to Trump in Isaiah, and Ezekiel 34 and 37 speaks of a great leader in the last days. Here in Moses 1:41 it says:

Moses 1:41 And in a day when the children of men shall esteem my words as naught and take many of them from the book which thou shalt write, behold, I will raise up another like unto thee; and they shall be had again among the children of men—among as many as shall believe.

This verse describes how, in the last days, God will raise up one likened to Himself, who revealed His words through another individual like him who will also be raised up. This seemingly references what Jesus told the Nephites in 3 Nephi 21. While many believe this refers to Joseph Smith, it does not.

This is what it says in

3 Nephi 21: 2 And behold, this is the thing which I will give unto you for a sign—for verily I say unto you that when these things which

SECTION 9 - ONE MIGHTY AND STRONG

I declare unto you, and which I shall declare unto you hereafter of myself, and by the power of the Holy Ghost which shall be given unto you of the Father, shall be made known unto the Gentiles that they may understand concerning this people who are a remnant of the house of Jacob, and concerning this my people who shall be scattered by them;

What's interesting here is that it discusses things He, Jesus, will speak about afterward. We have only a few chapters of information He delivered to those people. This is the coming forth from the large plates of Nephi and the sealed portion of the gold plates from which the Book of Mormon was translated. The things that were taught by Jesus were not revealed during Joseph Smith's translation of the Book of Mormon. This hints at a future event that comes under the hands of God's servant Donald Trump when the large plates of Nephi and the Brass Plates will come forth along with all of the records of the Nephites. Most likely, this will occur before Jesus opens the seventh seal of the sealed plates. This will be an astonishing day!

Several attributes associated with God's servant include: he is hidden (1 Ne 21:22). His image is marred more than any man (3 Ne 20:44). He shall speak before kings (3 Ne 20:44). He shall not cry or lift up his voice in the street (Isa 42:2). He is exalted, extolled, and very high (3 Ne 20:43). He is despised and abhorred (1 Ne 21:7). Later, he is revered and respected as he is the one who proclaims to Zion, "thy God reigneth!" (3 Ne 20:40)

How can God's servant do all of these things? How can he be a hidden, silent servant and still be both exalted and despised? Some people think that because he is hidden, we can't know who he is, and it certainly can't be Donald Trump since everybody knows who he is. How does this work? The answer is that he remains hidden until he is revealed. He isn't like the street preachers seeking only attention and money; his work is above all that, as he deals with high and important matters, such as bringing judgment to the Gentiles. Once it is shown that he is God's servant in the last days, everything changes. A world that despises him and mars him will eventually exalt him and respect him.

Another important example in the Book of Mormon that needs recognition is when King Mosiah and Alma act and perform their duties simultaneously. Both are prophets; one oversees the political realm, while the other manages the ecclesiastical side. This scenario is expected to occur again

SECTION 9 - ONE MIGHTY AND STRONG

soon. President Trump will oversee the political domain, and the President of the Church of Jesus Christ of Latter-day Saints will handle the ecclesiastical matters. This mirrors several instances in the Old Testament where a king and a prophet existed concurrently, such as David and Samuel.

Donald Trump is the one mighty and strong who must come forth in the last days as the champion of righteousness. Under his leadership, the House of Israel will be gathered, and those who have accepted the gospel in its fullness will be assigned inheritances in Zion under his direction. The creation of this marvelous city will take many years and will be unlike anything else in the world. It won't resemble Babylon; it will be Zion.

Every example of Babylon we see in the world resembles the others: giant, expensive skyscrapers reaching into the heavens to pretend to be closer to God. The cost per square foot of these steel and mirrored glass behemoths is staggering. All the surrounding buildings are crammed together, with every possible square foot utilized to its fullest for one reason only: money. The crowded streets, filled with honking yellow taxis, the fumes and pollution, the disease, the homelessness, the beggars on the street reaching out to those exiting their million-dollar cars who want nothing to do with them.

Zion will be nothing like that. Oh, there will be buildings, but they will all be devoted to temple worship and the things of God. There will be industry, manufacturing, production, and farming, but there won't be the dog-eat-dog world we are so familiar with. Let's imagine for a moment what it would be like during the millennium when all wickedness and sin are gone. Zion will be the example that will be duplicated all over the world. Joseph Smith drew a simple layout of the city's plans with 12 temples in the center, and then each home radiating outward, forming a patchwork of properties where they grow their own food and are independent.

Will there be a need for automobile production, shipbuilding, airplane manufacturing, farming equipment, medicine, etc.? What will science be like now that we have the sealed portion of the gold plates and the vision of the Brother of Jared available to all? What will history be like? We are promised that we will receive a white stone given to each of the faithful. What will we do with it? With Jesus Christ on the Earth, will there be a need to plant anything? Will everything be lush and green without snow, tornadoes, tsunamis, or earthquakes? Presumably, the Earth will be at rest because it will finally be free of wickedness, so it's doubtful that all of those damaging weather effects will continue to exist. Fossil records show pre-existing life, including fig leaves bigger than six feet across. Giant dinosaurs roamed the Earth, and tremendous whales swam the seas. While it is doubtful those will return, we are told:

> Isa 11:6 The wolf also shall dwell with the lamb, and the leopard shall lie down with the kid; and the calf and the young lion and the fatling together; and a little child shall lead them.
>
> 7 And the cow and the bear shall feed; their young ones shall lie down together: and the lion shall eat straw like the ox.
>
> 8 And the sucking child shall play on the hole of the asp, and the weaned child shall put his hand on the cockatrice' den.
>
> 9 They shall not hurt nor destroy in all my holy mountain: for the earth shall be full of the knowledge of the Lord, as the waters cover the sea.

We really have no way to conceive what that will be like, as we have no experience that even comes close to it. Our hustle and bustle, the chaotic craziness of our current lives, will be replaced with peace and harmony under the guidance of our God, Jesus Christ.

Zion will be the beginning of all this. It will be the aspect that begins to be translated into the Terrestrial world we will eventually inherit. Only those who are sufficiently righteous (or want to be) will be invited to participate because they have overcome this fallen world we are so familiar with. Donald Trump, the one mighty and strong, will be the primary leader organizing who receives what inheritance and where. This is the meaning of this chapter. We must do everything we can to be prepared for it.

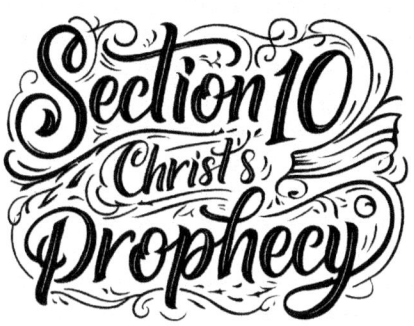

Section 10 - Christ's Prophecy in 3 Nephi 20-23

The prophecy given by Jesus Christ after his resurrection to the Nephites is one of the most remarkable prophecies in scripture. He discusses at length the words of Isaiah, along with Micah and others and mentions several significant events that are quoted word for word. Many people have discussed these verses and tried to understand what he's talking about. I will credit Victor Ludlow for structuring four chapters of scripture into a giant chiasmus. We can spend an enormous amount of time on these verses, but I want to focus on a couple of things. I need to give you all of the verses so you can easily review them.

Given the current organization, I would recommend going to their website to enhance your understanding of the structure.[21] It forms a large chiasmus with multiple aspects to explore. As I've mentioned before, one way to determine whether something was revealed by God is to check if it's written in chiasmus. Because it is structured this way, one can identify various center points of different chiasms within it. Although chiasmus is used in other literature, only God communicates in this manner with multiple layers of meaning in His words.

Please read this chapter, and if you wish, annotate it in your scriptures concerning the bullet points of each stanza. Begin with A for the first one, N for the middle one, and then proceed backwards. Although there are several chiasms from other scholars in these chapters, this one is a good overall starting point.

3 Ne 20:10... A Behold now I finish the commandment which the Father hath commanded me concerning this people, who are a remnant of the House of Israel.

B 11 Ye remember that I spake unto you, and said that when the words of Isaiah should be fulfilled—behold they are written, ye have them before you, therefore search them—

C 12 And verily, verily, I say unto you, that when they shall be fulfilled then is the fulfilling of the covenant which the Father hath made unto his people, O House of Israel.

D 13 And then shall the remnants, which shall be scattered abroad upon the face of the earth, be gathered in from the east and from the west,

SECTION 10 - CHRIST'S PROPHECY IN 3 NEPHI 20-23

and from the south and from the north; and they shall be brought to the knowledge of the Lord their God, who hath redeemed them.

E 14 And the Father hath commanded me that I should give unto you this land, for your inheritance.

F 15 And I say unto you, that if the Gentiles do not repent after the blessing which they shall receive, after they have scattered my people—

16 Then shall ye, who are a remnant of the house of Jacob, go forth among them; and ye shall be in the midst of them who shall be many; and ye shall be among them as a lion among the beasts of the forest, and as a young lion among the flocks of sheep, who, if he goeth through both treadeth down and teareth in pieces, and none can deliver.

17 Thy hand shall be lifted up upon thine adversaries, and all thine enemies shall be cut off.

18 And I will gather my people together as a man gathereth his sheaves into the floor.

19 For I will make my people with whom the Father hath covenanted, yea, I will make thy horn iron, and I will make thy hoofs brass. And thou shalt beat in pieces many people; and I will consecrate their gain unto the Lord, and their substance unto the Lord of the whole earth. And behold, I am he who doeth it.

20 And it shall come to pass, saith the Father, that the sword of my justice shall hang over them at that day; and except they repent it shall fall upon them, saith the Father, yea, even upon all the nations of the Gentiles.

G 21 And it shall come to pass that I will establish my people, O House of Israel.

22 And behold, this people will I establish in this land, unto the fulfilling of the covenant which I made with your father Jacob; and it shall be a New Jerusalem. And the powers of heaven shall be in the midst of this people; yea, even I will be in the midst of you.

23 Behold, I am he of whom Moses spake, saying: A prophet shall the Lord your God raise up unto you of your brethren, like unto me; him shall ye hear in all things whatsoever he shall say unto you. And it shall come to pass that every soul who will not hear that prophet shall be cut off from among the people.

24 Verily I say unto you, yea, and all the prophets from Samuel and

SECTION 10 - CHRIST'S PROPHECY IN 3 NEPHI 20-23

those that follow after, as many as have spoken, have testified of me.

25 And behold, ye are the children of the prophets; and ye are of the House of Israel; and ye are of the covenant which the Father made with your fathers, saying unto Abraham: And in thy seed shall all the kindreds of the earth be blessed.

26 The Father having raised me up unto you first, and sent me to bless you in turning away every one of you from his iniquities; and this because ye are the children of the covenant—

27 And after that ye were blessed then fulfilleth the Father the covenant which he made with Abraham, saying: In thy seed shall all the kindreds of the earth be blessed—unto the pouring out of the Holy Ghost through me upon the Gentiles, which blessing upon the Gentiles shall make them mighty above all, unto the scattering of my people, O House of Israel.

28 And they shall be a scourge unto the people of this land. Nevertheless, when they shall have received the fulness of my gospel, then if they shall harden their hearts against me I will return their iniquities upon their own heads, saith the Father.

29 And I will remember the covenant which I have made with my people; and I have covenanted with them that I would gather them together in mine own due time, that I would give unto them again the land of their fathers for their inheritance, which is the land of Jerusalem, which is the promised land unto them forever, saith the Father.

H 30 And it shall come to pass that the time cometh, when the fulness of my gospel shall be preached unto them;

31 And they shall believe in me, that I am Jesus Christ, the Son of God, and shall pray unto the Father in my name.

32 Then shall their watchmen lift up their voice, and with the voice together shall they sing; for they shall see eye to eye.

33 Then will the Father gather them together again, and give unto them Jerusalem for the land of their inheritance.

34 Then shall they break forth into joy—Sing together, ye waste places of Jerusalem; for the Father hath comforted his people, he hath redeemed Jerusalem.

35 The Father hath made bare his holy arm in the eyes of all the nations; and all the ends of the earth shall see the salvation of the Father; and

SECTION 10 - CHRIST'S PROPHECY IN 3 NEPHI 20-23

the Father and I are one.

36 And then shall be brought to pass that which is written: Awake, awake again, and put on thy strength, O Zion; put on thy beautiful garments, O Jerusalem, the holy city, for henceforth there shall no more come into thee the uncircumcised and the unclean.

37 Shake thyself from the dust; arise, sit down, O Jerusalem; loose thyself from the bands of thy neck, O captive daughter of Zion.

38 For thus saith the Lord: Ye have sold yourselves for naught, and ye shall be redeemed without money.

39 Verily, verily, I say unto you, that my people shall know my name; yea, in that day they shall know that I am he that doth speak.

40 And then shall they say: How beautiful upon the mountains are the feet of him that bringeth good tidings unto them, that publisheth peace; that bringeth good tidings unto them of good, that publisheth salvation; that saith unto Zion: Thy God reigneth!

41 And then shall a cry go forth: Depart ye, depart ye, go ye out from thence, touch not that which is unclean; go ye out of the midst of her; be ye clean that bear the vessels of the Lord.

42 For ye shall not go out with haste nor go by flight; for the Lord will go before you, and the God of Israel shall be your rearward.

43 Behold, my servant shall deal prudently; he shall be exalted and extolled and be very high.

44 As many were astonished at thee—his visage was so marred, more than any man, and his form more than the sons of men—

I 45 So shall he sprinkle many nations; the kings shall shut their mouths at him, for that which had not been told them shall they see; and that which they had not heard shall they consider.

J 46 Verily, verily, I say unto you, all these things shall surely come, even as the Father hath commanded me. Then shall this covenant which the Father hath covenanted with his people be fulfilled; and then shall Jerusalem be inhabited again with my people, and it shall be the land of their inheritance.

K 21:1 And verily I say unto you, I give unto you a sign, that ye may know the time when these things shall be about to take place—that I shall

SECTION 10 - CHRIST'S PROPHECY IN 3 NEPHI 20-23

gather in, from their long dispersion, my people, O House of Israel, and shall establish again among them my Zion; 2 And behold, this is the thing which I will give unto you for a sign—

L for verily I say unto you that when these things which I declare unto you, and which I shall declare unto you hereafter of myself, and by the power of the Holy Ghost which shall be given unto you of the Father, shall be made known unto the Gentiles that they may know concerning this people who are a remnant of the house of Jacob, and concerning this my people who shall be scattered by them;

M 3 Verily, verily, I say unto you, when these things shall be made known unto them of the Father, and shall come forth of the Father, from them unto you;

N 4 For it is wisdom in the Father that they should be established in this land, and be set up as a free people by the power of the Father, that these things might come forth from them unto a remnant of your seed, that the covenant of the Father may be fulfilled which he hath covenanted with his people, O House of Israel;

M 5 Therefore, when these works and the works which shall be wrought among you hereafter shall come forth from the Gentiles, unto your seed which shall dwindle in unbelief because of iniquity;

L 6 For thus it behooveth the Father that it should come forth from the Gentiles, that he may show forth his power unto the Gentiles, for this cause that the Gentiles, if they will not harden their hearts, that they may repent and come unto me and be baptized in my name and know of the true points of my doctrine, that they may be numbered among my people, O House of Israel;

K 7 And when these things come to pass that thy seed shall begin to know these things—it shall be a sign unto them,

J that they may know that the work of the Father hath already commenced unto the fulfilling of the covenant which he hath made unto the people who are of the House of Israel.

I 8 And when that day shall come, it shall come to pass that kings shall shut their mouths; for that which had not been told them shall they see; and that which they had not heard shall they consider.

H 9 For in that day, for my sake shall the Father work a work, which shall be a great and a marvelous work among them; and there shall be

SECTION 10 - CHRIST'S PROPHECY IN 3 NEPHI 20-23

among them those who will not believe it, although a man shall declare it unto them.

10 But behold, the life of my servant shall be in my hand; therefore they shall not hurt him, although he shall be marred because of them. Yet I will heal him, for I will show unto them that my wisdom is greater than the cunning of the devil.

G 11 Therefore it shall come to pass that whosoever will not believe in my words, who am Jesus Christ, which the Father shall cause him to bring forth unto the Gentiles, and shall give unto him power that he shall bring them forth unto the Gentiles, (it shall be done even as Moses said) they shall be cut off from among my people who are of the covenant.

F 12 And my people who are a remnant of Jacob shall be among the Gentiles, yea, in the midst of them as a lion among the beasts of the forest, as a young lion among the flocks of sheep, who, if he go through both treadeth down and teareth in pieces, and none can deliver.

13 Their hand shall be lifted up upon their adversaries, and all their enemies shall be cut off.

14 Yea, wo be unto the Gentiles except they repent; for it shall come to pass in that day, saith the Father, that I will cut off thy horses out of the midst of thee, and I will destroy thy chariots;

15 And I will cut off the cities of thy land, and throw down all thy strongholds;

16 And I will cut off witchcrafts out of thy land, and thou shalt have no more soothsayers;

17 Thy graven images I will also cut off, and thy standing images out of the midst of thee, and thou shalt no more worship the works of thy hands;

18 And I will pluck up thy groves out of the midst of thee; so will I destroy thy cities.

19 And it shall come to pass that all lyings, and deceivings, and envyings, and strifes, and priestcrafts, and whoredoms, shall be done away.

20 For it shall come to pass, saith the Father, that at that day whosoever will not repent and come unto my Beloved Son, them will I cut off from among my people, O House of Israel;

21 And I will execute vengeance and fury upon them, even as upon

SECTION 10 - CHRIST'S PROPHECY IN 3 NEPHI 20-23

the heathen, such as they have not heard.

E 22 But if they will repent and hearken unto my words, and harden not their hearts, I will establish my church among them, and they shall come in unto the covenant and be numbered among this the remnant of Jacob, unto whom I have given this land for their inheritance;

23 And they shall assist my people, the remnant of Jacob, and also as many of the House of Israel as shall come, that they may build a city, which shall be called the New Jerusalem.

D 24 And then shall they assist my people that they may be gathered in, who are scattered upon all the face of the land, in unto the New Jerusalem.

25 And then shall the power of heaven come down among them; and I also will be in the midst.

26 And then shall the work of the Father commence at that day, even when this gospel shall be preached among the remnant of this people. Verily I say unto you, at that day shall the work of the Father commence among all the dispersed of my people, yea, even the tribes which have been lost, which the Father hath led away out of Jerusalem.

27 Yea, the work shall commence among all the dispersed of my people, with the Father to prepare the way whereby they may come unto me, that they may call on the Father in my name.

28 Yea, and then shall the work commence, with the Father among all nations in preparing the way whereby his people may be gathered home to the land of their inheritance.

29 And they shall go out from all nations; and they shall not go out in haste, nor go by flight, for I will go before them, saith the Father, and I will be their rearward.

C 22: 1 And then shall that which is written come to pass: Sing, O barren, thou that didst not bear; break forth into singing, and cry aloud, thou that didst not travail with child; for more are the children of the desolate than the children of the married wife, saith the Lord.

2 Enlarge the place of thy tent, and let them stretch forth the curtains of thy habitations; spare not, lengthen thy cords and strengthen thy stakes;

3 For thou shalt break forth on the right hand and on the left, and thy seed shall inherit the Gentiles and make the desolate cities to be inhabited.

SECTION 10 - CHRIST'S PROPHECY IN 3 NEPHI 20-23

4 Fear not, for thou shalt not be ashamed; neither be thou confounded, for thou shalt not be put to shame; for thou shalt forget the shame of thy youth, and shalt not remember the reproach of thy youth, and shalt not remember the reproach of thy widowhood any more.

5 For thy maker, thy husband, the Lord of Hosts is his name; and thy Redeemer, the Holy One of Israel—the God of the whole earth shall he be called.

6 For the Lord hath called thee as a woman forsaken and grieved in spirit, and a wife of youth, when thou wast refused, saith thy God.

7 For a small moment have I forsaken thee, but with great mercies will I gather thee.

8 In a little wrath I hid my face from thee for a moment, but with everlasting kindness will I have mercy on thee, saith the Lord thy Redeemer.

9 For this, the waters of Noah unto me, for as I have sworn that the waters of Noah should no more go over the earth, so have I sworn that I would not be wroth with thee.

10 For the mountains shall depart and the hills be removed, but my kindness shall not depart from thee, neither shall the covenant of my peace be removed, saith the Lord that hath mercy on thee.

11 O thou afflicted, tossed with tempest, and not comforted! Behold, I will lay thy stones with fair colors, and lay thy foundations with sapphires.

12 And I will make thy windows of agates, and thy gates of carbuncles, and all thy borders of pleasant stones.

13 And all thy children shall be taught of the Lord; and great shall be the peace of thy children.

14 In righteousness shalt thou be established; thou shalt be far from oppression for thou shalt not fear, and from terror for it shall not come near thee.

15 Behold, they shall surely gather together against thee, not by me; whosoever shall gather together against thee shall fall for thy sake.

16 Behold, I have created the smith that bloweth the coals in the fire, and that bringeth forth an instrument for his work; and I have created the waster to destroy.

17 No weapon that is formed against thee shall prosper; and every

SECTION 10 - CHRIST'S PROPHECY IN 3 NEPHI 20-23

tongue that shall revile against thee in judgment thou shalt condemn. This is the heritage of the servants of the Lord, and their righteousness is of me, saith the Lord.

B 23: 1 And now, behold, I say unto you, that ye ought to search these things. Yea, a commandment I give unto you that ye search these things diligently; for great are the words of Isaiah.

2 For surely he spake as touching all things concerning my people which are of the House of Israel; therefore it must needs be that he must speak also to the Gentiles.

3 And all things that he spake have been and shall be, even according to the words which he spake.

A 4 Therefore give heed to my words; write the things which I have told you; and according to the time and the will of the Father they shall go forth unto the Gentiles.

5 And whosoever will hearken unto my words and repenteth and is baptized, the same shall be saved. Search the prophets, for many there be that testify of these things.

Now that we have these marvelous chapters organized in a chiastic structure, let's spend the next chapter understanding a bit more about this organization, how it affects us today, and how it fits into the events of the last days. This is an astonishing revelation. Jesus Christ himself speaks to the Nephites and shares some extremely powerful information. However, this information is for you and me; it wasn't for them. This is meant for our day. When I make a Part 2 of this book, I will spend more time on this.

I've always found it interesting that John the Revelator was entrusted with the mission to write the words of that prophecy in his book. We know that others have seen the same vision, such as Nephi, Isaiah, Jesus Christ, the brother of Jared, and others, but it is to John that the authority to write this in his unique way was given. Isaiah, of course, saw the same vision and spoke of many of the same things. In a way, they all give him the respect he deserves for this life mission.

Christ respects it and does not reveal everything in that vision. He shares some of its contents, and all of it complements what was written, but even he, the great creator and our eternal savior, maintains certain bounds around his words to avoid overstepping John's calling.

SECTION 10 - CHRIST'S PROPHECY IN 3 NEPHI 20-23

Now maybe I'm taking things a bit too far here, but I believe that each of us has a mission on Earth. It may not be as glorious or grand as revealing the entire series of events of the last days that was commissioned to John, but we all have something to accomplish. Some missions may be small or great, but they are still responsibilities given to us. Our patriarchal blessings are an excellent source of revelation regarding what the Lord has in mind for us. They may or may not reveal everything that we need to know, but they provide a good foundation. Even if your blessing says nothing regarding these matters, I personally believe that you have something that God wants you to do.

Each of us needs to learn what that is and do all we can to achieve it. Christ himself said that this was his gospel: to do the will of his Father. I've heard for many years that he accomplished his mission and we just have to accept that. Perhaps there's a profound lesson in that we also need to learn to do the will of our Father. When we follow his will, whatever that may be, we are following Christ and fulfilling our part of the gospel.

There's a connection to doing what God wants us to do because, in every case, it's for our benefit. Too many people I know have gone off and pursued their own desires. Sadly, I misunderstood something God wanted me to do, and I have profound regrets to this day. I know people who completely ignored their patriarchal blessings and did whatever they wanted. They may never know what blessings they could have received if they had followed His guidance.

When we work out our salvation with fear and trembling, we discover what God wants us to do and then do it. Some people have been called to be world leaders. Others have gained respect in business or industry. Some have performed great charitable works around the globe. Others have accomplished the incredible task of raising a family in righteousness. Everyone looks to the rich and famous and thinks that's what we should be doing, but is that what God wants you to do? I've seen individuals who spent their entire lives caring for a child born with cerebral palsy. Was that wasted? Oh, I think not! That was for them, for whatever reason, and the lessons they learned in the process led them to achieve eternal life.

God may or may not expect you to accomplish something great; rather, He desires you to do the specific thing He wants. There's no need for fear or

SECTION 10 - CHRIST'S PROPHECY IN 3 NEPHI 20-23

jealousy; it's all about faith. We may not have a mission as grand as that of John the Revelator, but if you both reach the Celestial Kingdom, it doesn't matter.

Now let's look at that prophecy of the Suffering Servant.

Section 11: The Suffering Servant

Section 11 - Suffering Servant

Isaiah states the following:

52:11 ¶ Depart ye, depart ye, go ye out from thence, touch no unclean thing; go ye out of the midst of her; be ye clean, that bear the vessels of the Lord.

12 For ye shall not go out with haste, nor go by flight: for the Lord will go before you; and the God of Israel will be your rearward.

13 ¶ Behold, my servant shall deal prudently, he shall be exalted and extolled, and be very high.

14 As many were astonied at thee; his visage was so marred more than any man, and his form more than the sons of men:

15 So shall he sprinkle many nations; the kings shall shut their mouths at him: for that which had not been told them shall they see; and that which they had not heard shall they consider.

Soon, many righteous will be called to flee Babylon, be perfectly clean, and be worthy of officiating in the priesthood. They will be involved in establishing the New Jerusalem or Zion. It will not be a hasty, haphazard event; it will be calm and organized. Just like when the Israelites left Egypt, the Lord will protect and guide them.

Verses 13-15 talk about the leader of this group, a servant who will be exalted and lifted up. Something about his image or our perception of him is marred, but the nations of the Earth will greatly respect him and pay attention to what he says. We often refer to him as the suffering servant.

The ultimate suffering servant is Jesus Christ himself, who suffered more than anyone could ever suffer, physically or spiritually, in the history of the world. Because of his tremendous gift to us, we are free from death. If we repent, we can be free from sin. Jesus went through a tremendous phase of condescension, being denigrated by the people and leaders of his day. They accused him of all manner of evil and wickedness. They claimed he had the devil. They brought him before phony courts that were utterly illegal in his day. He experienced the suffering of the atonement in the garden of Gethsemane and on the cross. No one even comes close to this suffering. But he overcame it all and, in the end, was victorious against everything that

SECTION 11 - THE SUFFERING SERVANT

could be thrown against him, and we are all blessed because of it!

Many of God's servants have been called to go through similar experiences. Abraham was commanded to offer up his son. Job loses everything but has it all return. Moses was cast out into the wilderness. Joseph Smith was severely beaten, tarred, feathered, and brought before numerous phony courts. There are many others, but Donald Trump is the one on which these verses are focused.

No one in world history has had their image tarnished more than Donald Trump. They have done everything possible to stop him, even resorting to attempted assassinations. They have dragged him into courts on numerous scandalous and false charges. They have tarnished his name and family. They have tried to shut down his businesses and produced all sorts of offensive videos, movies, and even horrifically degrading spectacles like a giant 35' tall inflatable Trump that was completely nude and hanging from a crane in southern Utah. Some comedians have even stooped so low as to depict them holding his bloody head after it had been severed from his body.

While Christ is the ultimate suffering servant because no one has endured more than he has in both physical and spiritual terms, Trump represents a suffering servant whose reputation and image have been tarnished. I repeat, no one in history has faced such abuse.

His visage is marred. His image is marred. Our perception of him is marred. The way they want people to view him, along with their perception of him, has been altered by the beastly media system they have owned since the early 1900s. They have done everything possible to portray him as evil, silly, mean, disgusting, immoral, degrading, demoralizing, greedy, boastful, and more. While it is true that he has been somewhat of a philanderer in his life and has made numerous offensive remarks, God has used similar types of people to perform His work in the past. Some of our founding fathers were philanderers themselves. Great prophets and kings in the Old Testament were the same way. Can you imagine how David would be perceived today?

God selects such individuals, urging us to look beyond the world's perception. It becomes a test to determine if we can heed the Spirit, feel the heart, and understand the will of God without being swayed by good looks, smooth words, or flashy details. Satan is a master of smooth talk. He pos-

SECTION 11 - THE SUFFERING SERVANT

sesses immense skill in persuading the masses to act according to his desires. He focuses on influencing through external or superficial means rather than genuine substance. He ensures no one is offended, using language that unites everyone rather than preaching the truth. His subtle tactics have been refined to a high degree in everything from advertising to the Halls of Congress. His deceit has influenced billions of people. In contrast, God's chosen servants deliver harsh words, likened to a sword that divides bone and marrow.

This closely resembles what Christ himself said about his mission:

> Matt 10:33 But whosoever shall deny me before men, him will I also deny before my Father which is in heaven.
>
> 34 Think not that I am come to send peace on earth: I came not to send peace, but a sword.
>
> 35 For I am come to set a man at variance against his father, and the daughter against her mother, and the daughter in law against her mother in law.

It's crucial that we have the spirit to see beyond outward appearances.

Christ discusses the Suffering Servant in depth in 3rd Nephi chapters 20-23 as shown in the previous chapter. The central verse of this section is 21:4, which addresses the establishment of a free people. These remarkable chapters are ones I could spend a significant amount of time on. In the first part of chapter 21, he mentions a sign being given so we may know when the Father's covenants are about to be fulfilled. As noted, verse 4 speaks of establishing a people as a free people so they may spread the gospel to the House of Israel. This mission was to be carried out by the Gentiles.

> 3 Ne 21:4 For it is wisdom in the Father that they should be established in this land, and be set up as a free people by the power of the Father, that these things might come forth from them unto a remnant of your seed, that the covenant of the Father may be fulfilled which he hath covenanted with his people, O House of Israel;

We've always been taught that this marked the establishment of the original constitution and the foundation of America, allowing Joseph Smith to provide a place for the emergence of the Book of Mormon. I now see this quite differently. God's servant, Donald Trump, will establish a free people

SECTION 11 - THE SUFFERING SERVANT

once he brings about God's kingdom on earth. ***Then, we will be free.*** The glorious establishment of America, from the pilgrims and explorers like Columbus, was a prophesied event in history. They sought religious freedom and the chance to achieve what they could not do under the bureaucratic systems in Europe. Nephi saw in vision the coming forth of America and its establishment as a powerful nation. As we have already noted, after the Civil War, we lost much of our freedom and have been slaves to the Gadianton Robbers ever since. It's surprising that this is never taught; in fact, the opposite has been promoted in everything we read and see about how blessed we are to be in a free country, while we are actually slaves.

But we can hardly do anything without government red tape standing in our way. We pay taxes on taxes on taxes and face a crazy bureaucracy that prevents us from growing gardens or collecting rainwater. Homeowners associations rake in millions of dollars yet spend only thousands on actual community benefits while bureaucrats comb the neighborhood for the slightest scratch in the paint. Property taxes are set by the city that collects them, and the value of your home is determined by them. You never fully own your home. I could go on and on about the reality that we do not live in a free country. Don't get me wrong, we are not like China or North Korea, but we are not free.

Look at how many people have been brought into our country illegally for specific purposes. One of these purposes was to alter the voter census to benefit Democrats. Another was to drive up housing prices, which have skyrocketed over the last couple of decades with no end in sight. Giant corporations are acquiring all the residential homes, forcing us to become renters. They are now purchasing trailer parks and raising rents for those who can only afford that. These corporations should have been broken up and classified as a monopoly, but because they have been paying politicians, they are not being held accountable. Isaiah warns us in,

> 5:8 ¶ Woe unto them that join house to house, that lay field to field, till there be no place, that they may be placed alone in the midst of the earth!

There has been an incredible misuse of the land. It is regarded solely as a means of profit, disregarding its potential to build families, self-reliance, a connection to God, pride of ownership, and everything else that comes with

SECTION 11 - THE SUFFERING SERVANT

owning private property. All you see being constructed right now are apartment complexes, which are no more affordable than homes. It's important to note the reason Isaiah warned that this would happen: the rich would end up isolated in their 28,000 square-foot mansions. The Lord denounces this. Our world praises this, seeks it actively, and says nothing against these abominable apartments that are crammed together like prison cells.

But that all changes under the law of consecration that will be established in Zion, where everyone will be assigned an inheritance. First, they must give everything they own, and they will receive back only what they need. But it remains theirs; it can never be taken away. That single fact alone will make a tremendous difference in how everything operates in that community. There's pride in ownership. There's responsibility and a desire to present their best selves. Call it peer pressure if you want, but if there are weeds and trash in the yard, everyone knows who to blame. That's not the case today. Nobody cares because they don't own it. They work so hard and for so long to give money to the true owner that they simply don't care.

This system, founded on freedom and personal responsibility within a community of people who care about each other and follow the laws, will foster unmatched prosperity never before seen in the world. When everyone thrives at the company they work for, everyone shows they care. Nothing is produced or shipped that hasn't been proven to be exactly as advertised and ordered. There will be no flaws deceptively sold to clients or customers. No tricks or shortcuts will be taken just to make a few extra dollars. The highest quality products ever produced by any company will emerge from this system.

He also discusses how kings will shut their mouths in his presence for matters they have not been told to consider. This concept is echoed in 3 Ne Chapter 20, Verse 45. This aligns with the principle of Chiasmus. He will sprinkle many nations, implying he will either bless numerous nations, gather them, or that many people will be astonished by him. Additionally, in 21:10, it speaks of how the life of his servant will be in his hands, and they will not harm him, though he will be marred because of them.

> 3 Ne 21:10 But behold, the life of my servant shall be in my hand; therefore they shall not hurt him, although he shall be marred because of them. Yet I will heal him, for I will show unto them that my wisdom is greater than the cunning of the devil.

SECTION 11 - THE SUFFERING SERVANT

11 Therefore it shall come to pass that whosoever will not believe in my words, who am Jesus Christ, which the Father shall cause him to bring forth unto the Gentiles, and shall give unto him power that he shall bring them forth unto the Gentiles, (it shall be done even as Moses said) they shall be cut off from among my people who are of the covenant.

All my life, I had been taught that this was Joseph Smith because verse 11 discusses how he would take the gospel to the Gentiles. How could it possibly be anyone else? He is the one to whom the gold plates were given to translate the Book of Mormon. He is the one who established the church in this last dispensation. He was the first prophet of that dispensation. From him has sprung everything that has occurred as the gospel has been preached worldwide. Who else could it be?

In November of 2023, I received a different interpretation of this. I kept looking at this over and over and reading it many times. Usually, when I have a question about a gospel principle, I read it multiple times until I finally understand it. I spent four weeks reading these verses but could not figure it out. He finally made me go to some other scriptures in Isaiah and Micah. It was then that I realized that this was not Joseph Smith.

1- Joseph Smith never spoke before kings.
2- He was severely hurt and injured.
3- Joseph's life was taken from him.
4- This latter-day servant would not be harmed or killed.
5- Therefore, it cannot be our beloved prophet, Joseph.

Trump's life is in God's hands, and even attempted assassinations have failed. So what does it mean about him bringing the gospel forth from the Gentiles unto the House of Israel? It implies that he is going to do a great and marvelous work. After establishing the New Jerusalem, or Zion, the world's nations will marvel at his accomplishments.

That which they had not seen shall they consider. He will open the doors to our missionaries worldwide, spreading the gospel to every nation, kindred tongue, and people. ***Hundreds of millions of people will join the church!!!!***

SECTION 11 - THE SUFFERING SERVANT

We are building temples at an accelerated rate worldwide and, in some cases, in places that can barely house a session! The term gentiles used here is the rest of the world. It also means that he will bring the gospel to the House of Israel and gather them to both the Zion in America and the Jews to Jerusalem. He will help build temples in both places.

The people of these nations will need the covenants of the temple in the same manner our pioneer forefathers did before crossing the plains. They did everything possible to get the Nauvoo temple operational so that they may receive those blessed covenants to give them the power they needed to endure the tribulations of crossing the plains. Those people who joined the church worldwide will also need those same covenants to endure the tribulations that will come before the 2nd coming.

This will be one of the most significant events in world history.

What's interesting is what occurs after he shares these revelations. While it is true that these elements were included because the fullness of the gospel is contained in the Book of Mormon, there is another reason why they are positioned and ordered as they currently are. Most of us look at these verses in the following chapters and perceive them as just some additional cleanup notes or as being haphazardly assembled in an unorganized manner. That would be a mistake. Allow me to explain.

After his profound exposé on the suffering servant, he then asks Nephi to bring forth the records so he can examine them. He discovers that they forgot to include the notation about those who are resurrected at the time of Jesus' coming. As a side note, this is clear evidence that his visit to the Nephites did not occur immediately after the calamities of chapter 8 in 35. There must have been a significant amount of time between that destruction and his appearance. Why would he be critical of Nephi if he forgot to write those things down but it only happened the day before? Nephi would be running around trying to help his family, binding up wounds, and getting everybody situated for recovery from the terrible destruction. He would not have had time to write anything down. That's why I think that this appearance of Jesus to the people occurred several months later, probably in the fall or even the next year.

Anyway, he goes over and has them record those events. The interesting thing is, though, that we don't have that record. It's not in the Book of Mor-

SECTION 11 - THE SUFFERING SERVANT

mon; it is on the large plates somewhere, which we will get someday. For now, all we have is a reference to their occurrence.

He then references Malachi, chapter 3, verse 24. He states that these words were given to Malachi by the Father, and he desires for them to possess this knowledge. He speaks of sending a messenger before his face and presents his profound prophecy:

> 3 Ne 24:1 Behold, I will send my messenger, and he shall prepare the way before me, and the Lord whom ye seek shall suddenly come to his temple, even the messenger of the covenant, whom ye delight in; behold, he shall come, saith the Lord of Hosts.
>
> 2 But who may abide the day of his coming, and who shall stand when he appeareth? For he is like a refiner's fire, and like fuller's soap.
>
> 3 And he shall sit as a refiner and purifier of silver; and he shall purify the sons of Levi, and purge them as gold and silver, that they may offer unto the Lord an offering in righteousness.
>
> 4 Then shall the offering of Judah and Jerusalem be pleasant unto the Lord, as in the days of old, and as in former years.
>
> 5 And I will come near to you to judgment; and I will be a swift witness against the sorcerers, and against the adulterers, and against false swearers, and against those that oppress the hireling in his wages, the widow and the fatherless, and that turn aside the stranger, and fear not me, saith the Lord of Hosts.
>
> 6 For I am the Lord, I change not; therefore ye sons of Jacob are not consumed.

He continues this chapter by discussing important principles regarding the significance of living tithing and the law of consecration. Quoting these words is particularly important at this time. There is a reason they are mentioned.

> D&C 64:23 Behold, now it is called today until the coming of the Son of Man, and verily it is a day of sacrifice, and a day for the tithing of my people; for he that is tithed shall not be burned at his coming.
>
> 24 For after today cometh the burning—this is speaking after the manner of the Lord—for verily I say, tomorrow all the proud and they

SECTION 11 - THE SUFFERING SERVANT

that do wickedly shall be as stubble; and I will burn them up, for I am the Lord of Hosts; and I will not spare any that remain in Babylon.

Those who complain about keeping the law of tithing will not be worthy of Zion. Just as keeping the Word of Wisdom is necessary for spiritual survival in the last days and to avoid being burned, paying your tithing serves the same purpose. Both are interconnected and are part of what makes one righteous and worthy of redemption and protection.

And he goes on:

> 3 Ne 24:13 Your words have been stout against me, saith the Lord. Yet ye say: What have we spoken against thee?
>
> 14 Ye have said: It is vain to serve God, and what doth it profit that we have kept his ordinances and that we have walked mournfully before the Lord of Hosts?
>
> 15 And now we call the proud happy; yea, they that work wickedness are set up; yea, they that tempt God are even delivered.

I believe this directly refers to upholding the law of consecration. People often resist it because they feel envious of those who have more than they do. They desire more than their neighbors possess. They complain, questioning what profit there is in having walked mournfully before the Lord of Hosts. This highlights the issue and serves as another indication of those worthy to be part of Zion. They cannot be consumed by this jealousy.

He then jumps right into Malachi chapter 4, talking about the day that comes, which will burn them as an oven. When Moroni appeared to Joseph Smith, he alluded to this, saying, "**They** that come shall burn them up."

> JS-H 1:37 For behold, the day cometh that shall burn as an oven, and all the proud, yea, and all that do wickedly shall burn as stubble; for **they** that come shall burn them, saith the Lord of Hosts, that it shall leave them neither root nor branch.

This most likely refers to Revelation Chapter 19, when all those who come with Christ will destroy the wicked and burn them up. He also promises that Elijah the prophet will come and turn the hearts of the fathers to the children and the hearts of the children to the fathers, while the righteous will be led like calves in the stall; they will be protected.

SECTION 11 - THE SUFFERING SERVANT

3 Ne 26 then provides a beautiful illustration of all his other teachings, which they couldn't even record a hundredth part of. Mormon states that he will only write what he has been commanded to write. He offers a marvelous blessing to the children who opened their mouths and spoke marvelous things!

> 3 Ne 26:16 Behold, it came to pass on the morrow that the multitude gathered themselves together, and they both saw and heard these children; yea, even babes did open their mouths and utter marvelous things; and the things which they did utter were forbidden that there should not any man write them.

3 Ne 27 covers his giving the name of the church as they had requested and he gives his apostles a commission to go forth and teach his word to everyone around them. He commands everyone to repent and come to him and be baptized in his name.

3 Ne 28 discusses the incredible blessing given to the Three Nephites: they shall not taste of death. They are translated, allowing them to go wherever they wish and perform God's duties anywhere on Earth. They are not subject to the trials and temptations of the devil. With God's permission, they can do anything they desire and have a 2000-year mission to try and bring people to Jesus Christ. This is likely similar to what John the Revelator also experienced when he took the book and ate it; at first, it was sweet because he had personally felt the love of Jesus Christ and wanted everyone else to feel that love too. However, it later turned sour due to widespread rejection. The three Nephites were removed from the people of Nephi because those people rejected these three disciples, even though they were over 300 years old.

Mormon provides several examples of how they used their power to overcome the opposition they faced. They were thrown into pits of the Earth and buried, but that could not stop them. They were cast into dens of lions and wild beasts, yet they played with them like a child. He stated that they were like angels of God and possessed the power of God to persuade anyone willing to listen to the truth of their message. He noted that they would be among the Gentiles and issued a grave warning to those who would not heed the words of Jesus. He mentioned that it would be better for them not to have been born. That's quite a harsh sentence.

SECTION 11 - THE SUFFERING SERVANT

In 3 Ne 29, Mormon shifts gears and speaks directly to the Gentiles, warning them that if they do not treat these matters with respect, they will face severe punishment. He cautions them against spurning at the doings of the Lord because the justice of God's right hand is coming upon them. And woe to those who deny the revelations of God, claiming that He no longer works through revelation, prophecy, gifts, tongues, or the Holy Ghost. This stark warning chapter serves as a wake-up call to anyone willing to listen that something significant is coming, and they need to be alert.

3 Ne 30 continues his urgent warning, imploring the Gentiles to repent, abandon their secret works of darkness, and turn to God so they may be counted among His people of the House of Israel.

4 Ne 1 recounts a beautiful era in which they lived in peace and harmony for over 300 years. Everyone followed the law of consecration, cared for their fellow man, and there were no wars or pestilence; this was what they had long sought. This fulfills the prophecy given by Nephi and Lehi regarding what would come upon their people. It was a glorious time, yet remarkably, it covers only a couple of pages while encompassing over 300 years.

Why has he arranged these chapters in this particular order? What is the point of providing a synopsis for each one of them, since aren't they just somewhat haphazard, like a quick attempt to fill a gap? Oh no. These are intentionally positioned for a specific reason. The order of these chapters is designed for us to understand the events that will unfold in the last days.

When God's suffering servant, Donald Trump, obtains his commission from God, everything changes. According to D&C 88:96, when the first trumpet sounds, all of the Lord's people will be caught up to Him. They will be spared from all the calamities that come upon this earth.

> D&C 88:96 And the saints that are upon the earth, who are alive, shall be quickened and be caught up to meet him.
>
> 97 And they who have slept in their graves shall come forth, for their graves shall be opened; and they also shall be caught up to meet him in the midst of the pillar of heaven—
>
> 98 They are Christ's, the first fruits, they who shall descend with him first, and they who are on the earth and in their graves, who are first caught up to meet him; and all this by the voice of the sounding of the trump of the angel of God.

SECTION 11 - THE SUFFERING SERVANT

And who are the ones that will be brought in and spared? Those who are worthy of entering the temple. It tells us right here:

> 3 Ne 24:1 Behold, I will send my messenger, and he shall prepare the way before me, and the Lord whom ye seek shall suddenly come to his temple, even the messenger of the covenant, whom ye delight in; behold, he shall come, saith the Lord of Hosts.
>
> 2 But who may abide the day of his coming, and who shall stand when he appeareth? For he is like a refiner's fire, and like fuller's soap.

In the original appendix to the Doctrine and Covenants, the Lord said this:

> D&C 133:2 The Lord who shall suddenly come to his temple; the Lord who shall come down upon the world with a curse to judgment; yea, upon all the nations that forget God, and upon all the ungodly among you.

Donald Trump is the messenger of the covenant, preparing the way for the Lord to come. If we closely examine the words in this verse, we see that when it states, "and the Lord whom you seek," the Hebrew word used for "Lord" is "adon," not Jehovah or Adonai, but adon. Although most people use it to mean the Lord our God, it can also refer to an individual who has been commissioned by God to accomplish His work. However, I believe we're discussing Donald Trump as the messenger and Jesus Christ as the Lord. Donald Trump is the messenger of the covenant, and when he arrives, he will refine and purify them.

> 3 Ne 23:3 And he shall sit as a refiner and purifier of silver; and he shall purify the sons of Levi, and purge them as gold and silver, that they may offer unto the Lord an offering in righteousness.

He will refine the Jews and purify the sons of Levi so that they may offer sacrifices in righteousness to the Lord in the temple he helps them build. This temple will be built in Jerusalem. The sons of Levi have been waiting all these years to perform their ancient sacrifices again, and this will occur through Donald Trump's administration and leadership.

This is the day for the tithing of my people and for sacrifice. Everyone has been looking forward to these sacrifices for thousands of years. Currently, there are several red heifers in Jerusalem waiting to be sacrificed for this

SECTION 11 - THE SUFFERING SERVANT

purpose, but the timing is not right yet. There must be a temple first. All of this land has to be returned to the Jews as promised under the Abrahamic covenant.

And back in America, only those who are worthy of being in the temple by paying their tithing, living the word of wisdom, and adhering to the law of consecration in Zion are part of this group. They will be in America, and it will be a tremendous day. They are not complaining against God about having to live this law and asking why are other proud people have more things? Nope, they are living it perfectly.

Like the three Nephites, they have progressed to a Terrestrial level of existence. They are the Kings and Queens of the Gentiles. Additional words from Jesus Christ will be disclosed, including those found in the sealed portion of the gold plates. Just as what occurred during Jesus's visit, we will also experience tremendous revelations of additional scripture.

The name of this church is most likely the Church of the Lamb or the First Born because they have obtained the level of existence required to achieve that status. They will live in tremendous peace and happiness for 1,000 years, and no weapon formed against them shall prosper. Our goal, as Kings and Queens, will be elaborated upon later.

Those who fight against Zion will receive the harshest punishments. Those who refuse to listen to his chosen servants and mock and scorn those who partake of the fruit will be a part of all the dire destructions throughout the Book of Revelation and the fall of Babylon, the Great and Abominable Church, the Great and Spacious Building.

The chapters are organized in a specific pattern so that we know what to expect. There's nothing random about it at all. God knew that we would have the book of Malachi in the Bible; yet, He places a couple of chapters here in the Book of Mormon for a reason. It isn't just a repetition of the message; it's a time frame for the coming forth of that message, His chosen messenger of the covenant.

Exciting times ahead!

Section 12
Moses

Section 12 - Moses

Moses grew up in the richest nation in the world at the time, and if we accept the portrayal in the movie The 10 Commandments (I know it's not 100% historically accurate on several points, but just go with me for a moment), he became an exceptional builder, organizer, and leader. He was not raised in righteousness but in worldly wisdom, he was raised in Pharaoh's court, receiving the best education in Egypt, and as a prince, he likely studied leadership, military strategy, and governance.

At 40 years old, he witnessed an Egyptian taskmaster beating a Hebrew slave and killed the taskmaster in the process. He realized that he had been seen, and fearing Pharaoh's retribution, he fled to Midian across the desert. When he arrived in Midian, he defended the daughters of Jethro, who gave him his daughter Zipporah in marriage, and they had at least two sons. He had previously been married to an Egyptian woman and was later criticized for this action for having married two women. He worked for Jethro for 40 years.

At 80 years old, he had his burning bush experience on Mount Sinai. A year later, he then used miraculous plagues and signs to persuade the Egyptians to release the House of Israel from bondage. The crossing of the Red Sea ultimately drowned the Egyptians as they attempted to pass through it

This calling on Sinai was given in a marvelous revelation revealed through the prophet Joseph Smith and is the original setting for the book of Genesis. Let's look at these words as shown in:

> Moses 1:1 The words of God, which he spake unto Moses at a time when Moses was caught up into an exceedingly high mountain,
>
> 2 And he saw God face to face, and he talked with him, and the glory of God was upon Moses; therefore Moses could endure his presence.
>
> 3 And God spake unto Moses, saying: Behold, I am the Lord God Almighty, and Endless is my name; for I am without beginning of days or end of years; and is not this endless?
>
> 4 And, behold, thou art my son; wherefore look, and I will show thee the workmanship of mine hands; but not all, for my works are without end, and also my words, for they never cease.

SECTION 12 - MOSES

5 Wherefore, no man can behold all my works, except he behold all my glory; and no man can behold all my glory, and afterwards remain in the flesh on the earth.

6 And I have a work for thee, Moses, my son; and thou art in the similitude of mine Only Begotten; and mine Only Begotten is and shall be the Savior, for he is full of grace and truth; but there is no God beside me, and all things are present with me, for I know them all.

7 And now, behold, this one thing I show unto thee, Moses, my son, for thou art in the world, and now I show it unto thee.

This astonishing experience on Mount Sinai revealed who he truly was and transformed him completely. He had been elevated as a man of the world, raised in the teachings of the world, but now he became a servant in the likeness of Jesus Christ.

This is a type and shadow of our modern-day Moses. Donald Trump will turn 80 on June 14, 2026. This is a time frame. Maybe he will have a burning Bush experience that will give him his calling and mission from God? He will get the power he needs to accomplish tremendous miracles assigned to him. Maybe he will become a translated being? Again, this is only conjecture, but we know that something is going to happen! He will be healed and everyone will know it!

SECTION 12 - MOSES

As Jesus tells us in

> 3 Nephi 21:10 But behold, the life of my servant shall be in my hand; therefore they shall not hurt him, although he shall be marred because of them. Yet I will heal him, for I will show unto them that my wisdom is greater than the cunning of the devil.

The marred servant will be healed! Everything he has endured, particularly during the previous eight years of tremendous abuse and opposition, will be washed away. Our modern-day Moses will most likely have a powerful encounter with God on his own Mount Sinai.

It is prophesied that a modern-day Moses will arrive before the coming of Jesus Christ. Christ identifies himself as the one prophesied to come forth as Moses in 3 Nephi 20:23, so most people do not go beyond that definitive description.

> 23 Behold, I am he of whom Moses spake, saying: A prophet shall the Lord your God raise up unto you of your brethren, like unto me; him shall ye hear in all things whatsoever he shall say unto you. And it shall come to pass that every soul who will not hear that prophet shall be cut off from among the people.

How are we to understand this? If Christ himself states that he's the one to come forth, surely that can't mean anyone else, right? Again, chiasmus is involved here. The corresponding verse is Third Nephi 21:11, which describes how his servant will bring the gospel to the Gentiles. Therefore, Jesus Christ is applying that scripture to himself **and** his servant. The servant acts under Christ's power and direction.

> 3 Ne 21:11 Therefore it shall come to pass that whosoever will not believe in my words, who am Jesus Christ, which the Father shall cause him to bring forth unto the Gentiles, and shall give unto him power that he shall bring them forth unto the Gentiles, (it shall be done even as Moses said) they shall be cut off from among my people who are of the covenant.

Donald Trump is the modern-day Moses. This is the one that Moses prophesied would come forth in the last days. He shall bring the gospel unto the Gentiles that Joseph Smith restored and as shown in the previous chapter, he is the suffering servant.

Donald Trump's name means "World Ruler who Triumphs." He over-

SECTION 12 - MOSES

comes everything that has been thrown against him, every opposition raised and every enemy defeated. Now we come to the central verse of the entire book of Revelation as outlined in the Joseph Smith translation:

Revelation 12: 9 And I heard a loud voice saying in heaven, Now is come salvation, and strength, and the kingdom of our God, and the power of his Christ;

Notice that the Kingdom of God is established to bring salvation to the world using "the power of his Christ." Christ means "anointed." Everything done with the power of God occurs through Jesus Christ. He's the one who performed the infinite atonement because he was the only one capable of overcoming such a monumental feat, doing so for the right reasons and out of his love for all of us, as well as his willingness to obey his father. Numerous books have been written about the majesty of Jesus Christ and what he has accomplished. No one can take his place, not even close.

Trump is the anointed one that brings this Kingdom to life. He isn't the woman, the manchild, Dragon, sun, stars, flood, or any other symbol; he's the directing hand. "Christ" is a title meaning "anointed one." All power from God comes through Jesus Christ, and so of course, Christ is the ultimate source of all of this, but Trump is in this sense, a Christ, an anointed one. Like John the Baptist, he has been anointed to perform a mission to prepare the world for Jesus Christ.

Let's reread 12:9 here changing one word:

"9 And I heard a loud voice saying in heaven, Now is come salvation, and strength, and the kingdom of our God, and the power of his "Anointed One"

Trump is the Anointed One!

All the events in the Book of Revelation come to pass through his anointed servant, Donald Trump. The establishment of the Kingdom of God is achieved through the power of Christ, and Donald Trump, is the anointed one chosen to fulfill God's word.

This marred servant has condescended to the trials and difficulties placed upon all of God's servants. All the phony trials, unjust actions against him,

SECTION 12 - MOSES

smears, and campaigns to diminish his stature and alter our view of him are well-known and should be documented. The Jews of Jesus' day sought a political savior. They wanted someone to rescue them from the oppression of Rome. They looked for another King David to come and, with the power of God, destroy their enemies. They completely missed the fact that they had strayed from God's teachings, priesthood, and ordinances, claiming that because of their lineage and connection to Moses, they were the chosen people of the Earth. Many of them were infuriated when Jesus came in and threatened their authority. He could perform miracles and even do so on the Sabbath. How dare he!

This loss of power in the eyes of the people threatened their position. It jeopardized their ability to control the populace. Soon after Christ's birth, King Herod, one of the world's most malevolent people, was visited by the Wise Men, and Herod felt threatened by a child Not long after His birth, probably around 2 years old, an angel warned Joseph to take Jesus and Mary and flee to Egypt. They had been given the financial means necessary by the gifts of gold, frankincense, and myrrh. We don't know when they came back, but they were protected for a time.

In some ways, this symbolizes what occurs in Revelation chapter 12. A woman gives birth to a man child, and an evil empire seeks its destruction. The woman and the child are taken up to heaven and spared from ruin. The Kingdom of God is born in our time, and an evil group will seek its downfall. They cannot allow anything to undermine their power or control or even pose a threat to it.

In the final days of Jesus's life, Caiaphas, the powerful and deeply corrupt Jewish leader, taunted him, seeking a miracle. However, Jesus paid him no attention, which infuriated Caiaphas. There's a picture on the side of a building in Jerusalem marking the location believed to be Caiaphas' house. He was an incredibly wealthy man and highly malevolent. While the leader of the Jewish church or synagogue, he might as well have been Satan himself. In the center of his living room was a hole that led down to a prison beneath his house, where prisoners were tortured for his entertainment. His 72-inch wide-screen television in the living room was an actual torture chamber.

This picture depicts Jesus Christ being lowered into a chamber with a

SECTION 12 - MOSES

strap wrapped around his chest and under his armpits. This story is not recorded in our current scripture. The purpose of discussing it here is to illustrate that Christ descended below all things. The most terrible thing these people could do was torture him and crucify him, but that did not signify descending below all things. Those events took place in the Garden of Gethsemane and on the cross. The weight of the universe rested upon his shoulders. No one else could bear that burden and survive. Because of the power of God he inherited from his Father, no one could take his life from him; he had to give it up willingly.

He became our savior—my savior and yours. Our actions and sins placed a burden on his shoulders. It will be for nothing unless we take advantage of that infinite gift. Turning to him is our only hope of being forgiven.

God's last-day servant Moses, the First Horseman, the Messenger of the Covenant, Donald Trump, has also condescended below all things, but in a different manner. Only his image and reputation are marred, as they cannot harm him physically. He is God's chosen political Savior for the world. He has endured a level of persecution, condemnation, and derision that no one else in history has faced. Part of the reason for this is the justification of what he must do to save the world. Just as Jesus freed us from sin and death, Donald Trump will free us from the Political bonds we are in to Babylon and set us up as a free people! (3 Ne 21:4)

His completely unjust treatment will now be directed at all those who condemned him. With the mighty power of God, he will cast the wicked into the dustbin of eternity. We've already discussed some of the dramatic actions that will be taken against those who have opposed him. The point I want to emphasize here is that he will have a significant impact on every nation on Earth.

SECTION 12 - MOSES

The First Horseman is present at the opening of the 7th Seal. He has been the instrument to initiate all of this gathering. Donald Trump, the Servant of God, stands alongside Jesus Christ and Michael, as well as many of the glorious prophets from the past and present. The people sing the song of Moses (Rev 15:3), they honor the political Savior of the world who has led them all to the Savior of humanity: Jesus Christ. They sing a song of him and of the Lamb. They proclaim how great and marvelous God's works are as they acknowledge everything He has done to bring this about. They honor the servant for what he has accomplished and what he endured to arrive at this point. He has united all the nations under his rule to turn them over to Jesus Christ. He has faced tremendous opposition and triumphed! And he triumphed because of the Lamb of God, whose power permeates the universe and on which all of those chosen by God may rely to achieve their blessings. It is a stunningly glorious experience filled with reverence and awe and gratitude!

MICHAEL or ADAM   JESUS CHRIST   DONALD TRUMP

As mentioned, Donald Trump means "world ruler who triumphs." He is the political Savior of every nation on earth and will make it possible for every person who desires the Kingdom of God to have it. The destruction of the American head of the beast is only the beginning. All world governments must come under his rule and control so that they can be given to Christ.

Before even taking office, he began discussing the acquisition of the Panama Canal and Greenland. He suggested Canada as a potential 51st state. No president has addressed such matters in a century. This is merely a glimpse of what is to come. Zion encompasses all of North, Central, and South America. Joseph Smith prophesied that one day, it would all trans-

SECTION 12 - MOSES

form into Zion. He is already starting to fulfill that prophecy. We have only witnessed the beginning of astounding events that are imminent.

I understand these are bold statements that might lead some to believe we should idolize him. Not at all. I'm simply highlighting what prophecy indicates will occur. These remarkably dramatic events aren't what most people typically consider. We spend our days fixating on minor issues that matter in our lives, but we rarely contemplate the broader perspective that God's servant must possess.

He is currently tasked with wounding the head of the beast as part of establishing the political Kingdom of God. During the campaign, he promised that everything would be revealed. All those who have gained political and economic power, believing they were safe within their concealed group of cohorts from being brought to justice, are scrambling in fear. The last thing they desire is to be exposed for what they have truly done. However, as prophesied, this exposure must occur, and everything will be revealed from the rooftops.

His desired cabinet appointees have all been installed, and each one of them has been tasked with uncovering and revealing secret documents that these leaders thought would never come to light. They are examining incredibly corrupt systems involving payments to our enemies and actions against our own country. The revelations regarding not only the amount of money but also the direction in which taxpayer money flows reveal a level of corruption that has never been seen before. In the process, most likely millions of government-connected jobs will be eliminated. Of course, this makes people upset, but all of these things must take place to save the country. America is currently built as the great and spacious building, high in the air and supported solely by debt and pride. All of that debt will cause it to collapse if not resolved. Let's examine a couple of points regarding how he will wound the head of the beast:

Suppose it is proven that Barry Sotero, known as Barack Obama, was fraudulently elected president of the United States under false pretenses and that we have been misled all these years. This would send shock waves throughout this country. If he is an illegitimate president, all the laws he signed are invalid.

When it is demonstrated that Joseph Biden was fraudulently elected in

SECTION 12 - MOSES

the 2020 campaign and somehow miraculously obtained 81 million votes through unlawful means, all the laws he enacted will be considered illegal.

Within a month of his election, President Trump issued nearly 100 executive orders that revealed information that had been off-limits for decades. Discovering that we have actually been funding the Taliban all these years while fighting them should make every American furious. Witnessing the government's involvement in child sex trafficking and drugs should ignite a revolution. Learning that much of the money spent on wars has returned as kickbacks to politicians to fuel more wars should infuriate the masses. This is an endless list of the corruption that the Gadianton Robbers have created to amass their wealth, power, and ability to act without consequences. Astonishingly, some individuals are upset with Donald Trump for exposing these truths and are doing everything possible to prevent him from fulfilling his divine mission.

During the Revolutionary War, most people in the country did not want to fight England because they were making too much money. They didn't want to change the status quo. George Washington and his Continental Army had to fight under extremely difficult conditions and struggled to gain support. The idea of fighting England was unpopular. Why change everything when they were earning more than they ever had before? It's estimated that less than 20% of the population supported the war. However, if it hadn't been for George Washington and his troops believing they had a divine mission to help establish the Kingdom of God, we would not be here today in the same condition. We would not have benefited from the remarkable developments that have occurred here in America.

But Donald Trump also faces tremendous opposition. People don't want to change the status quo. They resist living under laws, regulations, or a balanced budget. They want to act freely and minimize their obligations. However, Trump has a divine mission as the modern-day Moses, tasked with liberating the House of Israel from the bondage of the Egyptians. After his upcoming burning bush experience, he will perform remarkable miracles that will liberate hundreds of millions around the globe. They will be freed from their taskmasters and prisons, whether physical, financial, or mental. He will establish a free people, seen worldwide as the example that other countries will aspire to emulate.

SECTION 12 - MOSES

This will shake the whole foundation of what people believe the United States stands for. And because of the image that our biased beast media system has given everyone, there will still be people who won't accept it. They will resist because they must acknowledge that they lived and believed a lie.

> 3 Ne 21: 9 For in that day, for my sake shall the Father work a work, which shall be a great and a marvelous work among them; and there shall be among them those who will not believe it, although a man shall declare it unto them.

This tremendous disruption will have a remarkable effect on the entire world. When it is revealed that each of the other countries has also participated in illegal and corrupt activities, a revolution will occur. We can hardly comprehend such a disruption.

Donald Trump is the political savior of the modern world. I have been unable to tell anyone about this particular function because too many people I've talked to did not accept what I had even partially given. Trump's actions as God's servant will completely dwarf those events done by Moses 3300 years ago! He is the modern-day Moses prophesied by Moses himself.

3rd Nephi 21:4, talks about setting them up as free people. This passage references the First Horseman and Revelation 12-14. Revelation 12 describes how the Kingdom of God comes forth and is attacked by the Beast System. Revelation 13 is about the Beast System and describes tactics used by the devil and the Antichrist. It describes a seven-headed beast coming out of the water.

When Trump comes forth to establish the Kingdom of God, he destroys the United States Secret Combination. This is the wounding of one of the heads of the beast. This deadly wound causes the United States to go into tremendous turmoil because millions of government dependent workers will lose their jobs. Most likely the economy will be in shambles for a period of time. The power structure will be without their finances and support.

The elites will jump up and down and scream like never before and accuse everyone of committing treason if they support Donald Trump. In their eyes, he is now considered treasonous and a traitor to the country, and they will set themselves up to commit blasphemy by claiming that they are the actual chosen system of God. They will say, "We follow the original Constitution! We are the power structure that has been organized since the beginning of our country. Anyone against that must declare allegiance to us or not be allowed into our banking system!"

Blasphemy is assigning something to God that isn't God's. I had always thought this was something different, but the Antichrist comes in a suit and tie. The current Beast System of government is wicked to its core. It is corrupt beyond anything we have ever seen, and yet they will claim they are God's chosen.

Unfortunately, as the Book of Mormon and Isaiah consistently emphasize, many modern-day Gentiles who are church members will fall away. Fortunately, not all will, but due to their wealth and comfort, they do not strengthen their testimonies as they ought, missing out on their blessings. (See my chapter on why people leave the church).

Because the Gentiles rejected the gospel (as warned by Jesus) that was given to them, many members of the church fell away, and we are witnessing that now in our country. Many have failed to recognize the tremendous gift they've been given and have failed to nurture and water their tree of faith to stay on the straight and narrow path. They've stopped paying tithing. They've stopped keeping their covenants. They've stopped following the word of wisdom and have spoken out against the church in various ways. Many people have built up large followings on social media, and unlike any time in the past, they find support for anything they do or say. This makes it much easier to fall away.

Because of this fall, this brings up the prediction that Christ mentions about how the House of Israel will overrun the land and take the wealth given to the Gentiles for themselves. This will be a horrific time in our country. As bad as the Civil War was in the 1860s, it will pale in comparison to this. We have been watching this event begin right now as the porous southern border has allowed tens of millions of people to come into our country illegally. There are those in power who have paid them to come in and even prevented border security from doing their job. All manner of people have entered the country, whether they were deserving or not, and sadly, most of them appear to be criminals and low-lifes from countries around the world. Many were housed in hotels and places nationwide at taxpayer expense.

This is one of the reasons that Trump won the 2024 election, and he has spoken out vociferously against this. However, the Democrats have allowed

SECTION 12 - MOSES

this because they wanted to change the census and obtain more power and votes to remain in office. They were willing to give away the country to retain power. They wanted to have a forever Democrat party running every aspect of the government. It is one of the most treasonous things that has ever been done in our country! In fact, it has never been done in one's own country. This tactic has been used many times throughout history to destroy another country and bring its population down into submission. This time it will bring to pass the destruction of those who made a "covenant with death" as mentioned in Isaiah 28:14-18.

It's possible that very shortly, the illegal aliens will run freely throughout the country and take whatever the Gentiles have. There are shipping containers full of weapons and arms that will be given to these people when those who invited them stop paying them for staying here. Can you imagine such destruction? They fly here on planes and spend time in nice hotels. They're given weekly allotments for food and entertainment. They're given everything that they won't give our own homeless or veterans. But then, all of a sudden, that will stop. And now, there are tens of millions of people who cannot support themselves and are without the ability to buy food or even get a job. Then, they are given the ability to take whatever they want with free weapons.

> D&C 112:24 Behold, vengeance cometh speedily upon the inhabitants of the earth, a day of wrath, a day of burning, a day of desolation, of weeping, of mourning, and of lamentation; and as a whirlwind it shall come upon all the face of the earth, saith the Lord.
>
> 25 And upon my house shall it begin, and from my house shall it go forth, saith the Lord;
>
> 26 First among those among you, saith the Lord, who have professed to know my name and have not known me, and have blasphemed against me in the midst of my house, saith the Lord.

This is an astonishingly frightful scenario, and it fits right in with what Christ told the Nephites in 3rd Nephi 21:21: "And I will execute vengeance and fury upon them, even as upon the heathen, such as they have not heard." All this comes upon not only the gentile nation of America because they did not accept the gospel but mainly upon those who were once members of the church and had fallen away. Upon my house shall it begin like an F5 Tornado (whirlwind) sweeping across the plains of Kansas or Oklahoma, leveling everything in its path. But,

> Isaiah 3:10 Say ye to the righteous, that it shall be well with him: for they shall eat the fruit of their doings.

Our only hope lies in Zion. It will be a place of safety, protection, freedom, and beauty on Earth. I urge each of us to do everything possible to prepare for that day. While the greatest blessings are reserved for those who have stood firm and remained faithful, they are a part of Zion and are protected. God's protection will most likely cover the homes and buildings of righteous members outside of Zion. Some have seen visions of the future in which gangs of marauders avoid certain homes and areas.

Some people I've talked to about this scenario of him being the "arm of the Lord," as mentioned in several places in the Scriptures, question this because one of the definitions of that arm is that he will be "the righteous" or "righteousness." From our perspective, it's difficult to imagine him receiving that label due to his checkered past. But Isaiah tells us:

> Isa 62:1 For Zion's sake will I not hold my peace, and for Jerusalem's sake I will not rest, until the righteousness thereof go forth as brightness, and the salvation thereof as a lamp that burneth.
>
> 2 And the Gentiles shall see thy righteousness, and all kings thy glory: and thou shalt be called by a new name, which the mouth of the Lord shall name.
>
> 3 Thou shalt also be a crown of glory in the hand of the Lord, and a royal diadem in the hand of thy God.

When Isaiah appeared before the Lord in chapter 6, he cried out, "woe is me. I am undone." (Isa 6:5) He recognized that even he, the one we call the great prophet Isaiah, was not worthy. The angel came and through the atonement of Jesus Christ, touched his lips with a burning coal cleansing his soul, and he became God's chosen prophet, not only for the people of his day but for the rest of the world.

I assert that Donald Trump will experience something similar. He will have a burning Bush experience to cleanse his soul and make him the Lord's chosen vessel. This experience will give him the power and authority to accomplish everything God has planned for him. The example of Isaiah is a type and shadow for our day and will be similar to what Trump experiences,

SECTION 12 - MOSES

which will bring about the prophecy in:

> 3 Nephi 21:43 Behold, my servant shall deal prudently; he shall be exalted and extolled and be very high.
>
> 44 As many were astonished at thee—his visage was so marred, more than any man, and his form more than the sons of men—
>
> 45 So shall he sprinkle many nations; the kings shall shut their mouths at him, for that which had not been told them shall they see; and that which they had not heard shall they consider.

He says his servant shall be exalted, extolled, and be very high. First, he's a billionaire, which I believe is rare for God's servants in most of history. Usually, those of great wealth do not look to God or depend on him.

But I believe his being exalted and extolled is from Revelation 12 when he is whisked off to heaven. That's when he possibly receives his translation ordinance or burning bush experience. He, and all those who are part of Zion, will be translated like the 3 Nephites. He will be lifted up, exalted, extolled, and very high! He will have an experience similar to Isaiah and lifted up to God himself and learn that he is God's chosen servant!

His sprinkling of many nations can be translated as gathering many nations that will be amazed at him. He is well respected worldwide, except for a large portion of our own country. His establishment of Zion and the incredible prosperity after the Beast System is kicked out are excellent examples for the rest of the world, and they show great interest in these things. But they had never heard of it before. They had never seen this done and that which they had not been told so they consider.

But he will establish Zion and Jerusalem. He will create a tremendously functional constitutional government here in the United States, based on the Constitution, without all of its enumerable additions that are not according to God's law. This will cause tremendous prosperity in the country as the people in Zion follow God's laws. This will be the pivot point whereby the world's nations and kings will consider something they had not seen before. This is when they will allow the missionaries to come into their country because of the incredible example of what is happening in Zion.

While the rest of the world suffers under the tyranny of artificial intelligence capabilities controlling what everyone does, where they go, what

SECTION 12 - MOSES

they buy, what they read or watch, and whether they have the privilege to look out their windows or even live, those with deficiencies, illnesses, physical problems, and mental issues, as well as those who refuse to toe the line under those who decide who lives or dies, are left vulnerable. The entire world will exist under a crushing tyranny in a Babylonian beast system economy that is worse than anything ever seen in history.

This stands in stark opposition to the freedom of Zion, the only truly free place in the world, where individuals can own property and move as they please, surrounded by people who care for and love them. They seek to benefit each other because of total conversion that is not achieved by force, but through love and the willingness to serve our Savior, Jesus Christ. Donald Trump, the modern Moses, will lead all those who desire peace and freedom from across the globe, despite being opposed at every step; however, they will lose every time.

This astonishing event is part of the prophecy that people will never talk about the Red Sea again, as mentioned in,

> Jeremiah 16:14 Therefore, behold, the days come, saith the Lord, that it shall no more be said, The Lord liveth, that brought up the children of Israel out of the land of Egypt;
>
> 15 But, The Lord liveth, that brought up the children of Israel from the land of the north, and from all the lands whither he had driven them: and I will bring them again into their land that I gave unto their fathers.

The 144,000 mentioned in Revelation 7 appear during the 6th seal, when all the upheaval occurs. Many of these individuals were martyrs as part of the 5th seal, but as we learn in the Doctrine and Covenants, these people are high priests who go forth throughout the world and gather the elect, those who have not taken the Mark of the Beast, and bring them into Zion. Because they are part of Zion, most likely, they are translated beings, and they will have the authority of God to translate those they find and gather them back together as one.

> D&C 77:11 Q. What are we to understand by sealing the one hundred and forty-four thousand, out of all the tribes of Israel—twelve thousand out of every tribe?
>
> A. We are to understand that those who are sealed are high priests,

SECTION 12 - MOSES

ordained unto the holy order of God, to administer the everlasting gospel; for they are those who are ordained out of every nation, kindred, tongue, and people, by the angels to whom is given power over the nations of the earth, to bring as many as will come to the church of the Firstborn.

Notice that they are out gathering people to bring them into the highest orders of the Church of Jesus Christ of Latter-day Saints, the Church of the Firstborn. This is Zion. It is a part of those who have reached the level of spiritual maturity that they become the sons and daughters of God. This is beyond baptism, whereby he becomes our father. The firstborn son was his chosen one. Those who are part of the church of the firstborn receive the same inheritance as his firstborn.

The covenants of the Father in 3rd Nephi 22 and Isaiah 54 are an extremely beautiful concept. God does everything for His people, even though they may not be righteous, because of the covenants made to their ancient fathers. They received this tremendous blessing, which caused the Jewish people to wonder where all these individuals came from. They are of the House of Israel, spread all over the earth, and are part of the remarkable growth the church will experience soon. It's impossible to describe such a glorious event.

He will establish a free people. Zion will be the focal point of freedom, using the Constitution of the United States as its rule of law. That Constitution was inspired by God and is the law that will go forth from Zion. Being established as a free people allows all these dramatic events to unfold, including the gathering of Israel, the conversion of hundreds of millions of people, the construction of temples in Missouri and Jerusalem, the dismantling of the Beast System armies, and the defeat of all the corrupt Gadianton Robbers.

The Kingdom of God is now established and the people are free for possibly the first time in world history. It's impossible to overestimate just how powerful this event is. That's why it's the center verse in the Book of Revelation. That's why it's the center point in the chiasmus revealed through Jesus Christ. Being set up as a free people where only the righteous will be permitted to dwell, will bring peace to those who seek it.

As previously mentioned, Zion is populated by righteous individuals of every kind, whether mortal, angelic, translated, resurrected, etc. Those who are welcomed do not need to be members of the Church of Jesus Christ of Latter-day Saints. Although the church leadership will manage the affairs of Zion, individuals from all religions, nations, languages, and backgrounds will be present. The only thing they share is a desire to follow God, a promise to keep covenants, and a refusal to accept the Mark of the Beast.

The unrighteous will fight against it. Those who are consumed by power and money and care not for the things of God will fight against it. Those who do not repent of their sins and want to continue following their own God, will face the ravages of living outside of Zion. They will be subject to the Babylonian economy that is run by the Beast System with its counterfeit Utopian goals using force and the Mark of the Beast to control everyone.

This is what Donald Trump, the anointed one, our modern-day Moses, will achieve. Furthermore, there is another event in antiquity that serves as a type and shadow of something else he will do. He was prophesied by Isaiah, and his name is Cyrus.

Section 13 - Cyrus

In Isaiah 45 he prophesies of a person named Cyrus who will save the House of Israel.

> Isa 45:1 Thus saith the Lord to his anointed, to Cyrus, whose right hand I have holden, to subdue nations before him; and I will loose the loins of kings, to open before him the two leaved gates; and the gates shall not be shut;
>
> 2 I will go before thee, and make the crooked places straight: I will break in pieces the gates of brass, and cut in sunder the bars of iron:
>
> 3 And I will give thee the treasures of darkness, and hidden riches of secret places, that thou mayest know that I, the Lord, which call thee by thy name, am the God of Israel.
>
> 4 For Jacob my servant's sake, and Israel mine elect, I have even called thee by thy name: I have surnamed thee, though thou hast not known me.

King Cyrus brought the Jews out of Babylon and back to Jerusalem to rebuild the temple. The one mentioned in scripture who accomplished this work from 559 to 530 BC serves as a type and shadow of the future King Cyrus, Donald Trump, who will do the same, but on a much larger scale for the Jews scattered throughout the world. The Jews even minted a coin (image [22]) in April 2019 featuring Trump on one side and Cyrus on the other, as he was the first president to recognize Jerusalem as the capital of Israel. Trump is well-regarded by the Jews, and for good reason: he's their promised future deliverer.

He frees the captives and vanquishes their oppressors:

> Isa 45:13 I have raised him up in righteousness, and I will direct all his ways: he shall build my city, and he shall let go my captives, not for price nor reward, saith the Lord of hosts.
>
> 14 Thus saith the Lord, The labour of Egypt, and merchandise of Ethiopia and of the Sabeans, men of stature, shall come over unto

SECTION 13 - CYRUS

thee, and they shall be thine: they shall come after thee; in chains they shall come over, and they shall fall down unto thee, they shall make supplication unto thee, saying, Surely God is in thee; and there is none else, there is no God.

This is a stunning turn of events. All of those who had held power and control over God's people are now bowing down to Donald Trump and recognizing that God has directed his path. It's very likely that many of these will convert to the gospel. We are told in other passages that the lost 10 tribes will bring their wealth to Ephraim, and here we see the merchants of the Earth and men of stature, greatly humbled and recognizing God's hand.

Many people wonder why there's so much emphasis on covenants. Why would it matter to have a covenant given to a person who lived 5,000 years ago, and why would it have any effect on us today? Even if the people fall away for thousands of years, there comes a time when God will fulfill his covenant with his chosen leader. The only reason Noah was saved in the ark was because Enoch covenanted with God that he would do this.

> Moses 7:50 And it came to pass that Enoch continued his cry unto the Lord, saying: I ask thee, O Lord, in the name of thine Only Begotten, even Jesus Christ, that thou wilt have mercy upon Noah and his seed, that the earth might never more be covered by the floods.
>
> 51 And the Lord could not withhold; and he covenanted with Enoch, and sware unto him with an oath, that he would stay the floods; that he would call upon the children of Noah;
>
> 52 And he sent forth an unalterable decree, that a remnant of his seed should always be found among all nations, while the earth should stand;

God made a covenant with Enoch to keep people on Earth for as long as it stands. You and I are the fulfillment of this covenant; we wouldn't be here without it. However, Enoch sees that the Earth has been in pain for many years because of the wickedness upon it. The Earth is in great turmoil and suffering. Then, he pleads with God, saying:

> Moses 7:58 And again Enoch wept and cried unto the Lord, saying: When shall the earth rest?
>
> 59 And Enoch beheld the Son of Man ascend up unto the Father; and he called unto the Lord, saying: Wilt thou not come again upon the

SECTION 13 - CYRUS

earth? Forasmuch as thou art God, and I know thee, and thou hast sworn unto me, and commanded me that I should ask in the name of thine Only Begotten; thou hast made me, and given unto me a right to thy throne, and not of myself, but through thine own grace; wherefore, I ask thee if thou wilt not come again on the earth.

60 And the Lord said unto Enoch: As I live, even so will I come in the last days, in the days of wickedness and vengeance, to fulfil the oath which I have made unto you concerning the children of Noah;

In the last days, during this time of wickedness and vengeance, He will fulfill the oath made with Noah to keep his descendants on the Earth until the end. We are blessed to be alive because of Enoch! We have received tremendous covenantal blessings through him.

The lost tribes, the Jews, and all of the House of Israel are blessed today because of the covenant God made with the prophets of the past, including Enoch, Noah, Abraham, Moses, and others. Our modern-day Cyrus, Donald Trump, is moving forward to fulfill that covenant. He retrieves the lost tribes and brings them to America. He gathers the Jews scattered throughout the world and returns them to Jerusalem. Those who do not fall under that covenant do not share in that blessing. That is why we go out as missionaries to try to convert the world, because they are the ones who are blessed.

As the Lord stated to Joseph Smith in,

D&C 1:12 Prepare ye, prepare ye for that which is to come, for the Lord is nigh;

13 And the anger of the Lord is kindled, and his sword is bathed in heaven, and it shall fall upon the inhabitants of the earth.

14 And the arm of the Lord shall be revealed; and the day cometh that they who will not hear the voice of the Lord, neither the voice of his servants, neither give heed to the words of the prophets and apostles, shall be cut off from among the people;

15 For they have strayed from mine ordinances, and have broken mine everlasting covenant;

16 They seek not the Lord to establish his righteousness, but every man walketh in his own way, and after the image of his own god, whose image is in the likeness of the world, and whose substance is that of an idol, which waxeth old and shall perish in Babylon, even

SECTION 13 - CYRUS

Babylon the great, which shall fall.

The Lord is coming, and He is angry. His sword is bathed in heaven, and the arm of the Lord shall be revealed. This "arm" is Donald Trump. Those who do not heed God's servants will be cut off.

Why? Because they've created their own religions. They've shaped it the way they desire. They do not seek the Lord to establish His righteousness; instead, everyone devises their own God and beliefs. As a result, we arrive at the next verses that discuss what God is doing to save as many people as possible from their fallen condition before the complete destruction of the Earth:

> D&C 1:17 Wherefore, I the Lord, knowing the calamity which should come upon the inhabitants of the earth, called upon my servant Joseph Smith, Jun., and spake unto him from heaven, and gave him commandments;
>
> 18 And also gave commandments to others, that they should proclaim these things unto the world; and all this that it might be fulfilled, which was written by the prophets—
>
> 19 The weak things of the world shall come forth and break down the mighty and strong ones, that man should not counsel his fellow man, neither trust in the arm of flesh—
>
> 20 But that every man might speak in the name of God the Lord, even the Savior of the world;
>
> 21 That faith also might increase in the earth;
>
> 22 That mine everlasting covenant might be established;
>
> 23 That the fulness of my gospel might be proclaimed by the weak and the simple unto the ends of the world, and before kings and rulers.

He called upon his prophet Joseph Smith and gave him commandments. He sent forth the weak and simple Missionaries all over the Earth to bring the gospel covenant to them, that his everlasting covenant may be established with them, and that they may be blessed because of that same covenant.

SECTION 13 - CYRUS

An interesting side note is the number of times I've witnessed Christian bullies recording confrontations with our young missionaries, which highlights their lack of knowledge and experience. These individuals, usually men, are extremely abusive. They are loud, bold, and domineering. Many people online cheer them on and thank them for exposing how "wrong" they are. Viral videos are posted all over social media and receive rave reviews, yet they are merely condemning themselves.

God said he would send out the weak and simple to thresh the nations of the Earth.

> D&C 35:13 Wherefore, I call upon the weak things of the world, those who are unlearned and despised, to thresh the nations by the power of my Spirit;

This is a sign that they are on God's mission. They're young, inexperienced, hopeful, and not too tainted by the doctrines of the world. No, they don't know everything, and some of them look somewhat embarrassed, but they should rejoice, and know that justice will come in their defense.

> D&C 35:14 And their arm shall be my arm, and I will be their shield and their buckler; and I will gird up their loins, and they shall fight manfully for me; and their enemies shall be under their feet; and I will let fall the sword in their behalf, and by the fire of mine indignation will I preserve them.

Every one of those who has persecuted those poor young missionaries will be held accountable before God for such abuse. Everyone who cheered them on and didn't recognize God's servants, the weak and simple servants, will also face the justice of God.

Now, back to our main discussion.

The events involving Cyrus occurred long after Isaiah had died. He had clearly seen it in a vision, and most people regard that event as the fulfillment of his prophecy. However, Isaiah takes whatever he can from history and applies it to our time. The emergence of the modern-day Cyrus and the remarkable work he accomplishes will dwarf the Cyrus of old.

I have not spent much time in this book about Isaiah, as I have focused on the Book of Revelation. Avraham Gileadi[23] has done tremendous work with Isaiah, so I will leave that to him and others. God told me to read the

SECTION 13 - CYRUS

Book of Revelation, so that's what I'm focusing on, but this aspect of Cyrus is essential in our discussion.

In Christ's prophecy in 3 Nephi 22, he quotes the entire 54th chapter of Isaiah. This beautiful chapter about the gathering of the Jews and the House of Israel is astonishing. The Jews have felt abandoned like a widow, a rejected wife who never bore children. Now, all of a sudden, in a dramatic turn of events, there are hundreds of millions of covenant-keeping members of the House of Israel.

They dwell in the New Jerusalem of both the Eastern and Western Hemispheres. This is before Christ descends on the Mount of Olives and splits it in two. Why do I say that? Because of these verses in that chapter:

> 3 Ne 22: 15 Behold, they shall surely gather together against thee, not by me; whosoever shall gather together against thee shall fall for thy sake.
>
> 16 Behold, I have created the smith that bloweth the coals in the fire, and that bringeth forth an instrument for his work; and I have created the waster to destroy.
>
> 17 No weapon that is formed against thee shall prosper; and every tongue that shall revile against thee in judgment thou shalt condemn. This is the heritage of the servants of the Lord, and their righteousness is of me, saith the Lord.

When God says they will gather against them and that no weapon formed against them shall prosper, when does this occur? There must be a time when the covenant-keeping and spared Jewish and House of Israel members live in peace. Outside, there are all kinds of opposition and weapons. Nations are trying to destroy them while,

> 3 Ne 22:13 ... all thy children shall be taught of the Lord; and great shall be the peace of thy children.
>
> 14 In righteousness shalt thou be established; thou shalt be far from oppression for thou shalt not fear, and from terror for it shall not come near thee.

I will discuss this in more detail in the context of modern-day Zion, but I just want to get you thinking about it. In verse nine, he talks about the waters of Noah unto him. That is a reference to the covenant God made with Enoch to spare the people and visit them in the last days.

According to the Bible Dictionary, this is what the Abrahamic Covenant means: Abraham first received the gospel by baptism (which is the covenant of salvation). Then he had conferred upon him the higher priesthood, and he entered into celestial marriage (which is the covenant of exaltation), gaining assurance thereby that he would have eternal increase. Finally he received a promise that all of these blessings would be offered to all of his mortal posterity (D&C 132:29–50; Abr. 2:6–11). Included in the divine promises to Abraham were the assurances that (1) Christ would come through his lineage, and that (2) Abraham's posterity would receive certain lands as an eternal inheritance (Gen. 17; 22:15–18; Gal. 3; Abr. 2). These promises taken together are called the "Abrahamic covenant." It was renewed with Isaac (Gen. 26:1–4, 24) and again with Jacob (Gen. 28; 35:9–13; 48:3–4).

The portions of the covenant that pertain to personal salvation and eternal increase are renewed with each individual who receives the ordinance of celestial marriage (see D&C 132:29–33). Those of non-Israelite lineage, commonly known as Gentiles, are adopted into the House of Israel and become heirs of the covenant and the seed of Abraham through the ordinances of the gospel (Gal. 3:26–29).

Being an heir to the Abrahamic covenant does not make one a "chosen person" per se but does signify that such are chosen to responsibly carry the gospel to all the peoples of the earth. Abraham's seed have carried out the missionary activity in all the nations since Abraham's day. (Matt. 3:9; Abr. 2:9–11.)

To fulfill the covenant God made with Abraham—having particular reference to the fact that the literal seed of his body would be entitled to all of the blessings of the gospel (Abr. 2:10–11)—a number of specific and particular things must take place in the last days. The gospel must be restored, the priesthood must be conferred again upon man, the keys of the sealing power must be given again to mortals, Israel must be gathered, and the Holy Ghost must be poured out upon the Gentiles. All this has already taken place or is in process of fulfillment.

SECTION 13 - CYRUS

The lands that were promised Abraham included:

1-Modern Israel

2-Parts of Jordan, Syria, and Iraq

3-Land from the Nile River to the Euphrates River

Currently, the Jewish nation possesses only a small portion of what was promised to Abraham and his seed. The term " seed " specifically refers to those of the House of Israel, not Ishmael, as he will be another nation. Just as Cyrus brought the Jews back to Jerusalem and helped them build the temple and reclaim their land, Donald Trump will assist them in reclaiming all the land promised to Abraham, regardless of who owns it now. This will be a significant achievement in the history of negotiations. Most likely, it will lead to some sort of conflict because others will not want to give it up willingly without extraordinary compensation. However, it will be taken back, and because of this tremendous accomplishment, they will never speak of Moses or Cyrus again

Donald Trump has an extremely important role to play worldwide. Under his leadership, the nations of the Earth will be defeated. They will consider what they had not been told. He's preparing the Earth so that all nations will come under Jesus Christ's rule. Just like George Washington, who was shot at multiple times yet never killed despite losing seven horses and having bullet-riddled clothes, they can't kill Donald Trump either. "The life of my servant shall be in my hand." (3 Ne 21:10).

I hope you have accepted this so far. Everyone knows there's something different about him. Yes, he is brash and egotistical, but no one without a strong ego could have endured the astonishing amount of opposition he faced. Before his election, all of the charges against him were finally dropped. An examination of all the court filings and investigations revealed they had nothing against him. They completely corrupted the Lawfare system for political gain just as they had done against Jesus Christ 2000 years ago!

SECTION 13 - CYRUS

I mention this here because the Beast System will do anything to eliminate him. They have tried everything possible to stop the emergence of God's servant, who will save millions or possibly even billions of people desiring to enter into a covenant with God to be spared in the last days. This is the mission of God's Chosen Servant, the First Horseman!

In both negative examples from the Book of Mormon, societies destroy themselves through self-inflicted destruction that wipes out entire nations; we would find ourselves in the same situation. Satan desires nothing more than to ruin everyone. He does not want anyone to return to God. Just as God has used multiple leaders throughout history to fulfill His work, He is using Trump to do the same in the last days. Without his leadership, despite his egotistical nature, we would not be blessed. We would suffer at the hands of the Gadianton Robbers, foretold in the Book of Mormon to overrun the Earth and seek the destruction of all mankind.

> Helaman 2:13 states "And behold, in the end of this book (of Mormon) ye shall see that this Gadianton did prove the overthrow, yea, almost the entire destruction of the people of Nephi."

Moroni provides a grave warning: any nation that aids these secret combinations will incur the wrath of God. He particularly warns the Gentiles so that we might repent and be spared.

> Ether 8: 22 And whatsoever nation shall uphold such secret combinations, to get power and gain, until they shall spread over the nation, behold, they shall be destroyed; for the Lord will not suffer that the blood of his saints, which shall be shed by them, shall always cry unto him from the ground for vengeance upon them and yet he avenge them not.
>
> 23 Wherefore, O ye Gentiles, it is wisdom in God that these things should be shown unto you, that thereby ye may repent of your sins, and suffer not that these murderous combinations shall get above you, which are built up to get power and gain—and the work, yea, even the work of destruction come upon you, yea, even the sword of the justice of the Eternal God shall fall upon you, to your overthrow and destruction if ye shall suffer these things to be.
>
> 24 Wherefore, the Lord commandeth you, when ye shall see these things come among you that ye shall awake to a sense of your awful situation, because of this secret combination which shall be among

SECTION 13 - CYRUS

you; or wo be unto it, because of the blood of them who have been slain; for they cry from the dust for vengeance upon it, and also upon those who built it up.

25 For it cometh to pass that whoso buildeth it up seeketh to overthrow the freedom of all lands, nations, and countries; and it bringeth to pass the destruction of all people, for it is built up by the devil, who is the father of all lies; even that same liar who beguiled our first parents, yea, even that same liar who hath caused man to commit murder from the beginning; who hath hardened the hearts of men that they have murdered the prophets, and stoned them, and cast them out from the beginning.

Verse 25 indicates that their goal is to destroy all people; that is their objective. Why do you think there have been over 64 million abortions in the United States in the past 40 years? Why do you think there are so many toxins in our food, chemicals in the water, and pollution everywhere? Why do we hear horrific accounts of child sex trafficking and slavery in its many forms? Why do organizations claim that the Earth cannot sustain this many people and must be reduced by 95%? Why are there endless wars? Why the stream of violent videos and games? Why the constant support for riots and mobs, and the reduction of justice? Why the flood of drugs and the rescinding of laws preventing them? Why has the education system caused the nation's standing to drop from first in the world to 40th? Why the decline in health and the increase in cancer and other diseases?

It's all because they want to kill you or enslave you.

We should feel blessed to have him. As the popular meme states, with him pointing directly at us, "They aren't coming after me; they are coming after you. I'm just in the way." This is absolutely true.

Section 14 - Nephi, Mormon and Moroni's Warnings

Three primary authors of the Book of Mormon lived during a time when their nation faced destruction. The prophet, Mormon and his son Moroni, view events from a very distinct perspective. The same with Ether. Everything they write throughout the Book of Mormon reflects that viewpoint. Nephi was another primary author and he wrote everything in his books according to the vision he had seen of the future. Mormon understands what it's like to witness a nation completely self-destruct after forsaking God and choosing to follow its own paths.

Mormon has observed the consequences of the Gadianton Robbers taking over the government and ruling with cruelty. He has watched individuals apostatize and turn against what they once believed to be true. He has seen sin grow among the people and consume everything they do. He has witnessed how the nation, once enlightened by none other than Jesus Christ and his disciples, turned away from that light and knowledge into terrible darkness.

After his father passed away, Moroni was given the responsibility of completing the record and transporting it to a hill in upstate New York, where he would show it 1,400 years later to the young prophet Joseph Smith. Moroni is completely alone. He has no one to depend on. His entire family has been killed, and his enemies are determined to destroy him. His only comfort comes from the spirit of God and the angels who visit him. Besides them, he has no mortal friends.

Nephi sees that destruction but he also sees beyond it and the glorious future that awaits the righteous who are a part of Zion.

From these two perspectives, terrible destruction and glorious salvation, cover much of the Book of Mormon, they gathered everything they had witnessed and prepared it for us. Both of them highlight an important lesson we need to learn. By remaining faithful while everything else is completely destroyed around them, they offer us a truly unique viewpoint from which the Gentiles, members of the Church of Jesus Christ of Latter-day Saints, will also need to endure.

Mormon led the armies that he knew would fail until a certain point when, after winning a small battle, they boasted among themselves of their

SECTION 14 - NEPHI, MORMON AND MORONI'S WARNINGS

great strength and then did the unthinkable:

> Mormon 3:9 And now, because of this great thing which my people, the Nephites, had done, they began to boast in their own strength, and began to swear before the heavens that they would avenge themselves of the blood of their brethren who had been slain by their enemies.
>
> 10 And they did swear by the heavens, and also by the throne of God, that they would go up to battle against their enemies, and would cut them off from the face of the land.
>
> 11 And it came to pass that I, Mormon, did utterly refuse from this time forth to be a commander and a leader of this people, because of their wickedness and abomination.

Mormon would not support this action. He withdrew his leadership and spent the next several verses in this chapter lamenting how far they had fallen. He recites the number of things he had done to try to save them but in the end, they turned to vengeance and therefore:

> 16 And it came to pass that I utterly refused to go up against mine enemies; and I did even as the Lord had commanded me; and I did stand as an idle witness to manifest unto the world the things which I saw and heard, according to the manifestations of the Spirit which had testified of things to come.

They had completely denied the spirit and succumbed to revenge and vengeance. This turned into an endless cycle of attacks because someone was killed on their side, prompting retaliation against the other side. This spirals into extinction as they refuse to turn to God in the midst of terrible trials. This is part of the bottomless pit, the filthy water, the Justice of God upon the wicked.

War is not fun. Most of us have been fortunate not to have lived through wars, as we have not experienced conflict on our land during our lifetimes. We are used to relative ease, peace, and prosperity. We grumble when someone cuts in front of us on the freeway too quickly. We complain about everything.

But these people had fallen from a similar position. Over several years, they had rejected the teachings of Jesus Christ, and it's most likely that they had the sealed portion of the gold plates revealed to them. They were the

SECTION 14 - NEPHI, MORMON AND MORONI'S WARNINGS

words of the Brother of Jared from the vision he had received from God and recorded by Ether. They weren't sealed up by Moroni yet and this shows that they rejected great things, even the beloved disciples, who were now over 300 years old!

I'm always reminded of that scene and the Indiana Jones and the Last Crusade movie of the knight, who was 800 years old guarding the cup of Christ. Something is very apropos here to this Nephite and Lamanite culture and that's his paraphrased quote, "they chose...poorly."

A poor choice was getting caught in the cycle of vengeance. God then inspires Mormon to write these astonishing words amid this horrible scene:

> Mormon 3:17 Therefore I write unto you, Gentiles, and also unto you, House of Israel, when the work shall commence, that ye shall be about to prepare to return to the land of your inheritance;
>
> 18 Yea, behold, I write unto all the ends of the earth; yea, unto you, twelve tribes of Israel, who shall be judged according to your works by the twelve whom Jesus chose to be his disciples in the land of Jerusalem.
>
> 19 And I write also unto the remnant of this people, who shall also be judged by the twelve whom Jesus chose in this land; and they shall be judged by the other twelve whom Jesus chose in the land of Jerusalem.
>
> 20 And these things doth the Spirit manifest unto me; therefore I write unto you all. And for this cause I write unto you, that ye may know that ye must all stand before the judgment-seat of Christ, yea, every soul who belongs to the whole human family of Adam; and ye must stand to be judged of your works, whether they be good or evil;
>
> 21 And also that ye may believe the gospel of Jesus Christ, which ye shall have among you; and also that the Jews, the covenant people of the Lord, shall have other witness besides him whom they saw and heard, that Jesus, whom they slew, was the very Christ and the very God.
>
> 22 And I would that I could persuade all ye ends of the earth to repent and prepare to stand before the judgment-seat of Christ.

He informs us that we will stand before Christ to be judged for our

SECTION 14 - NEPHI, MORMON AND MORONI'S WARNINGS

deeds. Notice that he includes everyone who belongs to the human family, including those forces that enter the land and create significant challenges. Yet, the lesson is clear: we must not succumb to the cycle of vengeance and revenge.

Mormon also included a significant story in his book about a people who were converted so profoundly that they would even give up their lives instead of fighting back or retaliating. They wouldn't even defend themselves. These people are all converted through the great prophet Ammon and his brothers. Just look at the extent to which they would rather give up their lives than do anything to hurt those who attacked them:

> Alma 24:6 Now there was not one soul among all the people who had been converted unto the Lord that would take up arms against their brethren; nay, they would not even make any preparations for war; yea, and also their king commanded them that they should not.

The king gives a stirring sermon inspiring everyone not to take up arms and in one of the most amazing stories in all of scripture, this happens:

> Alma 24:20 And it came to pass that their brethren, the Lamanites, made preparations for war, and came up to the land of Nephi for the purpose of destroying the king, and to place another in his stead, and also of destroying the people of Anti-Nephi-Lehi out of the land.
>
> 21 Now when the people saw that they were coming against them they went out to meet them, and prostrated themselves before them to the earth, and began to call on the name of the Lord; and thus they were in this attitude when the Lamanites began to fall upon them, and began to slay them with the sword.
>
> 22 And thus without meeting any resistance, they did slay a thousand and five of them; and we know that they are blessed, for they have gone to dwell with their God.
>
> 23 Now when the Lamanites saw that their brethren would not flee from the sword, neither would they turn aside to the right hand or to the left, but that they would lie down and perish, and praised God even in the very act of perishing under the sword—
>
> 24 Now when the Lamanites saw this they did forbear from slaying them; and there were many whose hearts had swollen in them for those of their brethren who had fallen under the sword, for they re-

SECTION 14 - NEPHI, MORMON AND MORONI'S WARNINGS

pented of the things which they had done.

25 And it came to pass that they threw down their weapons of war, and they would not take them again, for they were stung for the murders which they had committed; and they came down even as their brethren, relying upon the mercies of those whose arms were lifted to slay them.

26 And it came to pass that the people of God were joined that day by more than the number who had been slain; and those who had been slain were righteous people, therefore we have no reason to doubt but what they were saved.

27 And there was not a wicked man slain among them; but there were more than a thousand brought to the knowledge of the truth; thus we see that the Lord worketh in many ways to the salvation of his people.

This people who had once been a ferocious and bloodthirsty tribe now has been so converted that they won't even defend themselves and they lay down and die at the hands of their own people. The astonishing benefit of this is that it helped convert those people who were attacking them, at least the ones who were actual Lamanites. The Amalekites and the Amulonites were so hard hearted that they would not feel that spirit. They were not stung for the murders they had committed. They were angry, but why?

One reason is outlined here:

Alma 24:30 And thus we can plainly discern, that after a people have been once enlightened by the Spirit of God, and have had great knowledge of things pertaining to righteousness, and then have fallen away into sin and transgression, they become more hardened, and thus their state becomes worse than though they had never known these things.

They had previously been taught the truth and had apostatized. This warning from Mormon and Moroni specifically targets the Gentiles. Not just any Gentiles; he's addressing those who have taken upon themselves the name of Jesus Christ and joined the Church of Jesus Christ of Latter-day Saints. He's warning us that we will face a tremendous battle, and upon those who are fully converted, the power of God will come down to protect and save them. For those who are not fully converted, they may be filled

SECTION 14 - NEPHI, MORMON AND MORONI'S WARNINGS

with the spirit of the adversary and seek revenge.

There will come a time when things will differ from how they are now. A civil war will engulf the nation. The prophecies of Christ in Luke 12 inform us that,

> Luke 12:53 The father shall be divided against the son, and the son against the father; the mother against the daughter, and the daughter against the mother; the mother in law against her daughter in law, and the daughter in law against her mother in law.

What could drive family members to fight each other to the death? I can't imagine a worse scene. It's horrifying. You know how there are several times in the Scriptures when prophets wrote down what they had seen as a burden? Daniel mentioned that his thoughts greatly troubled him but kept the matter in his heart (Dan 7:28). I believe I know what is causing all of this, but I will keep it to myself. I've tried to do what God asked of me here, but I cannot include this in the book.

The Prophet Mormon included their powerful story of the Anti-Nephi-Lehis for a special reason, which is more important than we often realize. Most read it and casually ponder the profound change and their conversion, but it also shows the "patience of the Saints" that we will need to endure in the future (Rev 13:10, 14:12). How long? Many people think it's going to be 3 ½ years, as mentioned in Revelation 13:5

> Rev 13:5 And there was given unto him a mouth speaking great things and blasphemies; and power was given unto him to continue forty and two months.

John the Revelator records these words:

> Rev 13:9 If any man have an ear, let him hear.
>
> 10 He that leadeth into captivity shall go into captivity: he that killeth with the sword must be killed with the sword. Here is the patience and the faith of the saints.

They express the same idea: If we seek revenge and vengeance, we will be destroyed. I'm not sure how it all connects, but the fact that Mormon and John are conveying the same message should serve as a clue. We will face tremendous challenges that we must not retaliate against. This will require incredible faith and patience as we wait for the Lord to execute His ven-

SECTION 14 - NEPHI, MORMON AND MORONI'S WARNINGS

geance on the opposition.

But amidst it all, during this world war that encompasses the earth, God's servant has a tremendous mission to fulfill. It is outlined in,

> Mormon 8:25 And behold, their prayers were also in behalf of him that the Lord should suffer to bring these things forth.
>
> 26 And no one need say they shall not come, for they surely shall, for the Lord hath spoken it; for out of the earth shall they come, by the hand of the Lord, and none can stay it; and it shall come in a day when it shall be said that miracles are done away; and it shall come even as if one should speak from the dead.
>
> 27 And it shall come in a day when the blood of saints shall cry unto the Lord, because of secret combinations and the works of darkness.
>
> 28 Yea, it shall come in a day when the power of God shall be denied, and churches become defiled and be lifted up in the pride of their hearts; yea, even in a day when leaders of churches and teachers shall rise in the pride of their hearts, even to the envying of them who belong to their churches.
>
> 29 Yea, it shall come in a day when there shall be heard of fires, and tempests, and vapors of smoke in foreign lands;
>
> 30 And there shall also be heard of wars, rumors of wars, and earthquakes in divers places.
>
> 31 Yea, it shall come in a day when there shall be great pollutions upon the face of the earth; there shall be murders, and robbing, and lying, and deceivings, and whoredoms, and all manner of abominations; when there shall be many who will say, Do this, or do that, and it mattereth not, for the Lord will uphold such at the last day. But wo unto such, for they are in the gall of bitterness and in the bonds of iniquity.
>
> 32 Yea, it shall come in a day when there shall be churches built up that shall say: Come unto me, and for your money you shall be forgiven of your sins.

In verse 25, it states that the prayers were on behalf of the one who should bring these things forward. Does that refer to Joseph Smith, or is it meant for someone else? Throughout my life, I've been taught that this refers to Joseph Smith because he is the one who brought forth the gospel.

SECTION 14 - NEPHI, MORMON AND MORONI'S WARNINGS

He translated the Book of Mormon, and angels from heaven restored the priesthood through him. He did everything possible to establish Zion during his time and faced countless persecutions before ultimately being killed. He certainly initiated the restoration of the gospel in the latter days, but as we observe, the context of these verses is different. It pertains to Donald Trump because of the subsequent events, and each of these occurrences aligns with our time far better than it did in Joseph Smith's era.

This is the day when the blood of Saints during the 5th seal of martyrs shall cry unto the Lord, and when churches become defiled and are lifted up in the pride of their hearts; when the preachers envy those who belong to their churches. When there are fires, tempests, and vapors of smoke in foreign lands. The 24-hour news channels tell us everything 24 hours a day, not weeks later like in Joseph's day! When there are wars, rumors of wars, and earthquakes in diverse places (the USGS website updates us within minutes on any earthquake occurring anywhere in the world!) There will be great pollution on the earth (there was very little pollution in Joseph's day compared to today, when some nations dump millions of tons of trash into the ocean each week!). All of these events emerged long after the book was translated. It is today. This is when the Book of Mormon is about to go forth in its grandeur under Donald Trump's administration.

Several other places in the Scriptures echo similar sentiments, indicating that these events will take place today or very soon. They did not happen in 1830. The Church of Jesus Christ of Latter-day Saints did not reach its first million members until 1947. Soon, millions of members may join each month! Isaiah, Mormon, Moroni, and other great prophets foresaw this. All of this occurs under Donald Trump's leadership, expanding on what Joseph Smith started!

The Gentiles in America, have been given a tremendous opportunity. They were given the gospel through the prophet Joseph Smith, but have they accepted it? Very few have. The rate of growth in the church outside of the United States dwarfs what is currently happening in our own country. But put this in the context of the first shall be last of the last shall be first. God gave America the opportunity to accept the covenant of the gospel that he is offered to his children in ages past. They didn't have to be of any tribe. They didn't have to show their genealogy connecting them to Moses. They were freely given an amazing opportunity.

SECTION 14 - NEPHI, MORMON AND MORONI'S WARNINGS

But Jesus warned us that they would reject it. This stark warning from Jesus himself teaching the Nephites needs to be considered in this context:

3 Ne 16: 4 And I command you that ye shall write these sayings after I am gone, that if it so be that my people at Jerusalem, they who have seen me and been with me in my ministry, do not ask the Father in my name, that they may receive a knowledge of you by the Holy Ghost, and also of the other tribes whom they know not of, that these sayings which ye shall write shall be kept and shall be manifested unto the Gentiles, that through the fulness of the Gentiles, the remnant of their seed, who shall be scattered forth upon the face of the earth because of their unbelief, may be brought in, or may be brought to a knowledge of me, their Redeemer. *(We have been given the gospel and have a mission to share it with the rest of the world in order that:)*

5 And then will I gather them in from the four quarters of the earth; and then will I fulfill the covenant which the Father hath made unto all the people of the House of Israel.

6 And blessed are the Gentiles, because of their belief in me, in and of the Holy Ghost, which witnesses unto them of me and of the Father. *(Great blessings are given upon those who are fully converted to the gospel!)*

7 Behold, because of their belief in me, saith the Father, and because of the unbelief of you, O House of Israel, in the latter day shall the truth come unto the Gentiles, that the fulness of these things shall be made known unto them.

8 But wo, saith the Father, unto the unbelieving of the Gentiles—for notwithstanding they have come forth upon the face of this land, and have scattered my people who are of the House of Israel; and my people who are of the House of Israel have been cast out from among them, and have been trodden under feet by them; *(But with great blessings comes great responsibility. If they sin against that gospel, they break their covenant with God and will face the consequences. They once scattered the Lamanites across this land. With astonishing power, they went wherever they pleased. Nothing could stop the Gentiles from defeating the American Indians. It's truly a sad situation when recounting this history. But let's continue reading.)*

9 And because of the mercies of the Father unto the Gentiles, and

SECTION 14 - NEPHI, MORMON AND MORONI'S WARNINGS

also the judgments of the Father upon my people who are of the House of Israel, verily, verily, I say unto you, that after all this, and I have caused my people who are of the House of Israel to be smitten, and to be afflicted, and to be slain, and to be cast out from among them, and to become hated by them, and to become a hiss and a byword among them—

10 And thus commandeth the Father that I should say unto you: At that day **when the Gentiles shall sin against my gospel**, and shall reject the fulness of my gospel, and shall be lifted up in the pride of their hearts above all nations, and above all the people of the whole earth, and shall be filled with all manner of lyings, and of deceits, and of mischiefs, and all manner of hypocrisy, and murders, and priestcrafts, and whoredoms, and of secret abominations; and if they shall do all those things, and shall reject the fulness of my gospel, behold, saith the Father, I will bring the fulness of my gospel from among them.

Do you realize what this means? Do you understand the gravity of this phrase: "I will bring the fullness of the gospel from among them"? They had been given the opportunity to accept the fullness of the gospel, but when they sin against it—when they reject the prophets and apostles of the Church of Jesus Christ of Latter-day Saints—when they denounce the Book of Mormon and fight against God's chosen people, they will lose their chance to be baptized and live with God again. The gospel will be returned to the House of Israel, and only the righteous Gentiles, the fully converted members of the Church who have not apostatized, will join them. They will receive the blessings of the gospel in their lives. They will all be part of Zion, under God's protection and grace.

But the rest of the Gentiles, the former members and the Christian world established here in America who rejected it, will be trodden down by the House of Israel (mostly Lamanites)! Just as the Gentiles once had tremendous power over the American Indians, everything will reverse. The Gentiles will lose their power and will be trampled underfoot. Everything they have loved, prayed for, and claimed that God delivered to them will be given to the House of Israel. They will lose everything.

I constantly ask the Christians, the inactive members of our church, and those who have apostatized to please come back. Time is running out because things are about to change dramatically and become irreversible. The

SECTION 14 - NEPHI, MORMON AND MORONI'S WARNINGS

justice of God will come down upon them in a manner never seen before, even among the heathen nations. It's not just the loss of the gospel; it's the loss of everything they have!

> 3 Ne 16:11 And then will I remember my covenant which I have made unto my people, O House of Israel, and I will bring my gospel unto them.
>
> 12 And I will show unto thee, O House of Israel, that the Gentiles shall not have power over you; but I will remember my covenant unto you, O House of Israel, and ye shall come unto the knowledge of the fulness of my gospel.
>
> 13 But if the Gentiles will repent and return unto me, saith the Father, behold they shall be numbered among my people, O House of Israel.
>
> 14 And I will not suffer my people, who are of the House of Israel, to go through among them, and tread them down, saith the Father.
>
> 15 But if they will not turn unto me, and hearken unto my voice, I will suffer them, yea, I will suffer my people, O House of Israel, that they shall go through among them, and shall tread them down, and they shall be as salt that hath lost its savor, which is thenceforth good for nothing but to be cast out, and to be trodden under foot of my people, O House of Israel.

Nephi saw the future and was shown a recurring pattern of the House of Israel turning against God's chosen leaders, causing everything to come crashing down, but everything changes in the end. This time, anyone who fights against Zion will be destroyed. God's kingdom will be on Earth, and the nations will fear to oppose it. They will be as fearsome as an army with banners! (D&C 5:14) They will possess God's power and His army. All of these Gentiles, whether they were once members of the church or not, who have been blessed with the blessings of America, God's chosen land, but turned against it and rejected it will fight against the House of Israel and the righteous members of the church, the fully converted Gentiles, and they will lose. They will plunge into a horrifying civil war, and this is what Mormon and Moroni were trying to warn us about. They urge us to repent, come to God, and not fight against His people.

While all of this is happening, the war is outside of Zion, and amidst the commotion and cataclysms of earthquakes, volcanoes, tsunamis, tor-

SECTION 14 - NEPHI, MORMON AND MORONI'S WARNINGS

nadoes, hurricanes, and flooding, there will be peace and harmony inside Zion. From the center of the country, where the New Jerusalem is being constructed, God's missionaries will go forth in search of those who are patiently enduring as saints. Not every church member will be present in Zion; some will be called there, while others won't. This act itself represents another aspect of the faith we need to embrace.

I think most people have a distorted idea of how the end of the world will unfold. They believe that the New Jerusalem is going to be built and that within weeks, the entire city will be completed. Every member of the church is expected to gather from all corners of the globe. There's a notion circulating that the Antichrist will leave America for Europe and ultimately make its way to Jerusalem, where Armageddon will take place. The world's economies will collapse, leading to the fall of Babylon, and Christ will appear. A massive earthquake will occur, sparing the Jews, while the wicked are consumed by fire and the Earth is renewed all within the next 5-7 years.

It's a lot more complicated than that. Many of these events will occur, while some will not, but hopefully by now, I presume you see that this can't happen this way. I submit that things will be very different. I believe there is a lengthy process ahead of us. Now, of course, I'm promoting Donald Trump as God's servant who is preparing the way for Christ's return. He's nearly 80 years old; things can't be that far off, right?

Suppose Trump were to see God, similar to Moses when he was 80 years old, or as Isaiah did in his ascension. Would he be given the power he needs to perform God's work? How long would he live on Earth after that? The beloved Nephite disciples remained on Earth for over 300 years before the wickedness of the people led to their removal. Once someone has this experience, everything changes, as we have seen from several previous prophets.

I assert that building the city of Zion will take time, and Donald Trump may oversee it as long as God wants him to. Just look at how long it has taken to refurbish the Salt Lake Temple. This monumental project began in 2019 and is expected to be completed in 2027. It will have taken eight years to refurbish and significantly expand the temple. I understand that everyone wants things to happen quickly. We don't want to confront the possibility of facing such difficult times—who would? We sincerely hope Zion will be

SECTION 14 - NEPHI, MORMON AND MORONI'S WARNINGS

here next year so we can raise our children there and be removed from the ravages of war; I understand. But Mormon, John the Revelator, and Moroni are telling us that we need to prepare ourselves.

It's highly conceivable that Donald Trump could be the last president of the United States of America. If he has a burning bush experience, as I've suggested, that might signal the end. Everything would begin to shift toward the Kingdom of God. The subjugation of all nations and their submission under his rule, to be handed over to Christ, would represent a major event in the world. Christ promised the Nephites that His servant of the last days would be healed. Somehow, something happens to Trump that makes him recognized as God's chosen servant and all of his terrible ordeal of being marred will be reversed. **He will be healed.**

> 3Ne 21:10 Yet I will heal him, for I will show unto them that my wisdom is greater than the cunning of the devil.

The nation was given an opportunity to move forward under God's Servant and to change things in the right way during Trump's first presidency in 2016. His plans were working very well, and the country benefited greatly, but the Beast system could not tolerate this. They introduced COVID-19 and did everything they could to remove him from office. They demonstrated their corruption by stealing the 2020 election. However, his second term will be different. He will be healed, exalted, and extolled, and everyone will know it. They will praise his name!

In the captivating audiobook "They Saw Our Day,"[24] Lance Richardson explores some of the Hopi Indians' prophecies regarding three significant shakings of the Earth. The first was represented by one hand, corresponding to World War I. The second, also marked by one hand, was World War II. However, the third shaking involved both hands. We are on the brink of witnessing this profound shaking of the Earth in numerous ways.

The entire idea of not seeking revenge for the hardships people face and encouraging them to pray for the person who will bring forth the Book of Mormon to the world amid those challenges has yet to occur.

And we need to get ready.

Section 15
Kings and Queens of the Gentiles

Section 15 - Kings and Queens of the Gentiles

I've mentioned before how valuable the Book of Mormon is for understanding Isaiah. Every chapter that quotes his words adds something significant to our understanding of the most important person of all time: Jesus Christ.

The prophet Jacob, Nephi's brother, offers astonishing insights into Isaiah 49:22-26 and inserts eight complete verses in the middle to help clarify another important event. And does he clarify it! I remember reading these two verses in Isaiah years ago in my Isaiah class, wondering why it said this:

> Isa 49:22 Thus saith the Lord God, Behold, I will lift up mine hand to the Gentiles, and set up my standard to the people: and they shall bring thy sons in their arms, and thy daughters shall be carried upon their shoulders.
>
> 23 And kings shall be thy nursing fathers, and their queens thy nursing mothers: they shall bow down to thee with their face toward the earth, and lick up the dust of thy feet; and thou shalt know that I am the Lord: for they shall not be ashamed that wait for me.

I was also reading a commentary on these verses. I don't remember who it was, but they mentioned that, *"the nursing fathers and nursing mothers, who are the Kings and Queens of the Gentiles, will someday bow down to the Jewish people and the House of Israel in the last days and lick the dust from their feet. They said it's the leaders of the nations on Earth—those who hold authority, those who rule over the rest—who are now subjected to the utmost humiliation and recognition of who God's chosen people are. Licking up the dust from their feet is just a visually graphic way of demonstrating such degradation."* That just didn't seem right. Whoever I read was unfamiliar with Jacob's remarkable addition that explains this verse.

He writes this in,

> 2 Ne 6:12 And blessed are the Gentiles, they of whom the prophet has written; for behold, if it so be that they shall repent and fight not against Zion, and do not unite themselves to that great and abominable church, they shall be saved; for the Lord God will fulfil his covenants which he has made unto his children; and for this cause the

SECTION 15 - KINGS AND QUEENS OF THE GENTILES

prophet has written these things.

13 Wherefore, they that fight against Zion and the covenant people of the Lord shall lick up the dust of their feet; and the people of the Lord shall not be ashamed. For the people of the Lord are they who wait for him; for they still wait for the coming of the Messiah.

The Kings and Queens do not bow down to the Jewish people or the House of Israel; instead, it is those who oppose Zion and the covenant people of the Lord who will face severe humiliation due to their actions. That makes a lot more sense. I mean, why have someone in the position of a king carrying a nursing infant and then, all of a sudden, be turned around to humbly bow in submission to it? But as we can see, that isn't the case, and for whatever reason Isaiah wrote it that way, Jacob clarifies it. It's those who fight against Zion who are subjected to such degradation.

So, who are the Kings and Queens of the Gentiles? Jacob tells us this in,

2 Ne 10:11 And this land shall be a land of liberty unto the Gentiles, and there shall be no kings upon the land, who shall raise up unto the Gentiles.

Since there will be no kings in this land, so who could He be referring to? Is it the leaders of the people, those who have been elected to office? Are they the titans of business and industry in our country? Are they the politicians, celebrities, billionaires, and others who seem to have so much influence worldwide? While it might be satisfying to see them all humiliated, that is not who He's speaking about regarding the Kings and Queens.

There can only be one answer: the Gentiles who are the members of the Church of Jesus Christ of Latter-day Saints, who attend the temple, and were anointed as kings and priests, queens and priestesses unto God while remaining faithful in every way are those Kings and Queens! They have found their fulfillment in the Church of the Firstborn, and are part

SECTION 15 - KINGS AND QUEENS OF THE GENTILES

of Zion, the New Jerusalem!

These aren't just casual members; they are fully converted and perhaps translated individuals who have attained a much higher standing through the gospel of Jesus Christ. This same gospel is extended to everyone, but not everyone takes advantage of it. These individuals have done so. They have become Kings and Queens. They have become like their Savior. Furthermore, they perform a monumental work of salvation across the Earth as they gather anyone willing to forsake their sins, abandon the world, refuse to take upon themselves the Mark of the Beast, and flee Babylon to join those in the New Jerusalem.

Because the Kings and Queens have gained this tremendous ability, they most likely resemble the three Nephites, traveling around the Earth with the power of God to accomplish His work of gathering. Jeremiah prophesied about their journey:

> Jeremiah 16:14 ¶ Therefore, behold, the days come, saith the Lord, that it shall no more be said, The Lord liveth, that brought up the children of Israel out of the land of Egypt;
>
> 15 But, The Lord liveth, that brought up the children of Israel from the land of the north, and from all the lands whither he had driven them: and I will bring them again into their land that I gave unto their fathers.
>
> 16 ¶ Behold, I will send for many fishers, saith the Lord, and they shall fish them; and after will I send for many hunters, and they shall hunt them from every mountain, and from every hill, and out of the holes of the rocks.

Due to the remarkable establishment of the New Jerusalem under Donald Trump's leadership, no one will ever again talk about Moses, who led the children of Israel out of Egypt. This astonishing future event is so grand and impressive that we can hardly comprehend it. From there, the Kings and Queens of the Gentiles become hunters and fishers of men.

This is most likely just another description of the 144,000 of Revelation 7 and 14. They go out and find the poor lost sheep anywhere in the world. They hunt them in every mountain, hill, and hole in the rocks. Nothing is left unturned. No one is left behind. They are like angels of God seeking out anyone who's left and are High Priests, who most likely go out with their

SECTION 15 - KINGS AND QUEENS OF THE GENTILES

wives! In D&C 77 it says:

> D&C 77:11 Q. What are we to understand by sealing the one hundred and forty-four thousand, out of all the tribes of Israel—twelve thousand out of every tribe?
>
> A. We are to understand that those who are sealed are high priests, ordained unto the holy order of God, to administer the everlasting gospel; for they are they who are ordained out of every nation, kindred, tongue, and people, by the angels to whom is given power over the nations of the earth, to bring as many as will come to the church of the Firstborn.

"These 144,000 are Gods, as the name on their forehead specifies; their callings and elections have been made sure; they are exalted personages; they are 'redeemed from among men.' (Revelation 14:4-5)" (Bruce R McConkie, A New Witness for the Articles of Faith, 640). Since we are talking about Kings and Queens of the Gentiles, it must also include women.

I need to comment on the lost 10 tribes, as there is a popular series of books claiming they left this earth soon after their expulsion from northern Israel and achieved a status similar to Enoch or Melchizedek in a different sphere than this planet. I disagree with this suggestion. Everyone is entitled to their own opinion, but here is why I disagree with that notion.

As previously mentioned, God works through covenants. Because the House of Israel failed to keep their covenant and remain righteous, the Lord used their scattering to spread the covenant by blood throughout the rest of the Earth, enabling anyone with that blood in them to receive this profound blessing. If they had left this planet, how could that blood covenant have been achieved? Additionally, why would we need these 12 groups of 12,000 people to search for them on Earth? I have asked this question before, and the answer has been that some remained; while that is a possibility, it doesn't make much sense. Consider a group of 300,000 to 500,000 people who were part of the 10 tribes taken by the Assyrian kings.

If some of them started achieving the previously mentioned translated state, why not all of them? Who would want to remain under the most brutal kings in history? No one would! They would all want to leave. If you were standing there, observing some of your friends disappearing or being loaded onto a spaceship, why wouldn't you go with them?

SECTION 15 - KINGS AND QUEENS OF THE GENTILES

Because of this, I do not believe they left; rather, they were scattered all over the Earth to fulfill God's purposes. The 144,000 go out to find them and bring them back into the covenant. They come from all tribes and are equally found throughout the Earth. Even though it states they come from the northern countries, it simply indicates where they were taken, and after 2,700 years, they have spread across the Earth.

Under Donald Trump's leadership, they will be found and miraculously returned to either Zion in America or Jerusalem. This is an astonishing and miraculous event witnessed by multiple prophets.

I loved the TC Christensen movie "Escape from Germany," which tells the astonishing tale of rescuing all the missionaries from Germany before Hitler invaded Poland. The prophet urged the mission president to evacuate the missionaries because Hitler was preparing to act. The mission president was utterly taken aback and caught off guard, as there was no indication in Germany that this would happen. Nobody was discussing it. Yet, here, the prophet of God provided them with the insight that it would occur.

Because of unusual circumstances, the mission president sent one elder to find all these other Elders in various cities in northern Germany. There was no other way to reach them. They couldn't call them on the phone, and there was no time to send any letters. Things were very different back then. The mission president had to leave and therefore blessed him, promised that he would achieve his goal, and encouraged him to listen to the Holy Spirit.

Although it is a low-budget movie, it's well done and tells a profound story. As you can guess, they managed to get all the missionaries out using some very unusual tactics. The account presented in the video is completely true, and I encourage you to watch it. It was Apostle Joseph Fielding Smith who met with the elder facing difficulties in finding these missionaries, but he assured him that World War II would not start until all the missionaries were safely out of Germany. The missionary questioned this intensely, wondering how saving just a few missionaries could make such a difference and prevent an entire war. But it did. The day after they evacuated all the missionaries, Germany invaded Poland, and everything fell apart.

The point of telling you the story is that it will be the same in the last days. The Kings and Queens of the Gentiles will go everywhere in the world, seeking out anyone worthy and ready to be gathered in Zion before

SECTION 15 - KINGS AND QUEENS OF THE GENTILES

the great burning of the Earth that destroys all the wicked. These Kings and Queens of the Gentiles, hopefully you and me, have an astonishing mission.

I'm going to speak from a position of hoping I can become one of them. What do we have to do to get there? What do you and I have to give up? What tiny grain of Babylonian sand is holding us back? Maybe it's a giant rock that we are carrying around, but whatever it is, I encourage everyone to turn to Jesus Christ and get ready.

The 144,000 is not an exact figure. It's simply a way to represent a very large number of people divided into twelves and searching for each of those under the covenant from the 12 Tribes! There could possibly be millions, as that's what it will take to find all of these individuals. This grand angelic missionary force, empowered by God, can do anything a king or queen can do. They will even possess the power to fight the armies of the world. Where do they derive that power? From the priesthood, the same priesthood that Melchizedek held!

Melchizedek's name means "King of Righteousness." The Kings and Queens of the Gentiles hold his priesthood, embodying the essence of righteousness. We are eternally grateful to the prophet Joseph Smith for restoring our understanding of Melchizedek, including his experiences and principles. There is a reason the priesthood bears his name, and this is something you and I are meant to achieve. There's also a reason this knowledge has been removed from the Bible; the last thing Satan wants is for us to realize our true power and potential.

So now please read this as if it was describing you.

JST Genesis 14: 26 Now Melchizedek was a man of faith, who wrought righteousness; and when a child he feared God, and stopped the mouths of lions, and quenched the violence of fire.

27 And thus, having been approved of God, he was ordained an high priest after the order of the covenant which God made with Enoch,

28 It being after the order of the Son of God; which order came, not by man, nor the will of man; neither by father nor mother; neither by beginning of days nor end of years; but of God;

29 And it was delivered unto men by the calling of his own voice, according to his own will, unto as many as believed on his name.

SECTION 15 - KINGS AND QUEENS OF THE GENTILES

30 For God having sworn unto Enoch and unto his seed with an oath by himself; that every one being ordained after this order and calling should have power, by faith, to break mountains, to divide the seas, to dry up waters, to turn them out of their course;

31 To put at defiance the armies of nations, to divide the earth, to break every band, to stand in the presence of God; to do all things according to his will, according to his command, subdue principalities and powers; and this by the will of the Son of God which was from before the foundation of the world.

32 And men having this faith, coming up unto this order of God, were translated and taken up into heaven.

33 And now, Melchizedek was a priest of this order; therefore he obtained peace in Salem, and was called the Prince of peace.

34 And his people wrought righteousness, and obtained heaven, and sought for the city of Enoch which God had before taken, separating it from the earth, having reserved it unto the latter days, or the end of the world;

35 And hath said, and sworn with an oath, that the heavens and the earth should come together; and the sons of God should be tried so as by fire.

36 And this Melchizedek, having thus established righteousness, was called the king of heaven by his people, or, in other words, the King of peace.

Everything written above is what we must do to become a King or Queen of the Gentiles.

There have been numerous superhero movies presented to the world that showcase various individuals with extraordinary powers due to unusual circumstances. Superman was born on another planet, while Spider-Man was bitten by a radioactive spider. I need not go down the list, as there are many, but we all marvel at these movies (pun intended).

SECTION 15 - KINGS AND QUEENS OF THE GENTILES

Young children envision having these powers, pointing their fingers and displaying great intensity in their facial expressions, hoping to achieve the same results. I remember watching a charming commercial featuring a young child dressed in a Darth Vader outfit, trying to use the Force to move objects. Nothing works as he wishes throughout the day, and he becomes discouraged. When his dad comes home in the new car (which is what the ad is all about), he notices the situation. The boy walks up to the car and points his fingers at it, and from inside, his father uses the new technological key fob to start the engine. The young boy reacts with total surprise, thinking he has actually turned it on himself. It's a delightful commercial that we can all relate to.

But this power of the priesthood, named Melchizedek, is far greater and is real. It operates by faith, righteousness, and the will of the Lord. Every one of the achievements listed by Melchizedek, and many more, will be performed again during the last great gathering period. We will need faith, power, and that priesthood. We will need faith to break mountains, divide seas, dry up waters, and turn rivers out of their course. To call down lightning from heaven, cause tornadoes to remove our enemies, earthquakes to swallow them up, hail to destroy their weapons, and rain to flood their camps. We will have to be able to fight entire armies of nations, fend off gangs of marauders and murderers, and defend our families. We will need the ability to divide the earth and break every band. To be released from prisons, to be invisible to enemies, to deflect their bullets and missiles and to repel every advancement. We will need his power to heal the wounded, cure the diseased, replace lost limbs, restore eyesight, replace lost blood and bring the dead back to life. We need the power to stand in the presence of God and to be translated.

Melchizedek sought and obtained the city of Enoch, and we will need to seek the New Jerusalem, the place where Enoch and his people will descend. Melchizedek was translated to achieve that status, and that is what we will need to do. We are informed that resurrection is a priesthood ordinance; I submit to you that translation is as well. This will occur through the Melchizedek priesthood! We have also been told that this key of the priesthood has not yet been given to mankind on earth, so I presume that the translation key has not either.

This is the type of faith we need. This is why we are told to think ce-

SECTION 15 - KINGS AND QUEENS OF THE GENTILES

lestial and set our sights on the things of God. Look up! Look to God! Flee Babylon and stop being entrenched in the things of the world. Stop being tempted by all the offerings of Babylon, with its shiny baubles, glamorous gowns, exciting nightclubs, and laser light shows and concerts. Put aside everything the world does to distract you from the faith you need to have.

I hope no one reading this feels depressed or thinks they could never attain such a lofty position. Your adversary wants you to feel that way. He doesn't want you to realize who you are and what your true potential is. He will do anything to undermine you. Enoch was slow of speech, yet he was sent to preach the gospel to a very wicked people. However, something about his faith, love, and actions changed everything because Enoch had that same power!

> Moses 7:13 And so great was the faith of Enoch that he led the people of God, and their enemies came to battle against them; and he spake the word of the Lord, and the earth trembled, and the mountains fled, even according to his command; and the rivers of water were turned out of their course; and the roar of the lions was heard out of the wilderness; and all nations feared greatly, so powerful was the word of Enoch, and so great was the power of the language which God had given him.
>
> 14 There also came up a land out of the depth of the sea, and so great was the fear of the enemies of the people of God, that they fled and stood afar off and went upon the land which came up out of the depth of the sea.
>
> 15 And the giants of the land, also, stood afar off; and there went forth a curse upon all people that fought against God;
>
> 16 And from that time forth there were wars and bloodshed among them; but the Lord came and dwelt with his people, and they dwelt in righteousness.
>
> 17 The fear of the Lord was upon all nations, so great was the glory of the Lord, which was upon his people. And the Lord blessed the land, and they were blessed upon the mountains, and upon the high places, and did flourish.

The fear of the Lord was upon all nations! No one wanted to come up against them because they got routed every time. The Lord came and dwelt among them! He will also come and dwell in the modern New Jerusalem

SECTION 15 - KINGS AND QUEENS OF THE GENTILES

of our day.

This marvelous revelation given from the Lord in 1831 to the Prophet applies to our day:

D&C 45:62 For verily I say unto you, that great things await you;

63 Ye hear of wars in foreign lands; but, behold, I say unto you, they are nigh, even at your doors, and not many years hence ye shall hear of wars in your own lands.

64 Wherefore I, the Lord, have said, gather ye out from the eastern lands, (in our day this would be the whole world) assemble ye yourselves together ye elders of my church; go ye forth into the western countries (the world again), call upon the inhabitants to repent, and inasmuch as they do repent, build up churches unto me.

65 And with one heart and with one mind, gather up your riches that ye may purchase an inheritance which shall hereafter be appointed unto you.

66 And it shall be called the New Jerusalem, a land of peace, a city of refuge, a place of safety for the saints of the Most High God;

67 And the glory of the Lord shall be there, and the terror of the Lord also shall be there, insomuch that the wicked will not come unto it, and it shall be called Zion.

68 And it shall come to pass among the wicked, that every man that will not take his sword against his neighbor must needs flee unto Zion for safety.

69 And there shall be gathered unto it out of every nation under heaven; and it shall be the only people that shall not be at war one with another.

70 And it shall be said among the wicked: Let us not go up to battle against

SECTION 15 - KINGS AND QUEENS OF THE GENTILES

Zion, for the inhabitants of Zion are terrible; wherefore we cannot stand.

71 And it shall come to pass that the righteous shall be gathered out from among all nations, and shall come to Zion, singing with songs of everlasting joy.

If you have to read those verses again, please do. These astonishing things await us in our day. The inhabitants of Zion, the Kings and Queens of the Gentiles who are part of the New Jerusalem, have greater power than any Marvel movie character. And this is real power, not something obtained through strange or unusual means. This is power from God because of our faith, righteousness, and dependence on our Savior, Jesus Christ. This is the power that we need to search for and obtain. Remember, Enoch's city became so righteous that it was taken from the Earth, and the New Jerusalem will be spared from all of the cataclysms that come upon the rest of the Earth. Enoch's city will also return to the Earth and join with those who inhabit the New Jerusalem. It will be a glorious day and it will last for 1000 years!

Remember that song from 1971 by the group Ten Years After with the line, "I'd love to change the world, but I don't know what to do, so I'll leave it up to you." The entire song laments the problems in the world, but they don't know how to fix them. Numerous other songs express the same sentiment, yet every solution they propose is man-made and ultimately ineffective.

The whole point is that when we change ourselves—let me rephrase that—when we allow Christ to change us into who we are ordained to be, his Kings and Priests, his Queens and Priestesses, we will change the world. Enoch changed the world. Melchizedek changed his world as he sought the city of Enoch after the flood and obtained it.

No worldly government or program will create the Utopian society everyone claims to want; they all rely on force and coercion. Communism, Socialism, Marxism, and all the other ideologies that exist essentially do the same thing. They employ force to supposedly share the wealth. It has never worked, and it will never work. These ideologies were all proposed by Lucifer in the premortal world, and God warned everyone not to heed him. Unfortunately, a third part of his children did listen to him, and despite

SECTION 15 - KINGS AND QUEENS OF THE GENTILES

all the warnings God provided, they still chose Lucifer, fully aware of the consequences.

Babylon operates in a similar way. It relies completely on force and coercion. The monstrous digital banking system is set to create chaos worldwide. Unless they accept that Mark, no one will be able to buy or sell anything globally, except in Zion. I am confident that some form of artificial intelligence will be utilized to manipulate people in the future and guide them along specific paths. I have been studying this remarkable technology for a few years, and it continues to amaze me. I use it every day at my job, and it enables me to accomplish more tasks in one day than I could have completed in weeks.

But there is a negative side to it all that will be unavoidable.

Our only hope is Zion. I've said this a dozen times in this book, and I hope it finally gets through to somebody. We are so distracted from what God wants to give us. He wants to give each of us a white stone, and we know that within that white stone is the ability to learn everything in the world from his godly perspective.

> Rev 2:17 He that hath an ear, let him hear what the Spirit saith unto the churches; To him that overcometh will I give to eat of the hidden manna, and will give him a white stone, and in the stone a new name written, which no man knoweth saving he that receiveth it.

Instead, we spend many hours each day looking at our cell phones, learning everything from a worldly perspective, and in fact, it contains some of the most degenerate things in the history of the world. I'm not saying cell phones are inherently evil because it can be used for positive purposes, but I argue that much of it is a colossal waste of time and distracts us from who we can become.

That stone contains a new name personalized to you. This extremely personal gift, similar to the Liahona mentioned above, has tremendous revelatory power to guide us in everything we do. In Revelation 19:12, Christ himself is shown to have a name that no one else knows about him.

> Isaiah 62:2 And the Gentiles shall see thy righteousness, and all kings thy glory: and thou shalt be called by a new name, which the mouth of the Lord shall name.

SECTION 15 - KINGS AND QUEENS OF THE GENTILES

The Kings and Queens of Zion have also received a new name.

Donald Trump has a significant mission. I've said that he represents the First Horseman in Revelation 6, providing various examples of his remarkable mission. It's possible that the Horseman does not refer solely to him but rather to a group, as very few individuals are mentioned in the Book of Revelation aside from God the Father, Jesus Christ, and John the Revelator. Most instances refer to groups of people, governments, Gentiles, apostates, etc. I know people try to identify who each of the ten horns could be, including the Stout Horn, which likely refers to an individual. We understand that the Antichrist exists based on other writings in Scripture. He is described as the man of sin (2 Thes 2:3), perdition, and Isaiah likens him to the Assyrian.

I believe the Kings and Queens of the Gentiles may be united with the First Horsemen to bring about this tremendous change in America and the world. He's wearing a crown of victory[25], on a white horse which signifies that he is ordained by God. The Kings and Queens of the Gentiles are also ordained by God to go forth conquering and to conquer and this is done through the priesthood named after him whose name means the King of Righteousness.

This group of Kings and Queens, who attend the Temple, hold the priesthood, and faithfully keep their covenants, are part of this dramatic event. They help establish the Kingdom of God on Earth, opposing Satan's Babylonian system. The great Dragon will do everything possible to prevent that man-child, the Kingdom of God in its infancy, from growing. The Kings and Queens of the Gentiles will need to use their priesthood power to withstand the onslaught of the Dragon. Michael and his angels are said to be the ones who fight the Dragon and defeat him. I submit to you that those angels include the Kings and Queens of the Gentiles.

They go in search of those who are like infants and know nothing about the promises made to them. They don't know anything beyond their experiences. They are unaware of the possibilities of Zion, freedom, love, or forgiveness and are not members of the church. A child has no clue about the value of things or which direction to take. In this case, they are like babes in their arms. The Kings and Queens of the Gentiles find those who have not known the covenant blood promises given to their ancient fathers but

SECTION 15 - KINGS AND QUEENS OF THE GENTILES

possess a heart and mind eager to be righteous. Everyone is invited.

I've mentioned my opposition to timelines because it's impossible to give any kind of sequence that means anything. A couple of overarching events do happen, such as the establishment of Zion, Armageddon, and Christ's return to save the Jews. I know this is going to fly in the face of what a lot of people think, but my dream about the red velvet book (in Section 18) and everything falling all over the ground showed me that everything is coming. It's all a mess, and there is no order.

Nobody likes that, yet everyone buys books presenting a complex array of dates and events aligned with celestial signals. I believe some of them are accurate, but nearly everything else cannot be fitted into a timeline for how many timelines have we seen come and go over the last 50 years? There are many things to come that just don't fit most of the timelines that I've seen. I'm not saying they're wrong but I just want people to prepare themselves for the possibility of everything I've been speaking about taking a couple of decades to accomplish.

The Church currently has almost 18,000,000 members and yet there are almost 8,000,000,000 people on earth. That equates to .00225% of the population! While there are probably 4 billion people that have never heard of the name of Jesus Christ, there are probably 6 billion people that have never even heard of the name of the church! How can we possibly get everything done, get everyone ready, gathered, baptized, etc. before the final destruction of the world at Jesus Christ magnificent return in the next 5-10 years? This is going to take a while. It doesn't matter if it's broadcast all over the world on television or via the Internet, every one of those people need to have the opportunity to hear the gospel and to be baptized.

Let's suppose that 1 billion people join the church. If we wanted to baptize all of them in one year, doing it every day for 365 days, that would mean 2,739,726 baptisms per day! If we did this over a 10-year period, that would be 273,972 baptisms per day (91,324 per day over 30 years!), and mind you, that is for 365 days a year. If there are 30,000 chapels in the world, and each chapel were to baptize nearly 10 people per day, it's important to note that not all of them have a baptismal font. Yes, of course, there are lakes, rivers, and oceans, but it seems impossible to fit all of these requirements into most of the current timelines, which end within 10 years.

SECTION 15 - KINGS AND QUEENS OF THE GENTILES

The point I'm making is that there are many things yet to happen before Christ appears to the entire world. Zion will play a very significant role in this as the Kings and Queens of the Gentiles travel across the Earth, seeking those who are ready to accept the covenant of the gospel. Please note that none of the figures mentioned above account for the time needed to teach all the lessons. I'm assuming that only one out of eight people will accept this. Is that high or low? In most missions, that would be an extremely high number, considering one out of eight people they taught getting baptized.

But how many righteous Kings and Queens are currently able to do that? I don't know the answer, but I know that not everyone in the church is. Of course, we know that the House of Israel will come and help build a New Jerusalem, and the lost tribes will be gathered together to participate in these marvelous changes. If 2 million members of the church qualified to become Kings and Queens in Zion, that would equate to teaching 4000 people each!

It appears that large groups of people will reach the city of Zion over a period of time. They seem to be guided there in an organized manner from all around the world. God leads them from both the front and the rear, much like Moses led the children of Israel. Most likely, the first to arrive will be members of the church mostly under the title of Ephraim, under the direction of the prophet and apostles. We currently own almost all of the land needed to accomplish this major task and I believe there are still proof of ownership that go clear back to the original settlers but are currently held by members of the church, mostly in Utah. It's possible that those original land deeds may help acquire additional land for Zion.

Then, as each of the groups come in,

D&C 133:16 Hearken and hear, O ye inhabitants of the earth. Listen, ye elders of my church together, and hear the voice of the Lord; for he calleth upon all men, and he commandeth all men everywhere to repent.

17 For behold, the Lord God hath sent forth the angel crying through the midst of heaven, saying: Prepare ye the way of the Lord, and make his paths straight, for the hour of his coming is nigh—

18 When the Lamb shall stand upon Mount Zion, and with him a hundred and forty-four thousand, having his Father's name written on

SECTION 15 - KINGS AND QUEENS OF THE GENTILES

their foreheads. *(Note, although 144,000 are gathered and go forth throughout the world in the sixth seal in Revelation chapter 7, these are sixth seal events referenced in Revelation 14 and occur at the same time as the fall of Babylon. They did not happen in 1831 when this revelation was given. This is a prophecy of the future.)*

19 Wherefore, prepare ye for the coming of the Bridegroom; go ye, go ye out to meet him.

20 For behold, he shall stand upon the mount of Olivet, and upon the mighty ocean, even the great deep, and upon the islands of the sea, and upon the land of Zion.

21 And he shall utter his voice out of Zion, and he shall speak from Jerusalem, and his voice shall be heard among all people;

22 And it shall be a voice as the voice of many waters, and as the voice of a great thunder, which shall break down the mountains, and the valleys shall not be found.

23 He shall command the great deep, and it shall be driven back into the north countries, and the islands shall become one land;

24 And the land of Jerusalem and the land of Zion shall be turned back into their own place, and the earth shall be like as it was in the days before it was divided.

25 And the Lord, even the Savior, shall stand in the midst of his people, and shall reign over all flesh.

26 And they who are in the north countries shall come in remembrance before the Lord; and their prophets shall hear his voice, and shall no longer stay themselves; and they shall smite the rocks, and the ice shall flow down at their presence.

27 And an highway shall be cast up in the midst of the great deep. *(Note: there has been a lot of speculation as to what this great highway means when the rocks are smitten and ice flows down. Let me make it very simple for you. This shows a dramatic change in the earth, possibly the polar reversal that changes the location of the north and south poles, causing tremendous earthquakes and polar ice to melt. The land will be brought back together into one and everyone who is gathered will be spared from the flooding just like Moses leading the children of Israel through the Red Sea through the actions of the Kings and Queens of the Gentiles using the Melchizedek Priest-*

SECTION 15 - KINGS AND QUEENS OF THE GENTILES

hood!)

28 Their enemies shall become a prey unto them,

29 And in the barren deserts there shall come forth pools of living water; and the parched ground shall no longer be a thirsty land.

30 And they shall bring forth their rich treasures unto the children of Ephraim, my servants.

31 And the boundaries of the everlasting hills shall tremble at their presence.

32 And there shall they fall down and be crowned with glory, even in Zion, by the hands of the servants of the Lord, even the children of Ephraim.

Our modern-day Moses will be part of that assembly. However, it also seems that a significant number of righteous individuals will not relocate to Zion. Some will stay where they are; that's where God wants them for reasons unknown.

In January 2019, President Nelson advised members to remain in California despite the severe wildfires they had faced and the ongoing political and social issues in the state. Over the past couple of years, California has experienced a wide variety of weather: rain, heavy snowfall, tornadoes, the costliest fires in U.S. history, and droughts. I'm certain there will be more serious earthquakes since it is the second most seismically active state in the nation.

But he instructed people to stay there. A similar situation will occur with the establishment of Zion.

But let's be clear, there will soon be a significant division among all people, and I encourage everyone to reflect on themselves and understand where they stand. These words from the prophet Jacob are profound:

2Ne 6:13 Wherefore, they that fight against Zion and the covenant people of the Lord shall lick up the dust of their feet; and the people of the Lord shall not be ashamed. For the people of the Lord are they who wait for him; for they still wait for the coming of the Messiah.

14 And behold, according to the words of the prophet, the Messiah will set himself again the second time to recover them; wherefore,

SECTION 15 - KINGS AND QUEENS OF THE GENTILES

he will manifest himself unto them in power and great glory, unto the destruction of their enemies, when that day cometh when they shall believe in him; and none will he destroy that believe in him.

15 And they that believe not in him shall be destroyed, both by fire, and by tempest, and by earthquakes, and by bloodsheds, and by pestilence, and by famine. And they shall know that the Lord is God, the Holy One of Israel.

Those who fight against Zion will be humiliated to the point of licking up the dust of their feet, while those who are faithful will not be ashamed. They continue to await the coming of the Messiah. These events, like many others I have pointed out, demonstrate that there is a time frame within which we must endure the trials and tribulations that lie ahead. The opposition fights against them. This isn't merely a skirmish or a schoolyard scuffle; this is war. This is persecution. This is an all-out attack on the church and everything it teaches.

This doesn't happen in a day, week, month, or year. Several years of this must be endured. However, we are promised that none who believe in Him will be destroyed. That's a bold promise: "None will He destroy who believe in Him." (2 Ne 6:14)

While those who don't believe will face destruction from various forces, including the events I've just outlined that have occurred in California, they will know that it is the Lord God of Israel who has orchestrated it. I cannot definitively say whether these devastations or fires are the judgments of God or merely part of the natural processes in our world. Many righteous individuals were gravely impacted by these occurrences. Certainly, wicked individuals also suffered, but I do not claim the authority to declare that these are God's judgments. Only the prophet has that right.

The purpose of sharing all this is that we don't really know where we will each end up in the future. Will we be in the first group that is completely safe and spared in Zion? Will we belong to the second group that is still righteous but must remain where they are hopefully with a "Dome of Protection"? Will we fall into the third group of those severely punished because they once believed but have since fallen away and thus face the greatest consequences? Or will we find ourselves in the last group that seeks to destroy everything God is establishing?

SECTION 15 - KINGS AND QUEENS OF THE GENTILES

I'm determined to be a king in the first group. I'd prefer to wear a crown rather than lick up dust, but I know I have a long way to go. This book has provided a fantastic experience for me. I hope it has been worth the purchase. I understand it raises many questions and doesn't answer everything, but I hope I've helped somehow.

If there's anything to be credited, please thank God for that because He taught me what to say. If anything is wrong, blame me.

SECTION 16 - VISION OF THE TREE OF LIFE

Section 16 - Vision of the Tree of Life

Nephi is the author of the first and second books that bear his name. He writes this after arriving in the promised land and while serving as its king. This occurs 30 years after his father and family left Jerusalem. He reflects on his past 30 years of experiences and the visions he has received. I suggest that the entirety of First and Second Nephi is written from the perspective of the insights those visions provide. He selects specific events and quotes particular scriptures that we can use in our day to guide our decisions.

He envisions the tree of life on a much larger scale than his father did. He is not permitted to share the final part of his vision, leading many to wonder what he is omitting. However, once you grasp the concept of his writing the books with this vision in mind, you'll realize he left nothing out. He adhered to the angel's command and did not include it as revelation. Instead, he drew on examples from his family and scriptures that had already been written to fulfill the revelation for us.

The prophet Lehi in the Book of Mormon had an astonishing vision of seeing the Tree of Life and how it represents Jesus Christ, His love, mercy, and mission to the world. Lehi wandered through a dark period, guided

SECTION 16 - VISION OF THE TREE OF LIFE

by an angel, and saw the Tree. He partakes of the fruit, filling him with exceedingly great joy; it is the most desirable of all things. This is Jesus Christ. This is the gift of salvation and exaltation available because of the atonement of Jesus Christ. This is the forgiveness of sins, the washing away of guilt and pain, and the peace and love that fills a person's soul who does everything required to partake of that fruit.

It is a complete and unconditional repentance, the overcoming of trials, sins, addictions, and everything else that afflicts us, followed by baptism by someone with the proper authority to wash away all our sins. We are given the gift of the Holy Ghost to help guide us throughout the rest of our lives to stay on that path. It's impossible to overstate the love someone feels after having that experience.

Lehi wishes to share this with his family, calling out loudly to his wife, Nephi, and Sam to come to him and enjoy the fruit. They all join him and share the same experience, guided by their prophet and leader, who directed them toward this path.

Lehi seeks out his two other sons, Laman and Lemuel, beckoning them to come and partake of the fruit as well, but they refuse. They wander off into the darkness. Lehi then sees a rod of iron that extends toward the Tree, following a straight and narrow path. We later understand this to represent the word of God and the covenants people must make to reach that Tree. Massive numbers of people try to find that path, yearning for the blessed gift of joy and freedom from sin that partaking of the fruit offers. However, a mist of darkness comes and blinds them to where the path is or where it leads.

Many individuals never find the path, and among those who do, some relinquish the rod of iron and end up drowning in a foul river nearby. A select group reaches the end and enjoys the fruit of the Tree, yet they feel shame for their actions because a building across the river attracts scornful onlookers who point fingers and mock them for what they have taken and done. Others are seen enjoying the fruit, overwhelmed with joy and gratitude for their experience. They feel a deep sense of peace, reflecting their development, joy, and love. They have triumphed over life's obstacles and challenges to reach this point.

The great and spacious building on the other side of the river has no

SECTION 16 - VISION OF THE TREE OF LIFE

foundation. It is high in the air and filled with people dressed in very fine clothing. These individuals want nothing to do with overcoming their sins or addictions. They want to indulge in the wickedness of the world. The whore who sits upon the beast of Revelation holds a cup filled with filthiness from which everyone partakes. This is the type of crowd in that building. There's all manner of activity and buying and selling. The whole aim is to get rich and famous and to have more than everyone else. It's a grand and glorious time for everyone inside, and the last thing they desire is to see someone be humble and content with just some fruit from a Tree. How boring. How demeaning. How could they possibly want to miss out on all our concerts, pride, and the exciting life we live? How could they ignore our Oscars and Emmys, our Pulitzers and medals of honor? How could they seek to be known, having the most views, likes, and shares? It's far more important that we have millions of followers and would do anything to gain them, including selling our own souls. Can they not see what they're missing out on?

I'm jumping the gun here.

In the end, the building comes crashing down, killing everyone. The destruction is immense, and the only people left are those standing next to a beautiful Tree. Nephi then desires to have the same vision for himself. Anyone who seeks the things of God can have the same experiences as those who lead the church. These visions, dreams, visitations, angels, and the voice of God are not limited to the prophets and apostles of our church. Any member may receive them; their reception depends only on the worthiness, sincerity, desire, and purity of the recipient. It's their heart that matters. What they set their hearts upon makes a difference.

Nephi wants to see the same thing, and God grants him this wish with an exceptional twist. He sees how this affects the entire history of the world from that point on. He sees the future. This is approximately 587 BC, and he sees everything moving forward.

He is fortunate to experience the Tree firsthand. Through its marvelous words, he recognizes that this symbolizes the love of God, Jesus Christ, bestowed upon the world so that they may be forgiven for their sins and avoid the tremendous judgment that falls upon those who do not repent. It brings great joy to the soul. He grasps the condescension of God in how

SECTION 16 - VISION OF THE TREE OF LIFE

Jesus Christ, who is Jehovah in the Old Testament—the one who created the Earth, by whose power everything exists—holds the Earth in its orbit around the solar system and how, in such an exalted position, he was born in the most humble of circumstances.

He sees him going forth among the children of men, with 12 Apostles going forth among the world to teach God's message of believing in him and repenting. He sees Jesus being baptized even though he's the only person in the entire history of the Earth who didn't need to be baptized. He sees the Holy Ghost come upon him, and then the 12 apostles go forth amongst the people, healing all manner of sicknesses, casting out devils, and performing innumerable miracles in front of everyone.

But then he sees that the Son of God was judged by the world in a large and spacious building. He observes that everyone in this building fights against the House of Israel, resulting in the tremendous fall, crash, and destruction of the people within it. He leaves us with this final word regarding this episode: "thus shall be the destruction of all nations, kindreds, tongues, and people that fight against the twelve apostles of the Lamb."(1 Ne 11:36)

Let's take a moment to reflect on what he just described. He sees the people among whom the Son of God would be born and perform his astonishing atonement for mankind, and how they would reject him, crucify him, and kill him. As we know, in 70 AD, the Roman emperor Titus came in and utterly destroyed Jerusalem. It happened on the exact same day of the calendar as when Jerusalem was destroyed in 587 BC which was the 9th of Av (Tisha B'Av) in the Hebrew calendar. These people, who are supposed to be the house of God, the House of Israel, were actually located in the great and spacious building. They allowed their pride in their position to distance them from the humility required to partake of the fruit of the Tree.

As a side note, we know that a small group of Christians followed Jesus's command to flee into the mountains when they saw these signs approaching. They reached Pella, and kept alive some of the oral traditions of Jesus's teachings. It's possible that this is a group that is a type and shadow for those who escape to Zion in the last days.

Nephi sees his people after they arrive in the promised land, many generations having passed since his time. He observes the same events that occurred in the other section. He notices the mist of darkness over the land

SECTION 16 - VISION OF THE TREE OF LIFE

and witnesses lightning, thunder, and earthquakes, along with tumultuous noises and great disturbances in the cities that have been built. A profound darkness envelops the land, and he realizes it is the terrible judgments of the Lord.

But then he sees the Lamb of God descending from heaven and appearing to his descendants. He sees 12 disciples chosen by him and the marvelous blessings that have allowed the people to live in incredible peace and harmony for four generations. This astonishing experience is truly unique in history. Jesus visits them often. Three of those 12 disciples are given the gift of never needing to face death. They are not subject to pain, sin, or Satan.

The sad part is that Nephi observes the people doing the exact same thing: they rose up in great pride, denied Christ and the twelve apostles, and fought against them. They sold themselves for money and claimed that salvation could be found in this church or that church. They dwindled in unbelief and were filled with pride and vain imaginations. They succumbed to the multiple temptations of the devil, which overpowered them. They gathered together in tremendous multitudes for war. He sees that river of filthy water, which symbolizes the depths of hell. I submit to you that this pit is war, because that's exactly what happened; they devolved into a massive, terrible civil war.

The Book of Mormon also contains another record of other people who were brought to America about 1,500 years before Nephi and his people. They arrived here in a marvelous manner, as the great prophet had witnessed tremendous visions. The Brother of Jared wrote what became the sealed portion of the gold plates that we have discussed in detail here. The important point is that these people also came to America, and in the brief record of the Book of Ether, we see a roller coaster of righteousness and wickedness over at least a 1,500-year period that culminates in a horrific civil war that wipes everybody out.

There are two world wars yet to come, with the second emerging from the first. The first occurs during the time of the Four Horsemen and the opposition that Donald Trump faces in establishing the Kingdom of God. They do everything they can to destroy it. Many martyrs are created during this terrible time. The Saints are commanded to flee Babylon and gather to Zion. However, once they are all there, the bottomless pit is opened, and God's

SECTION 16 - VISION OF THE TREE OF LIFE

army goes out to destroy the Dragons' minions. With tremendous military power, they sweep across the Earth, enduring a period of five months during which those who have received the Mark of the Beast are tormented and cannot die. As stated elsewhere in this book, this is meant to compel them to repent. Sadly, most will not repent, and this leads to a 13-month war that culminates in Armageddon.

Even though I'm calling them two different world wars, they are, in reality, the same one. However, a significant shift occurs when God's destroying angel Abaddon opens that pit, and they have the power of God to destroy those who oppose his work. This is all outlined in Revelation 9 and Isaiah 13.

But back to Nephi's vision. He greatly lamented the loss of his posterity to such terrible destruction. It pained him deeply to see what they had chosen. This loss must have been devastating to his soul. He knew the judgments of God had come upon them because of their choices, but he truly wished they had made better choices.

He then observes the nations and kingdoms of the Gentiles, primarily in Europe. He sees the formation of a great church that was more abominable than all the churches that slaughtered the faithful, tortured them, and imprisoned them in captivity. He perceived that the devil was its founder and that it sought after gold and silver, as well as worldly possessions. It pursued the admiration of the world and aimed to destroy the saints of God.

Nephi sees Columbus and other settlers arriving in America. He witnesses them being guided by the hand of God, carrying with them a book of great value. We know that this is the Bible, and for the most part, they were God-fearing people seeking religious and economic freedom from the tyranny of European nations. He recognizes God's hand in helping them win battles against more powerful adversaries. He also observes that the Gentiles have taken away many plain and precious truths from the Bible, blinding their eyes and hardening their hearts. This was all orchestrated by the great and abominable church.

Nephi sees that these Gentiles destroy the descendants of his seed (1 Ne 13:14). They have tremendous power over them and smite them greatly, and he says that it is the justice of God upon them. However, he notices that his descendants have written a book and called upon them to come forth in

SECTION 16 - VISION OF THE TREE OF LIFE

the last days to tell the world about what happened to them. God extends mercy to the Gentiles and grants them this tremendous power to overcome them and the opportunity to experience revelatory power similar to that which has been given to the House of Israel, the Jews, and the Nephites, all of whom have lost it because of sin and wickedness. (1 Ne 13:39)

This is far more significant than we realize. The record they bring, known as the Book of Mormon, testifies to the truth of the Bible. It restores many of the plain and precious truths that have been taken away from the Bible. It was inspired by God to come forth in the latter days to give the Gentiles an opportunity to participate in the salvation of mankind. This is a tremendous gift that God has provided in these last days; however, we know that the Book of Mormon is not well received and is, in fact, greatly mocked, including a Broadway play that uses its name in blasphemy.

Nephi promises that the time will come when Christ will manifest himself to the Jews and the Gentiles, and then he will manifest himself to the Gentiles and then to the Jews. The first shall be last and the last shall be first. If the Gentiles hearken unto the Lamb of God as revealed through the prophet Joseph Smith, they shall be numbered among the House of Israel. They will be blessed forever. They will not be brought down into captivity. They won't be confounded. That great pit—war—which has been dug by the great and abominable church founded by the devil shall be filled by those who dig it (1 Ne 14:3). They will not suffer the destruction of everything they have been blessed with if they will but accept the gospel as revealed through the prophet Joseph Smith in the latter days.

God promises that it will be well with the Gentiles if they keep their covenant. But then a stark warning: woe be unto the Gentiles if they harden their hearts against the Lamb of God! He promises that a great and marvelous work will come forth, dividing the people either by convincing them of peace and eternal life or delivering them down into captivity and destruction. The great and abominable church is the opposition that the righteous Gentiles face in the last days. There are only two churches: the church of the Lamb of God and the church of the devil. (1 Ne 14:10)

Sadly, he sees that the number of people in the Church of the Lamb is few, but they were also spread across the face of the Earth. Now, the great wind-up scene unfolds as the nations and kingdoms of the Gentiles fight

SECTION 16 - VISION OF THE TREE OF LIFE

against the Lamb of God. This is just as it happened with Jesus when the Jewish nation fought against Him and His apostles, of whom all were killed except John. Similarly, the people of Nephi turned against what they had been blessed with, fighting against the Lamb of God and facing destruction in a civil war. Likewise, the Jaredites experienced a civil war after denying everything that had been given to them.

These events will occur again. A marvelous moment takes place in 1 Nephi 14:25 when God tells Nephi that he will witness the vision of the end, the final scenes of world history, but he cannot write them down. He explains that these visions were reserved for his apostle John, as he was foreordained to record this account. This is clearly the book of Revelation. However, I hope you recognize a pattern here in relation to what occurs or will occur in our day.

I've often pondered what it is that he was not allowed to write because he says clearly:

1 Ne 14:16 And as there began to be wars and rumors of wars among all the nations which belonged to the mother of abominations, the angel spake unto me, saying: Behold, the wrath of God is upon the mother of harlots; and behold, thou seest all these things—

17 And when the day cometh that the wrath of God is poured out upon the mother of harlots, which is the great and abominable church of all the earth, whose founder is the devil, then, at that day, the work of the Father shall commence, in preparing the way for the fulfilling of his covenants, which he hath made to his people who are of the House of Israel.

Then the angel informs him that he is not permitted to write the rest, and Nephi complies with this command. However, I also believe the spirit guided him to write the additional chapters so that those who are attuned to the spirit can witness the same things and serve as a second witness to what the revelation describes. Lets go through each of them and see if we can discover something.

In Chapter 15, Nephi speaks to his brothers and explains the symbolism of the tree of life, the iron rod, the filthy water, and other elements. Each of these holds great significance, and essentially, he discusses what we must do to become a part of Zion in that day. While the rest of the world will be

SECTION 16 - VISION OF THE TREE OF LIFE

in turmoil and at war, we are to hold onto the iron rod. We must be baptized, receive the gift of the Holy Ghost, and cling to the iron rod until we reach and partake of the fruit of the tree. This symbolizes coming unto Jesus and recognizing who He is. Partaking of this fruit is available to anyone who chooses to follow this path and is far more significant than many people realize. This is what everyone in the world needs to do to survive the last days and become part of Zion.

Nephi goes on to share the significance of the river of filthy water which I interpret to mean war. Somehow, there is a great flame that is bright, representing the justice of God, yet it is also a terrible hell. A significant division exists among the people, who must choose either the church of the Lamb or the church of the Devil. The vast majority are in the great and spacious building, which is destined to collapse. This building opposes the most precious fruit, and those within it scornfully point their fingers at those who partake of it.

This was a hard thing for Laman and Lemuel to accept, and in chapter 16, they complain that these are harsh words. They are the words of God. There are people in our day who refuse to give up their sins, turn their hearts to God, and come to Him. They would rather indulge in the pleasures of the great and spacious building. However, that building will come to an end.

Chapter 16 also includes the marvelous story of the Liahona and how it guided them to the promised land. The reality is they were not acting as one, which is why they wandered through the desert for eight years. We will face the same issue if we are not united as a people. We need to be united as a husband and wife, as a family, as a ward, as a stake, and as a church. If we are not united, we will not achieve Zion. Zion is the ultimate goal, and those who live in it are united. This will be a significant test for us in our day as we strive to overcome the world and the basic needs of living. Someday I will write a book about this chapter alone because of its significance.

Chapter 17 outlines the ship's construction so they can cross the ocean to the promised land. They were not to rest until they reached that land. A very similar story occurred with the Jaredites as they lingered on the shore for four years. This serves as a type and shadow of our day. We may need to create something to reach Zion. Whether it's building a ship, a tent trailer, or a motor home, that choice will be up to each of us. But the reality is that

SECTION 16 - VISION OF THE TREE OF LIFE

we will need to leave behind what we currently love to reach Zion. This will not be a luxurious cruise or an exotic vacation. For some, it will be simple, as they are already prepared. For others, it will be an arduous journey.

Chapter 18 states that even after everything, some still do not have their hearts fully set on Zion. This is a new land and a different way of living. Things will be very different from what we're familiar with. We must humble ourselves and recognize God's hand and blessing in what He is doing for us, even though it may not feel like a blessing at the moment. We will have left our comfortable lives and will now have to start anew. But if we are righteous, we will make it through it.

Chapter 19 discusses his vision of the life of our Savior, Jesus Christ, and how, after everything God has done for them, they now trample Him underfoot and kill the very God who gave them everything they have. This rejection of our Savior, Jesus Christ, continues today. People scoff at those who appreciate His simple teachings. They want to be part of the current trend of "prosperity gospel" teachings. Nehor was prominent in the Book of Mormon for teaching this principle. He was killed for the murder of a man of God, but this did not deter his teachings. People prefer good preachers who can deliver powerful sermons and deserve to be compensated for their work. Some of the televangelists of our day fly on multiple private jets, claiming that Jesus has blessed them for sharing the gospel. No. They are Satan's minions deceiving the masses under these false concepts of the philosophies of men mingled with scripture.

Chapter 20 then explores the fulfillment of the rest of the vision he received from the angel. He specifically addresses members of the Church of Jesus Christ of Latter-day Saints, as noted in verse one. He warns that there are those who are part of the church and refer to themselves as citizens of the holy city, but they do not rely on the God of Israel. This chapter is a harsh reminder for those of us in the latter days who claim to be saved because we have been baptized under authority, yet do not uphold our part of the covenants we make. He then informs us that he has foretold several things due to this lack of covenant fulfillment keeping.

But because of his namesake, he will not give it to another. We have been transgressors from the womb. He will defer his anger for his namesake, and we will not be cut off; instead, we will suffer for the things we

SECTION 16 - VISION OF THE TREE OF LIFE

have not done. He's going to refine us in a furnace of affliction. He will not allow his name to be polluted, and he commands all of us to assemble so he can declare these things. Everything could have been as peaceful as a river for us, our righteousness could have been like the waves of the sea, and our seed could have been as numerous as the sand, but many have apostatized and gone against what they knew to be true. Therefore, he commands us to flee Babylon. He will lead us out of the desert and cause water to flow so that we may not die of thirst.

He told us all this beforehand because he knew that we are obstinate and have an iron neck. We do not bow down to him in worship and praise as we should.

Nephi then quotes Isaiah chapter 49, which is the quintessential chapter in all of Isaiah discussing his chosen servant of the last days, even Donald Trump. The House of Israel is scattered all over the world, and they need to be gathered for the last time. In his servant's mouth come forth sharp words—a man who has been made like a polished shaft in a quiver (Rev 6:2 shows the First Horseman has a bow!). God declares that he is his servant, and even after all he has accomplished during his first presidency and the difficult trials of the condescension phase, enduring the ridiculous and unconstitutional lawfare, he is called to do a great thing. He was worried that he hadn't achieved what he needed, but now he has a great work.

It may be a light thing to gather the tribes of Israel and restore the Jews, but he will also be a light to the Gentiles. Many people in his country despise him, and even some distant nations. However, kings shall see him and relinquish their kingdoms. Princes will bow down in worship, recognizing God's servant. The day of salvation is at hand, as he foretold. He has given the servant due to the covenant he made with his people and prophets from long ago, to establish the Earth and enable them to inherit the desolate land granted so long ago. He will free prisoners from all over the world, both those in physical and spiritual bondage. He will lead them like sheep to be fed in the pasture of God. They will not hunger or suffer because of the terrible events occurring elsewhere; he will guide them by springs of water.

And just as the Red Sea opened, creating a highway for the children of Israel to enter the promised land, multiple highways will be made available for all those whom Donald Trump leads out of their lands to Zion. This

SECTION 16 - VISION OF THE TREE OF LIFE

will eclipse the Red Sea experience, making it is never spoken again. They will come from far in the north and the west, and they will sing joyful songs. They shall suffer no more, for God has comforted His people. They may have believed that God had forgotten them, but He did not. Just as a mother cannot forget her nursing child, He will not forget them because of the atonement of Jesus Christ, who has made all this possible, and it is engraved in the palms of His hands.

Donald Trump is God's servant who fulfills that covenant and leads them like Moses to Zion. As they move forward, those who sought to destroy them will be laid waste. When they arrive in the promised land, once dirty and forgotten, he will adorn them beautifully like a bride on the most glorious day of any woman's life. Everything that appears wasted and desolate will be transformed into God's glory. They will have countless children to help expand throughout the country. What began as a small place will grow to encompass all of the Americas.

The Jews of the covenant will wonder where in the world all these people came from. She thought she had lost all her children and her eternal covenants, claiming she was desolate, tossed to and fro, and left alone. But God reminds her that He lifted His hand to all those who had received the covenant and brought them to Zion. He did this through the Kings and Queens of the Gentiles, the righteous covenant temple-attending members of the Church of Jesus Christ of Latter-day Saints, who achieved the glory that was offered. They went out and gathered the House of Israel as nursing fathers and nursing mothers, carrying infants. They rescued them from those who would hold them in captivity. They saved God's children, and in return, those who sought their destruction will turn upon themselves, experiencing the most violent acts of war and cannibalism ever seen.

In Chapter 22, Nephi explains these matters and illustrates how they relate not only to his time but also to the last days—our time. He prophesies that after the House of Israel has been nurtured by the kings and queens of the Gentiles, he will establish them as a standard, which is something that will emerge in the last days.

None of these things can happen unless he bares his arm in the eyes of all nations. He is going to use Donald Trump, the most recognized figure in the world, to fulfill God's covenant. He will lead them out of captivity,

SECTION 16 - VISION OF THE TREE OF LIFE

and the great and abominable church will turn against itself and wage war among its own. Every nation will be at war against another, but God will remove those who are unwilling to accept this covenant. Anyone who fights against Zion will be destroyed, and that great and spacious building will come crashing down earth.

Satan will be bound by God's destroying angel Abaddon and will have no power because he will be sealed in the bottomless pit. The wrath of God will be unleashed upon the children of men because He will not allow the wicked to destroy the righteous. He will preserve the righteous by His power, and the righteous need not fear because they will be saved, even as if by fire.

Then blood and fire and vapor of smoke will come upon the Earth against anyone who hardens their heart against Jesus Christ. The righteous will not perish, but those who fight against Zion will be cut off. The Lord will prepare a way for His people to fulfill the words of Moses, saying that the prophet of the Lord your God will raise up a Moses like me to deliver the people, and anyone who does not hear that prophet, Donald Trump, will be cut off from among the people. Yes, 1 Nephi 22:22 states that this prophet is the Holy One of Israel, even Jesus Christ; we know that He is speaking about Himself **and** His servant in the last days from 3 Nephi 21:15. This is a dual prophecy that will be fulfilled in our day.

Then every church built for personal gain will collapse and be destroyed. Those who seek the lust of the flesh and worldly desires in the great and spacious building—the great and abominable church, Mystery Babylon, the great Beast System—will be destroyed, while the righteous will be led as calves to the stall, receiving rain, dominion, mind, and glory. He will gather them from the four corners of the Earth; because of the righteousness of the people, they will have no power over them.

The pattern Nephi observed of the gospel being given and restored to the Earth at various times in history, where God has planted the tree of life for people to partake of, has consistently been destroyed by those who have fought against the House of Israel. This happened to the Jews, and it occurred with the Nephites and Lamanites; however, in the last days, all who oppose the House of Israel will be destroyed. Those who are part of Zion, the tree of life, and God's covenant will endure every attack from the Beast

SECTION 16 - VISION OF THE TREE OF LIFE

System that seeks its destruction. Every nation on Earth will come under the authority of him who has been ordained to accept that rule and turn it over to Jesus Christ.

For the first time in history, God's complete kingdom will be on Earth, and Satan's will be obliterated!

In every one of those examples, the gospel was given to a people, but due to sin, pride, and the wealth of the world, they migrated to the great and spacious building. Many individuals felt ashamed of partaking of that fruit and fell into forbidden paths. The great apostasy is occurring right now, even though some believe it refers to the period between the death of the apostles and the restoration of the gospel. I contend that this is not accurate. One cannot be considered an apostate unless they have learned the truth and then turned away from it. For at least 1,800 years, those people did not have the opportunity to learn the truth. They could not have apostatized because they never learned it. This great apostasy that Paul describes as occurring in the last days will indeed happen in our time because people will have learned the truth and chosen to go against it.

> 2 Thes 2:3 Let no man deceive you by any means: for that day shall not come, except there come a falling away first, and that man of sin be revealed, the son of perdition;
>
> 4 Who opposeth and exalteth himself above all that is called God, or that is worshipped; so that he as God sitteth in the temple of God, shewing himself that he is God.

Those who fight against Zion, along with those who leave the church and the covenants they have made, are the ones who have migrated to the great and spacious building. For whatever reason, like the ones I've discussed in the chapter on why people leave the church, they have lost the spirit and are therefore at risk of becoming part of that building, which will eventually collapse and endanger everyone inside. This is when the Earth burns at the coming of Jesus Christ.

Nephi saw all of these things in that vision, and he was not allowed to share the insights regarding God's servant, the First Horseman, Donald Trump, because that was ordained by God for John the Revelator to reveal. However, the same principles had been spoken about by Isaiah and

SECTION 16 - VISION OF THE TREE OF LIFE

other prophets. Therefore, he did not disobey the command at all; rather, he became a second witness by using principles and specific examples from his life that we can apply to our day. First Nephi is far more important than most people realize. It serves as a handbook and a pattern for those who are commanded to leave Babylon and flee to Zion. It shows us the challenges we will face and the attitude we must adopt regarding this tremendous change that is about to take place. We will all need to travel to Zion under the direction of the prophet of the day.

And may I point out that I am not suggesting that anyone will receive a personal revelation to leave their home and travel to Missouri. I am not qualified to make such a statement. We do know what Christ said in,

> 3 Ne 21:28 Yea, and then shall the work commence, with the Father among all nations in preparing the way whereby his people may be gathered home to the land of their inheritance.
>
> 29 And they shall go out from all nations; and they shall not go out in haste, nor go by flight, for I will go before them, saith the Father, and I will be their rearward.

It will be organized! The leadership will never falter, and we must follow whatever guidance they provide. They have not instructed us to travel to Missouri; that has not been communicated as a direction. I think it is dangerous for some people to claim that we need to do this, but I cannot speak for them either.

We need to wait until the Lord's direction is revealed through His chosen servants. Something will happen to Donald Trump that will lead to his recognition for who God has ordained him to be. He will be healed. He will be elevated, exalted, and extolled all over the world. He will be the divisive figure who separates the wicked from the righteous. Exactly how that ties in with Zion and the Church of Jesus Christ of Latter-day Saints and their leadership, I don't know. All I know is that great and marvelous things are coming, and we need to prepare in every way we can.

The Church of the Lamb, whose numbers are few, is armed with righteousness and power in great glory. This group of people does not fall away or oppose the Lamb of God, even though some do apostatize and suffer the wrath of God. The entire Book of Revelation is the culmination of the Kingdom of God being established, and we understand that it is through Donald

SECTION 16 - VISION OF THE TREE OF LIFE

Trump's administration and leadership that the political kingdom is formed, and Zion, or the New Jerusalem, is built upon the American continent. The righteous members of the Church, those willing to live the law of consecration, do not give in to the temptations and wiles of the devil. They navigate through the mist of darkness and partake of the Tree of Life in its fullness. They are blessed with the power of God and are safe and secure in Zion.

But God works through a covenant, and the work of the Father will commence in that day, fulfilling the promises made thousands of years ago to their ancient forefathers. God promised them that they would be blessed in many ways, and in the last days, everyone who is of the House of Israel and who is willing to accept these blessings will be gathered to Zion.

This will lead to wars and rumors of wars against the great mother of harlots. This bottomless pit of war will transform the Earth. The righteous members of Zion, from the Church of the Firstborn, will be granted immense power not only to endure the assault of the wicked who seek its destruction, all of whom belong to the great and abominable church, but they will also have the power to gather and seek out those under covenant.

This represents the 144,000, the Kings and Queens of the Gentiles.

As we have observed in other scriptures examined in this book, this process begins when God establishes the Gentiles as a free people under Donald Trump's leadership. This is not simply the founding of America; it represents a re-establishment of the nation with all the original intentions envisioned by our founding fathers.

The most significant event in world history after the atonement of Jesus Christ is about to take place: the reestablishment of the full Kingdom of God. Once this occurs, the entire world—particularly those who belong to the church of the devil—will attempt to destroy it, but will fail miserably. This time, the devil will not prevail.

This time, the righteous members of the church will remain steadfast and receive God's power to overcome everything that opposes them. Many will be killed and martyred for the glory of God and to bring about the justice that will be enforced on those who fought against them. At times, individuals must die to reveal the wickedness of the opposing side. Everyone desires to be among those who survive in Zion and witness its incredible beauty, safety, and peace. However, we are shown that not everyone will

SECTION 16 - VISION OF THE TREE OF LIFE

be present. The fifth seal represents the day of martyrs, during which, in response, those who belong to the Church of the Devil will kill those who belong to the Church of God but are not in Zion.

These topics are challenging to discuss, as no one wants to engage with them. However, when viewed through the eyes of God, whose thoughts are higher than ours, even those who die as martyrs are greatly blessed. We understand that life is not all there is; we will live for eternity in a realm of glory that depends on our faithfulness here. Those who face such difficult circumstances are promised eternal blessings. Mortality is merely a blip in the timeline of eternity. Typically, we focus on what is right in front of us and seldom consider beyond a few years. Very few of us reflect on the eternal consequences of our choices; otherwise, we would make different decisions.

However, let there be no mistake: there are those outside of Zion who will also receive the power of God to overcome their enemies. We are instructed that we cannot judge anyone who has passed away in these last days as being one of the wicked. That is not our place. We do not know the reasons why some are saved and others are not; our role is simply to remain faithful.

The primary goal of this chapter is to demonstrate how the Book of Revelation aligns with Nephi's vision and the extraordinary glory and power of what is nearly upon us. We need to prepare ourselves. I propose that the spiritual readiness required to withstand what lies ahead is more crucial than most of us recognize.

Yes, we need to prepare in every way possible, including food storage and financial reserves. We've been hearing this for the past hundred years or so, but spiritual preparation is even more crucial. Look, I've been a prepper from the start. I've had dreams about what's coming and have tried to do everything I can to get ready for those challenges, but spiritual preparation is the most important aspect.

Let me provide a partial list of what I believe this involves. At the most fundamental level, it requires the faith necessary to accept the gospel as revealed and taught by the authorized servants of the Church of Jesus Christ of Latter-day Saints. Those who possess this level of faith have chosen the straight and narrow path and are clinging to the rod of iron. However, that

SECTION 16 - VISION OF THE TREE OF LIFE

is only the beginning. There is much more to follow.

Walking along the straight and narrow path while holding the rod of iron signifies growth, spiritual maturity, and the capacity to resist the temptations of the world. It involves accepting the injustices that come our way and facing life's challenges. It means overcoming opposition, doubts, fears, and anti-Mormon literature. It signifies advancing in gospel knowledge and strengthening our testimonies and relationship with God. It also entails growing in revelation and spiritual gifts. This journey includes overcoming addictions, addressing challenges in raising a family, remaining faithful to our spouses, and, most importantly, keeping our covenants no matter what happens.

It means nurturing and watering our Tree of Faith until we are certain for ourselves that Jesus exists and that He is our Father.

The culmination of this growth is the understanding that Jesus Christ lives, has paid for your sins, and has granted you salvation. That's the goal for all of us—or at least it should be. What's amazing, though, is that even after we reach this state, the temptations don't disappear. The darkness and mockery from those in the great and spacious building persist. The temptations are much more subtle than they were along the path. They can manifest as thoughts of loyalty or distrust. Even the mere notion of becoming great or prideful can lead us astray. Lehi's vision illustrates that there are those who, even after they reach the end and know Christ, will fall away, and I submit to you that the main cause of their falling away is pride.

We must remain vigilant at every step, even after reaching the end. However, the purpose of this chapter is to demonstrate that everyone in the world must follow the same path during these last days. Each person must come to the Church of Jesus Christ of Latter-day Saints and accept and live the covenant given through authorized servants. We read the Bible and observe the sacrifices and rituals performed in the tabernacle of Moses. Yet those same rituals are practiced today, in their perfected form, in the temples of God. We cannot be saved without these covenants.

However, as mentioned, even some who have reached the highest levels of participation in these covenants fall away. A friend of mine recently shared with me about a temple sealer who appeared on one of these podcasts to discuss how and why he left the church. He then jokingly remarked

SECTION 16 - VISION OF THE TREE OF LIFE

in a casual manner, "I guess that makes me a son of perdition." It is distressing to see people leave the church over minor issues. When we compare our current circumstances to what the physical problems our pioneer ancestors endured 175 years ago, there is truly no comparison. They faced much greater challenges, even simply staying alive. However, that struggle brought them closer to God.

In our age of comfort and abundance, it's easy to forget God. In a way, we face a much greater challenge than our pioneering ancestors because we have a phone in our hands all day, providing access to anything we desire. Unfortunately, many people use their phones primarily for distraction and entertainment.

To all my friends who are not members of the Church of Jesus Christ of Latter-day Saints, whether you are Christian, Buddhist, Muslim, or belong to another religion: I recognize that what I'm sharing here may not resonate with some of you. I'm not criticizing you or your beliefs; as I've pointed out earlier in this book, all religions have experienced God's influence in their lives. We are living in the last days, and everyone who has embraced God's truth at any level must ultimately accept and live by the full principles of the gospel. This is the same message Jesus shared during his time, inviting others to follow him. That call required leaving behind what they were comfortable with, including their previous understandings, and it necessitated a profound transformation in their hearts.

Not only that, but the world mocks everything we teach, and there is considerable controversy surrounding all aspects of joining this church. It would have been much easier if Joseph Smith had simply stood up and declared, "I've had a vision from God; come join my church." Instead, we faced an astonishingly unusual situation of presenting a book written on gold plates, revealed by an angel. If that were the only controversy, it might suffice, but it isn't. There are thousands of contentious issues surrounding membership in the Church of Jesus Christ of Latter-day Saints.

In these final days, we are introduced to a controversial figure: Donald Trump, who is positioned to help restore the political Kingdom of God. Make no mistake, he lacks the ecclesiastical authority of the prophets and apostles of the Church of Jesus Christ of Latter-day Saints. He has a mission to address political aspects, and all of this will be combined in a way that

SECTION 16 - VISION OF THE TREE OF LIFE

currently remains unrevealed. I have shared numerous insights in this book on how this operates, but I'm simply asking you to set aside your doubts and fears, put away your preconceived notions, read the Book of Mormon, and discover for yourself if it's true. Because if it is true, everything changes.

Once you recognize its truth, you have the opportunity to pursue the straight and narrow path and be baptized to initiate that process. What more is there? The world will be destroyed. If we are not part of Zion, the New Jerusalem, and the Church of God, who are we? There will only be two churches. Who wants to belong to the other one? Some of those people associated with that church are those who consciously deny the spirit of God they experienced while reading the Book of Mormon. They resist it and face the consequences of such actions. The rest never read it and had no interest in it.

Many people I've spoken with demand physical proof of the Book of Mormon. They insist on archaeological evidence of the cities mentioned in the book. They want something that can be verified through the five senses: sight, smell, taste, hearing, and touch. So let me ask you, is that the only way to determine if something is true? Is that how you have discovered the truth of everything you know? I hope you realize that's not the case.

We have direct physical proof of the gold plates given to Joseph Smith. Three Witnesses saw the plates, saw the angel Moroni, and heard the voice of God commanding them to testify to the world. We also have eight additional witnesses who saw the plates. They felt and held them in their hands. They did not see an angel or hear the voice of God.

Here we have two groups of people in entirely different circumstances who knew the plates were real. Those tuned into spiritual things will recognize and appreciate the dramatic events of the first group. Those who are scientifically minded should have no problem accepting the experience of the second group because it meets all of their requirements. However, both of these events still require you to have faith because faith is the only way we're going to learn the truth about anything.

The astonishing events about to unfold in our world are expressed in unusual figurative language, to say the least. The Book of Revelation has been preserved so that we may understand His will. The pattern depicted in the Book of Mormon through the visions of Nephi and Lehi is destined to repeat, with one significant exception: **Zion will not be destroyed.** God's Kingdom will not face destruction as it has numerous times throughout history, except for the cities of Enoch and Melchizedek! Only with Zion will there be the power of God to overcome the armies of the world that seek to annihilate it. Only the righteous will be spared, while everyone else will suffer like never before.

Section 17
Why People Leave The Church

Section 17 - Why people leave the Church

Anyone who leaves the Church of Jesus Christ of Latter-day Saints does so for the exact same reason as anyone else who has left.

Yes, they do.

They may say they had discovered something they didn't like in church history. They think they have found something they think no one else knows about. Maybe they read some anti-literature and caused doubts in their mind.

They may say they disagree with what a previous prophet did or said, whether true or not. They may claim that God would never allow a true Prophet to do such a thing.

They may claim that they were offended by a member. Maybe someone looked at them weirdly or didn't invite them to their Christmas party. Perhaps no one ever came to Minister to them or recognized something they did or brought them meals during a difficult time when those same people took care of the Johnsons who weren't nearly as bad off.

Maybe they were defrauded of money by a member. Maybe their child was abused by a member. Maybe their spouse beat them, or got fired from their job which was owned by another member.

Maybe their husband had a high church calling and was caught cheating and having an affair. Maybe they decided to change genders or went to live with someone of the same gender.

Maybe they didn't like the Church's Doctrine, Policy, or Proclamation. Perhaps they disagreed with something the Prophet or Apostles said.

Maybe they were upset with a group or organization the Church supported.

Maybe they broke sacred covenants and allowed Satan to take control of their lives.

Maybe they were deceived by a Facebook Group claiming secret

SECTION 17 - WHY PEOPLE LEAVE THE CHURCH

knowledge or persuaded to follow someone committing Priestcraft like Nehor or Korihor.

Suppose they turned to the occult or Eastern Religions for solace and felt something. How can this be?

Maybe they got rich, greedy, full of the world's cares, and lost the spirit.

Maybe they stopped praying, reading their scriptures, attending church, keeping the word of wisdom, or paying their tithing and didn't feel like doing it anymore.

Maybe they became so educated they thought they knew more than God or at least a better way to do things.

Perhaps they developed a large following on Facebook or Instagram and people started praising them for their extensive knowledge. Satan tempted them with pride that eventually brought their downfall.

Perhaps they started seeing faults in their Bishop or Stake President and criticizing their decisions.

Maybe they prayed and prayed and never got an answer, even for something important, and eventually, they just gave up.

Maybe they suffered an illness for many years and couldn't understand why God allowed them to suffer for so long. Perhaps it was their spouse or child that suffered.

Maybe they saw another member get drunk, drink coffee, vape, be unsportsmanlike in a basketball game, or do something else that showed they were a hypocrite.

Maybe they couldn't overcome an addiction, they got involved in porn, committed a crime, or know of a member that caused the death of someone because they fell asleep at the wheel, or worse, had a DUI.

Perhaps they just forgot about what they promised to do or failed to follow their Patriarchal Blessing and things looked hopeless. Maybe they were embarrassed to come anymore because of something they did.

There are a million claims about why they left the Church, but there is only one real reason.

SECTION 17 - WHY PEOPLE LEAVE THE CHURCH

Only

SECTION 17 - WHY PEOPLE LEAVE THE CHURCH

One

SECTION 17 - WHY PEOPLE LEAVE THE CHURCH

Let's do a little self-analysis here. If you're not a 100% tithe-paying, Word of Wisdom-following, commandment-keeping, temple recommend holding, temple attending, fully engaged in your calling, reading your scriptures, and saying your prayers every day kind of person, what are your reasons? Are you totally active, somewhat active, completely inactive, or have you entirely apostatized from the church and are now fighting against it? Before we continue, I want you to answer this question for yourself. This is not a test. No one is going to see it. Please fill in the blanks as they are introspective statements.

I am _____ percent active.

The problem I have with not being 100% active is

_____
_____
_____
_____
_____

Are you ready for the answer as to why they are all inactive to any degree because of the exact same reason?

Alma 32:38-40 tells us that those who have fallen away from the church and lost their testimonies was because they neglected their tree of faith:

> 38 But if ye neglect the tree, and take no thought for its nourishment, behold it will not get any root; and when the heat of the sun cometh and scorcheth it, because it hath no root it withers away, and ye pluck it up and cast it out.

> 39 Now, this is not because the seed was not good, neither is it because the fruit thereof would not be desirable; but it is because your ground is barren, and ye will not nourish the tree, therefore ye cannot have the fruit thereof.

> 40 And thus, if ye will not nourish the word, looking forward with an eye of faith to the fruit thereof, ye can never pluck the fruit of the tree of life.

SECTION 17 - WHY PEOPLE LEAVE THE CHURCH

> *They failed to nurture and water their tree of faith!*

This marvelous chapter on Faith, the first principle of the gospel, should be studied extensively and is worth reviewing often. It not only tells us how to increase our faith but how to tell if anything is true and is something we can put our faith in. There's nothing wrong with having doubts, but what we do with those doubts will affect our eternal future.

This chapter also warns of the consequences of failing to continue the path once started. Just as planting an apple seed will eventually develop into an apple tree that produces fruit, Faith is the same thing. It takes years to pluck fruit from the Tree of Faith, and it's entirely dependent on a person's belief and the type of soil in their soul. It's also reliant on the Lord's timing rather than their own. We don't determine when answers come!

Everyone will face the "Heat of the Sun" to test their Faith, sometimes multiple times. But if their ground is barren, if they failed to nurture and water the tree, they yank it out and claim it wasn't true, but that is false.

The problem is they KNEW it was true; they just failed to keep watering it, and it died.

Jesus taught us in the Parable of the Sower exactly where every person on this planet fits when it comes to acceptance of the gospel and their faith. It's in Luke 8

> 4 ¶ And when much people were gathered together, and were come to him out of every city, he spake by a parable:
>
> 5 A sower went out to sow his seed: and as he sowed, some fell by the way side; and it was trodden down, and the fowls of the air devoured it.
>
> 6 And some fell upon a rock; and as soon as it was sprung up, it withered away, because it lacked moisture.
>
> 7 And some fell among thorns; and the thorns sprang up with it, and choked it.
>
> 8 And other fell on good ground, and sprang up, and bare fruit an

SECTION 17 - WHY PEOPLE LEAVE THE CHURCH

hundredfold. And when he had said these things, he cried, He that hath ears to hear, let him hear.

9 And his disciples asked him, saying, What might this parable be?

10 And he said, Unto you it is given to know the mysteries of the Kingdom of God: but to others in parables; that seeing they might not see, and hearing they might not understand.

11 Now the parable is this: The seed is the word of God.

12 Those by the way side are they that hear; then cometh the devil, and taketh away the word out of their hearts, lest they should believe and be saved.

13 They on the rock are they, which, when they hear, receive the word with joy; and these have no root, which for a while believe, and in time of temptation fall away.

14 And that which fell among thorns are they, which, when they have heard, go forth, and are choked with cares and riches and pleasures of this life, and bring no fruit to perfection.

15 But that on the good ground are they, which in an honest and good heart, having heard the word, keep it, and bring forth fruit with patience.

I had previously asked you where you fit regarding your activity level in the church. After reading this parable, we learned a few things about these four groups of people. The first group never allows the gospel into their hearts or minds at all. If you're reading this book, I'm pretty sure you're not in that group. We can see it all around us: people whose only desire is something for themselves, and they will do anything to get it. They don't care about anyone else unless they can use them. Every attempt to share the gospel with them is ignored and even resisted.

SECTION 17 - WHY PEOPLE LEAVE THE CHURCH

The second group hears the word with gladness. There's something truthful about it. They recognize by the spirit that this is good. But it doesn't last long. It doesn't even have time to get into their souls. Something comes up, and they kill it before it has a chance to grow. Whether it's a distraction, a sin, or a desire of the world, they leave it. God tried to give them a chance, but they refused.

The third group is the one I believe most people in our country belong to. They receive the word with joy, love the Bible, and enjoy attending megachurches. They shout and exclaim how great God is, yet they don't do much beyond that. They're primarily one-day-a-week worshipers, and the rest of the time, they only care about worldly matters. They resist missionaries because it implies they need to do something more. They're the ones who explain that all you need to do is believe in order to be saved. They pick and choose which scriptures to obey while ignoring the rest. They sing and pray together but also witness Christian bullies attacking missionaries from the church. They drive fancy cars and live in nice homes, claiming they've acquired these things because of their faith in Jesus. They avoid accepting the gospel because it feels like too much work. They continue to believe the falsehoods spread about the church, as it makes their lives easier.

The fourth group is the smallest group, the ones who accept the gospel as taught by the missionaries. They have good hearts and want to do their best. They bear the fruit of repentance and are patient with one another. They seek the welfare of those around them and always strive to do their best. They keep their covenant, the commandments of God, and only seek His will. It's not that they lack trials or difficulties to overcome—everyone does— but they use their faith in Jesus Christ to overcome those challenges.

So, which group are you in? I hope it's the fourth group. However, we live in a time that was prophesied to witness a significant apostasy in the last days. Most people believe that the great apostasy happened after the apostles died, leading to almost 2000 years without the spirit and the Holy Ghost guiding His prophets. It is true that, as far as we know, there were no other prophets on Earth beyond Moroni in 421 A.D. I might be mistaken here, but that's what we have on record so far. Joseph Smith didn't arrive until 1820, and because of this, many consider that this long period represents the great apostasy.

SECTION 17 - WHY PEOPLE LEAVE THE CHURCH

I suggest that we consider this from a different perspective. Paul teaches this profound principle in,

> 2 Thes 2:1 Now we beseech you, brethren, by the coming of our Lord Jesus Christ, and by our gathering together unto him,
>
> 2 That ye be not soon shaken in mind, or be troubled, neither by spirit, nor by word, nor by letter as from us, as that the day of Christ is at hand.
>
> 3 Let no man deceive you by any means: for that day shall not come, except there come a falling away first, and that man of sin be revealed, the son of perdition;
>
> 4 Who opposeth and exalteth himself above all that is called God, or that is worshipped; so that he as God sitteth in the temple of God, shewing himself that he is God.

He's discussing the second coming of Jesus Christ. Many people assumed it would occur soon after his resurrection, but they did not fully understand the scriptures. They gathered together, striving to live their best lives under the apostles. Paul teaches here that there will be a falling away first. Yes, this includes the 1800 years previously mentioned, but I'm suggesting that this actually refers to our day.

The vision of the tree of life provides a prime example of what apostasy entails. Once those who have reached the tree and partaken of the fruit become ashamed due to the ridicule from those in the great and spacious building. Remember, the vision of the tree of life is a repeating pattern that fits into every segment of history, as Nephi discovers. The great apostasy occurs when someone who has partaken of the fruit falls away. For 1,800 years, no one partook of the fruit; it wasn't available. The great apostasy that Paul speaks of is our day, and many who have partaken of the fruit have fallen away because they feel ashamed in a world filled with pride.

These verses from Paul discuss a Man of Sin who will be revealed, the son of perdition who opposes everything God does. He mentions that part of the emergence of this Man of Sin is a significant falling away. He's referring to the church in our time. This falling away is occurring right now. Satan whispers to us very subtle and clever things:

You can take it easy; everything is fine.

SECTION 17 - WHY PEOPLE LEAVE THE CHURCH

You don't need to read the scriptures every day. Just do it when you have time.

You don't have time to pray; there are too many things you need to complete, and wasting time in prayer will not help you. You never get an answer anyway, so what's the point?

Oh look, it's Stake Conference this weekend; let's take a little vacation.

You do not have to go to church every single week. You can miss one once in a while.

You have accomplished great things in life; you don't need God anymore.

You know you feel the Spirit much more in the wilderness than in a church building.

No one comes to minister to you; why should you go minister to anyone else?

The church doesn't need your tithing; you can stop paying it. Just think of what else you could buy with that money!

If you try to share the gospel with your neighbors, they're just going to think you're weird.

You don't need to wear your garments all the time; they are inconvenient; besides, you don't like the material, and they just don't fit right, interfering with the latest clothing styles.

Having a cup of coffee isn't going to keep you out of the celestial kingdom.

Go ahead and go to the store on the Sabbath; it doesn't matter anymore. Everybody does it.

It's no problem watching TV and especially sports on Sunday. Besides, the best games are on Sunday!

Now please stop listening to him. Lets get back to the right spirit. This could clearly be a very long list, but it all starts with a small thought—a wedge of doubt—that, if left unattended, will destroy our tree of faith.

In April 1966, President Spencer W. Kimball delivered a memorable address quoting an account by Samuel T. Whitman entitled "Forgotten Wedges." President Thomas S. Monson then revived that story in April 2002[26] with a talk entitled "Hidden Wedges" about how someone had left a wedge in the crook of a tree while splitting wood and forgot all about it. He kept thinking about going to get it but always put it off. Eventually, the tree grew so large that it completely enveloped the wedge; however, a large storm came and broke off one significant limb from the tree. Now out of balance, the rest of the tree split into pieces. Upon investigation, they discovered that the wedge, which had been there all those years, was the cause of its destruction.

SECTION 17 - WHY PEOPLE LEAVE THE CHURCH

In a similar way, Satan puts a wedge in our hearts and in our faith by putting a simple thought that, if not removed, will destroy our tree of faith. If we fail to remove that wedge, it can lead to far more significant things, and we see people all the time who actively seek to destroy the church. Once that spirit enters their hearts, very few come back. Some do, though, and it's usually due to an extremely difficult problem they face in life because of their decisions. We welcome them back just as Joseph Smith welcomed back his accusers, who caused so many problems. I've talked with members who left, and they discussed how hard it was to leave, even saying it was the most challenging thing they had ever done.

Of course it was! They were fighting against the Holy Spirit, who was trying to persuade them to stay! They went against years of testimony, service, instruction, firesides, Sacrament talks, partaking of the Sacrament, General Conferences, pioneer history, parental love, Primary, Sunday School, young men/women activities, Scout camp, Girl's camp, reading Scriptures, and feeling that Spirit 10,000 times! It's hard to kick against all that, yet somehow they do anyway. They get it stuck in their heads that something isn't right or the way they want it, and so they pack up and leave.

Some leave very gradually over time, but their hearts remain set. Some leave in a great huff and ensure that everyone knows what they've done. They broadcast it to the entire world, and in this strange time we live in, they can find a support group for any reason they depart. Dozens, hundreds, or even thousands of others will be there to offer their condolences and congratulations. And some will make a great deal of money in the process!

But the only way back is to repent and humbly admit they made a mistake. They CAN come back, and we want them back!

But many will continue doing what they want to do. Self-justification is a common tactic that we've all used at some time in our lives to justify our actions. It's a part of pride. We don't like to admit we were wrong. We especially don't like it when someone points that out. We will sometimes do anything to avoid that!

But self-justification won't work at the Judgment Bar of God. Scripture tells us that once we are in that situation and have not repented, we will wish an entire mountain could fall upon us and hide us from His presence! Imagine desiring a trillion tons of dirt to squish us instead of being in front of God! No wonder there will be weeping and wailing and gnashing of teeth! Now is the day to repent because whatever spirit we create in this life goes to the other side.

There is a current trend of digging up actions of past Church leaders and saying, "There's no way the Church is true! Look at what he did!" Yes, many have done things they probably shouldn't have done. So have you. But their actions, as egregious as they may be, have no bearing on the truthfulness of the Book of Mormon. Besides, you weren't there. You don't know the situation. You don't even know if it was reported correctly. Even if it was 100% true, I recommend letting God be the Judge instead of you trying to do His job.

Some members self-justify not returning because of the actions of members when they left. Perhaps they got yelled at, shunned, ignored, cast out, or even disowned by their family or Ward, but that self-justification doesn't work either. Only humility will. They will be judged for their actions, and you will be for yours (see previous paragraph about judging).

Sadly, members who yank out the dead sapling or tree leave the Church but can't leave it alone. At first, they may gently walk out the door and leave a letter explaining their reasoning, but soon, they actively seek to destroy the Faith of others and become a significant opposition to the Lord's work and mission. Some even boldly post their reasons on YouTube to make money, all the while gaining support from others who have also left and furthering the great apostasy just mentioned.

They follow the same path as their adversary and support his cause! Why allow him to direct your actions?

While Alma tells us in the verses above that if they continue, they will NEVER be able to partake of the Tree of Life; repentance must be part of the process. They can turn to God and be forgiven with humility and acknowledgment of their actions. Alma himself was on that path. He repented and became a great leader. (But don't expect the same experience as Alma! Few people realize just how traumatic those three days were!)

I pray that we all recognize our position in the Tree of Faith-growing process and take action to further the goal of partaking in that fruit by nurturing the tree of Faith within us daily. If we have uprooted it and claimed

SECTION 17 - WHY PEOPLE LEAVE THE CHURCH

it wasn't true, I pray we will humble ourselves and place the blame for our inactivity or opposition exactly where it belongs: on ourselves.

We are responsible for our spiritual growth. We need to recognize this to grow to our full potential. God will help you! He WANTS you to succeed! And active members should do all they can to welcome them back!

One of the biggest reasons people leave churches is that they suppose life will be easy if they follow the gospel. Since they are having a problem, they either assume the church is not true or ask why bad things happen to good people. This question has been asked numerous times and featured in multiple books and movies. Atheists love to ask why there is suffering. According to their reasoning, if God really existed, there would be no suffering.

We all encounter this because we strive to do our best, yet something unfortunate occurs. Everything I mentioned earlier is just a small grain of sand on a vast seashore of similar challenges. We each face our own trials and tests and wonder why.

Perhaps we feel we are doing everything possible. We believe, work hard, strive, read our scriptures, and pray, yet terrible things happen. Some of these challenges are astonishingly difficult. While I have faced many of my own issues in life, often due to my own mistakes or poor choices, there is a reason we all encounter trials, even when we are trying to do our best.

Remember, God's ways are higher than our ways, and His thoughts are higher than our thoughts. So why would He do this? Why would He allow such hardships in our lives instead of rewarding those who follow Him with great blessings and deep joy?

Regardless of our station in life, we need to strengthen our faith. Faith is one of the most powerful forces we will ever need in eternity. It was through faith that God created this Earth. Faith is power. Faith is dynamic and alive. If we wish to become like Him, we must have that same faith.

We love movies like Star Wars and imagine having "the Force," pointing our fingers at something, and moving it without actually touching it. There has been much discussion regarding this, with some people claiming it's wizardry and others asserting it's about the priesthood and the power

SECTION 17 - WHY PEOPLE LEAVE THE CHURCH

of God.

What I dislike about movies' portrayal of such things is that the evil side, the dark side, has almost the same level of power negatively for control and personal gain as the good side does positively. While it is true that Satan has power given to him, enabling him to commit his terrible deeds, it pales in comparison to the power of God. Satan has only been granted enough power to serve as our tempter and adversary. Without any power, we would face no opposition and experience no temptation.

The only true positive power in the universe is faith in Jesus Christ—faith in His name and belief that turning to Him will empower us to repent, overcome trials, endure great difficulties, and face numerous other challenges in life, including the small list above and many more.

If we come across someone who has stumbled or fallen away. How should we respond? What can we do to help bring that person back to what they know is true? Let me show you how not to approach this situation.

The gospel embodies love and care for others. Jesus Christ exemplifies faith, hope, charity, and love, serving as the perfect model of these virtues. While he is indeed a God of justice, demonstrated by his act of overturning the tables in the temple, he remains the ultimate representation of love.

If you have a loved one who has fallen away or is in the process of doing so, I can tell you from personal experience that the only way they will come back is through love. Yelling at them does nothing. Ruining a relationship is one of the worst things you can do during these difficult times. I can share numerous examples of how I and others have made mistakes. Just remember the story of how Ammon reached the hearts of the Lamanites through service and love before he could teach them with the spirit (Alma 18). That example applies to our families as well. We may feel fearful, nervous, and angry about what we see happening, but we cannot let those emotions take over. It will ruin everything for years to come.

The whole point of this is that we, as parents, fear our children's choices, yet we must allow them to make those choices. They may need to learn things the hard way, just as we did.

For anyone else reading this who might be inactive, or for those of you with children or loved ones who are, I hope this serves as a valuable lesson.

SECTION 17 - WHY PEOPLE LEAVE THE CHURCH

We strive to teach the correct principles, and God will judge and hold us accountable if we fail to do so. We are not responsible for their choices, and we must allow them to make those decisions independently. Our role is to love them and hope that, in time, they will return.

The fear we have is that they may never return. We've known people who have died without reconciling with God. But that's their choice. No amount of force will ever bring them back. Perhaps I'm wrong, and someone may send me a note explaining how they approached things differently, but this is my experience. I've known several others who grew angry at their children and completely distanced themselves because of the choices those children made. I don't believe that's the right choice. I don't think it's a wise decision. As parents, we look to the future and desire a celestial eternity with our children, and we fear losing that, which can lead to anger over their actions. However, we can't view it that way. We must exercise our faith and hope, allowing them to learn on their own.

A good friend of mine told me that his daughter approached his wife and said she no longer believed the church was true. His wife replied, "OK. Let me know when you're ready to come back." He was stunned because he would not have reacted like that. His daughter eventually returned and is now more committed than ever. She faced extremely difficult times, but that's part of mortality. We have to learn the consequences of our own decisions.

The good news is that Jesus Christ will always be there, and anyone can turn to Him whenever they wish. We each decide what rock bottom is, how high we will stand, and how low we will go. He will be there if we turn to Him. If we don't receive the answers we want, in the manner we desire or within the expected time frame, please understand that you may not have done anything wrong. Yes, sometimes these trials are tougher than we can imagine, but please use them to strengthen your faith. If you spend years fasting and praying for relief for your child, spouse, or loved one from a disease or another issue, and it doesn't come to pass, don't turn away from God. Just know that He will take away all the pain you suffer, the fears, the loss, and the tremendous difficulties. He will take it upon Himself. He already has if you will accept it! Your Savior, Jesus Christ, knows more about the situation than you do. He knows you better than you know yourself.

SECTION 17 - WHY PEOPLE LEAVE THE CHURCH

Of course, it's easy to write this in a book and tell everyone to just have faith during the trials they face, but I know what I'm talking about. I look around and see people who have gone through tremendous ordeals, and I marvel at the kind of individuals they are for enduring such challenges. We all know individuals who complain and moan about the smallest issues. They become angry and lash out at everyone, seeking attention and sympathy for their struggles. At the same time, there are others who have battled cancer three times, lost children or spouses, gone bankrupt, faced serious abuse, been in severe car accidents, etc., and yet they maintain the sweetest disposition. They are filled with love and gratitude and genuinely want to know how others are doing. They care about those around them.

Our trials and difficulties in life shape us into who we are. If we turn to Christ, these experiences can mold us into who He desires us to be. The great Apostle Peter expressed this best.

> 1 Peter 4:12 Beloved, think it not strange concerning the fiery trial which is to try you, as though some strange thing happened unto you:
>
> 13 But rejoice, inasmuch as ye are partakers of Christ's sufferings; that, when his glory shall be revealed, ye may be glad also with exceeding joy.
>
> 14 If ye be reproached for the name of Christ, happy are ye; for the spirit of glory and of God resteth upon you: on their part he is evil spoken of, but on your part he is glorified.

He encouraged us to view these fiery trials not as strange, unusual, or out of the ordinary for anyone else, but as reasons to rejoice in them. Be happy! Rejoice in knowing that God has chosen you, loves you, and wants you to grow and become more like Him. By doing so, we give Him more glory.

> 1 Peter 1:7 That the trial of your faith, being much more precious than of gold that perisheth, though it be tried with fire, might be found unto praise and honour and glory at the appearing of Jesus Christ:
>
> 8 Whom having not seen, ye love; in whom, though now ye see him not, yet believing, ye rejoice with joy unspeakable and full of glory:
>
> 9 Receiving the end of your faith, even the salvation of your souls.

SECTION 17 - WHY PEOPLE LEAVE THE CHURCH

10 Of which salvation the prophets have inquired and searched diligently, who prophesied of the grace that should come unto you:

11 Searching what, or what manner of time the Spirit of Christ which was in them did signify, when it testified beforehand the sufferings of Christ, and the glory that should follow.

The end of our faith, the culmination of our trials, and the final blessing we receive for successfully overcoming the challenges we face is nothing short of the salvation of our souls. Christ's atonement was worth it. He saved you. You triumphed over the trial through His name and are blessed with eternal salvation. You glorify Him when you turn to Him and deepen your faith, succeeding because of Him. Don't be ashamed. Glorify God.

1 Peter 4:16 Yet if any man suffer as a Christian, let him not be ashamed; but let him glorify God on this behalf.

17 For the time is come that judgment must begin at the house of God: and if it first begin at us, what shall the end be of them that obey not the gospel of God?

18 And if the righteous scarcely be saved, where shall the ungodly and the sinner appear?

19 Wherefore let them that suffer according to the will of God commit the keeping of their souls to him in well doing, as unto a faithful Creator.

So why did I write a lengthy chapter on testimonies, apostasy, overcoming trials, facing opposition, and using love and concern to bring people back? What could this possibly have to do with a book about the claim that Donald Trump is God's prophesied servant? How in the world is this connected? There's a far deeper connection than you realize.

Peter presents a twofold prophetic insight. Within just a few years after Peter's time, following his martyrdom in 70 A.D., Jerusalem would be utterly destroyed. God's incredible judgment would be unleashed upon those who had the opportunity to accept the gospel offered by God's only begotten Son, Jesus Christ. They had the covenant; they were part of the chosen generation, significantly blessed with immense responsibilities and opportunities. Yet, they rejected it and even killed their God. No other nation on earth would have executed their Redeemer (2 Ne 10:3).

SECTION 17 - WHY PEOPLE LEAVE THE CHURCH

However, that isn't the only occasion when this prophecy has an effect. The Lord has stated in,

> D&C 112:25 And upon my house shall it begin, and from my house shall it go forth, saith the Lord;
>
> 26 First among those among you, saith the Lord, who have professed to know my name and have not known me, and have blasphemed against me in the midst of my house, saith the Lord.

This is all coming back again in our time—sooner than most people realize. Everything you have read in the rest of this book addresses this concept in its terrible majesty and incredible glory. A great and terrible day lies before us. A magnificent work is about to emerge.

The gospel has been delivered to the Gentiles, as prophesied in various places in the Scriptures. The members of the Church of Jesus Christ of Latter-day Saints, are the Gentiles referred to. God is stating that it shall begin upon His house. Why? That's the question we need to ask ourselves.

Each of us needs to reflect on our actions and consider where we stand. How strong is our faith? How determined are we to uphold the commandments and our covenants? How often do we criticize church members, our local church leaders, or the prophet and apostles? Are we truly the light upon the hill, or the salt that has lost its flavor and is thus good for nothing but to be thrown out and trampled underfoot? Do we continue to strive to be better than our neighbors and spend our time on trivial matters? And most importantly, are we acting as one, which is the requirement for Zion?

Our only hope for the future lies in Zion, as a tremendous division is imminent, separating the righteous from the unrighteous. In the coming days, there will be only two churches: the Church of the Lamb and the Church of the Devil. Additionally, there will only be two economies: Zion and Babylon.

I pray that each of us will humble ourselves and be protected by the covenants of Zion. I also don't want to seem like someone who can't fall, as that would be prideful and dangerous. Anyone can fall. My faith will be tested just like yours. We all need more faith. I pray we will all turn to Jesus Christ to guide us in the right direction, forgive others, and overcome past decisions, actions, and personal hypocrisy. I pray we will do something ev-

SECTION 17 - WHY PEOPLE LEAVE THE CHURCH

ery day to nurture that Tree of Faith and draw closer to God. We will need every ounce of faith we can possibly acquire to face and overcome the tremendous challenges ahead of us. No matter where you stand in relation to the tree of life, partaking of its fruit and remaining near the tree is the only way to be saved in the coming days. It doesn't have to physically be in Jackson County, Missouri; you can be anywhere in the world and still remain close to the tree, but everything else will come crashing down.

###

Do you know someone who could benefit from this chapter? Perhaps they are dealing with a family member who has gone astray. Maybe they have gone astray themselves or know someone who has. We are living in the last days, and the prophesied great apostasy is upon us. Maybe this chapter could help them. I'm confident it can also assist those who want to learn how to deal with someone and answer their questions. As you have read, many people have become quite angry, even with loved ones, for whom they have felt betrayed.

If you enjoyed this chapter and know of someone who might benefit from it, I've made it available for instant download without any sign-up required. I've chosen a simple, memorable link that's easy to share. Obviously, in book form, you can't click on a link, but you can type it or send it via text message, and it will be delivered instantly.

Many incredible prophecies in the Scriptures are about to unfold. I don't know the exact percentage, but someone conducted a study on all prophecy in our standard works, and they claimed that about 85% of all prophecy points to our time. While much of it refers to Christ's first coming, it also pertains to his imminent return in our time, and the role Donald Trump plays as His foreordained Servant, much like John the Baptist.

Thank You!

Kelly Smith

Here is the link to share or scan this code:

https://First-Horseman.com/faith

Section 18 - Conclusion

Remember this statement in the Foreword of my book?

"Shortly after President Nelson was named the 17th president of the church, he provided this brief statement in an interview with the newsroom during his visit to Chile in October 2018:

> "We're witnesses to a process of restoration. . . If you think the Church has been fully restored, you're just seeing the beginning. There is much more to come. ... Wait till next year. And then the next year. Eat your vitamin pills. Get your rest. It's going to be exciting." (9)

I have shown throughout this book that numerous aspects are set to be restored, including the Political, Economic, and Social elements of the Kingdom of God, which are connected to the existing Ecclesiastical portion. Each of these represents a significant step in the complete restoration of God's kingdom.

> Elder Neil A Maxwell said in 1977, "... All the easy things the Church has had to do have been done. From now on it is high adventure!" (Wherefore, Ye Must Press Forward [1977], 81–84).

Since President Nelson has been named prophet, a story appeared in the Church news about how there have been 99 announcements and changes since he became the prophet five years prior to the date of the article in January 2023. There have been more changes in the years following.

Some of those include the ministering program, multiple temples, ending the relationship with the Boy Scouts, the first volume of the Saints series, home-centered church-supported gospel study, the discontinuation of church pageants, an online missionary recommendation process, authorizing missionaries to communicate with their families each week, waiting for temple sealings after civil marriages were discontinued, a new Book of Mormon video series, the discontinuation of the Young Men presidency which was turned over to the Bishopric, revised temple questions, a new missionary handbook, adjustments to ceremonial temple clothing, a new general handbook, a new church symbol, the bicentennial proclamation of the restoration of the fullness of the gospel of Jesus Christ, several policy changes, modifications to the Salt Lake Temple for earthquake preparedness, greatly expanded genealogy programs, discontinuing time-only marriages in the temple, the establishment of multiple social media accounts, donations to the World Food Program, a new Strength for Youth guide, changes in the temple ceremony, and many more.

I believe that most of these changes are still related to the ecclesiastical portion of God's kingdom. When we consider what needs to be done for the other three aspects of the kingdom, we realize that a lot remains to be accomplished. None of this will happen instantly or overnight; it will require years of adjustment, training, and adaptation. Embracing these changes will necessitate a great deal of open minds and hearts. Look at the resistance that has emerged regarding these changes from President Nelson; some people have even left the church because of them!

Every one of the other three aspects of God's kingdom requires monumental changes, especially considering what has transpired throughout history. As a Church, we have been unsuccessful in implementing those changes. We have attempted to live the Law of Consecration, the United Order, the Kirtland Safety Society, Orderville, and other initiatives multiple times, but they did not succeed. Zion is characterized by one heart and one mind, with no poor or rich among its members; this harmony is achieved through righteous individuals willing to adhere to the law without seeking to be superior to their neighbor. This particular aspect may be the most challenging to live out, given its history of failure, not only within our 200-year past since the restoration began but also in ancient times. It was only completely successful on two occasions, and once for a brief period; every other attempt has not succeeded. This will present a significant challenge, but it may be a necessity, as the alternative leads to the most oppressive tyranny ever witnessed on this earth. Never before have we had the means to monitor every single aspect of a person's life, especially regarding their financial activities.

The political kingdom restored through the First Horseman, Donald Trump, will be the most explosive, as it will require tremendous changes that differ from past changes. This isn't so much a change of heart but a change in acceptance, support, and attitude. When people are fighting for their lives and the lives of their families, they are much more willing to follow a strong leader with a vision who has been given direction from God. When we observe the number of countries coming under Donald Trump's control, some might claim he is just another Hitler, Stalin, or one of the

SECTION 18 - CONCLUSION

other terrible dictators from the past. It could be true if not for his ordination and calling from God to bring all these kingdoms under his rule so that they may be turned over to Jesus Christ. The hard part will be getting the testimony of that mission. Once we understand that mission, it will become much easier, but people will struggle to overcome their biased views of him and what we are used to.

The social aspect will also face challenges because, as previously mentioned, this is the time when men are demeaned and feminism has deeply rooted itself in the minds of both men and women. A return to a patriarchal order will meet strong resistance, as evidence illustrates how a distorted view of this has been detrimental to women worldwide. God's patriarchal order is the best thing for women because it is founded on love, freedom of choice, and priesthood power. When men commit to leading with genuine love, there will be no abuse or the power-hungry, ultra-controlling mindset that is often criticized as wrong. Just because men are physically stronger than women does not grant them control over them in such a manner. That strength is intended to provide for and protect, not to abuse.

President Nelson was right. The restoration of the Church will require massive changes in all our lives. Why do you think he has continually urged us to develop the spiritual strength and testimony we need to overcome the difficulties of our time? This has been a constant theme of his since his installation as our prophet. He has reminded us many times to think celestial and to attend the temple as often as possible, with the promise that there is nothing better we can do to draw closer to God. A study of all his words, especially since becoming the prophet, would probably be advisable.

The restoration of the gospel is not over. There are decades of work ahead of us, as none of these things will occur with the flick of a finger. The resistance to these changes will be immense. Each of them will require great faith, and the fact is that some people simply don't like change. We will need to adapt to a new church culture that aligns with the principles God will restore to the Earth. Changing culture is the hard part. We are accustomed to doing things a certain way and following a pattern. That pattern will change. I don't think any of us fully recognize the magnitude of these changes. I'm uncertain how many of us are truly ready for them. But that's why President Nelson urged us to take our vitamins. We will need them.

SECTION 18 - CONCLUSION

And all of this is meant to bring us unto Jesus Christ and the major wind up scenes in Revelation starts with the establishment of the Political Kingdom of God under Donald Trump's hand. Donald Trump is God's prophesied servant who will arrive in the last days. He is the First Horseman who sets everything else in motion in the Book of Revelation. He assists in establishing the Kingdom of God and creating a tremendous culture, just as John the Baptist was ordained to do.

Here was John the Baptist's ordination:

D&C 84:28 For he was baptized while he was yet in his childhood, and was ordained by the angel of God at the time he was eight days old unto this power, to overthrow the kingdom of the Jews, and to make straight the way of the Lord before the face of his people, to prepare them for the coming of the Lord, in whose hand is given all power.

John the Baptist was ordained to overthrow the kingdom of the Jews,

SECTION 18 - CONCLUSION

but Donald Trump was commissioned to overthrow the kingdoms of the world. Under his leadership, the stone cut from the mountain without hands destroys the governments of nations across the globe. He has done this to prepare the way of the Lord, not for his own glory.

Donald Trump is the prophesied Cyrus who emerges to acquire the entire land promised to Abraham, fulfilled in our day, and bestowed upon the Jews. He is the Messenger of the Covenant who will come suddenly to the temple. He will construct their temple in Jerusalem, refine the sons of Levi, who will offer an offering in righteousness. He is the suffering servant who endured more image-marring than anyone in history; yet, God healed him.

He is the foretold King David, who will sit on his throne and rule over the entire world, eventually handing that throne to Jesus Christ. He will overthrow all nations just as the stone cut out of the mountain without hands, as seen by the prophet Daniel. All nations will fall under his reign. The "Davidic Servant" is not named David, he is named Donald Trump. David means "beloved" and God's suffering servant is beloved by God.

He is the prophesied Moses who has his own Mount Sinai experience and will afterwards gather the entire House of Israel in a manner far more marvelous than the parting of the Red Sea long ago. It will be so extraordinary that they will never speak of the first Moses again. He will perform incredible miracles, just as Moses did, to fulfill God's purposes. He will stand beside Jesus Christ and Michael while everyone sings the song of Moses, expressing gratitude for what he has done to realize God's plans. It is impossible to fully describe all the things that will be under his leadership.

As the First Horseman who initiates the tremendous events recorded in the Book of Revelation, Donald Trump impacts all of humanity. His establishment of the Political Kingdom of God inflicts a deadly wound on the Beast System dominating America. This deadly wound is eventually healed and transforms into the terrifying beast seen by Daniel and Ezra. Its rise triggers the greatest world war that the Earth has ever witnessed and creates a significant division among the people. Yet, under Donald Trump's leadership and the divine power bestowed upon those in Zion, the Kings and Queens of the Gentiles, along with the tremendous army of God and the incredible cataclysmic destruction by meteors and other heavenly events, they will dismantle the Beast System. Jesus Christ and his army of celestial

SECTION 18 - CONCLUSION

beings consume everything and rid the world of all evil, thus ushering in a millennium of peace and happiness never before seen on Earth.

His leadership will transform the world and better prepare it to welcome our Savior, Jesus Christ. Those who follow the missionaries, repent, and join the Church of Jesus Christ of Latter-day Saints will be saved in Zion. The city is protected from all nations of the earth facing destruction. And much destruction is coming as recorded in scripture!

Many great prophets received books from celestial sources. Moses was given the Ten Commandments, though that may be another illusion in the future. The Brother of Jared was granted the Urim and Thummim and a vision of the world, which led to the creation of the sealed book. This book is sealed to be revealed at the opening of the seventh seal and contains the history of the entire earth.

Ezekiel was given a book that revealed the coming destructions in,

> Ezek 2:9 ¶ And when I looked, behold, an hand was sent unto me; and, lo, a roll of a book was therein;
>
> 10 And he spread it before me; and it was written within and without: and there was written therein lamentations, and mourning, and woe.

In the very first chapter of the Book of Mormon, the great prophet Lehi was also given a book about the abominations in Jerusalem and the destruction that would come upon the people.

> 1 Ne 1:11 And they came down and went forth upon the face of the earth; and the first came and stood before my father, and gave unto him a book, and bade him that he should read.
>
> 12 And it came to pass that as he read, he was filled with the Spirit of the Lord.
>
> 13 And he read, saying: Wo, wo, unto Jerusalem, for I have seen thine abominations! Yea, and many things did my father read concerning Jerusalem—that it should be destroyed, and the inhabitants thereof; many should perish by the sword, and many should be carried away captive into Babylon.

John the Revelator was also given a book that symbolized a daunting mission he had to undertake during a time of significant turmoil on Earth. He would prophesy once more among all the people of the Earth:

SECTION 18 - CONCLUSION

> Rev 10:9 And I went unto the angel, and said unto him, Give me the little book. And he said unto me, Take it, and eat it up; and it shall make thy belly bitter, but it shall be in thy mouth sweet as honey.
>
> 10 And I took the little book out of the angel's hand, and ate it up; and it was in my mouth sweet as honey: and as soon as I had eaten it, my belly was bitter.
>
> 11 And he said unto me, Thou must prophesy again before many peoples, and nations, and tongues, and kings.

Limhi sent a group of people to find those in Zarahemla who might be able to save them from the Lamanites, who had imposed a 50% tax on the people. They dispatched 43 men who eventually discovered 24 gold plates and were extremely curious about what was written on them. They were found among the completely destroyed people, with bones scattered throughout the area. They wanted to know what was on this record! They perceived it as a warning that the same fate could befall them if they did not repent! This record documented the rise and fall of the Jaredites, including the sealed portion of the gold plates.

> Mosiah 21: 25 Now king Limhi had sent, previous to the coming of Ammon, a small number of men to search for the land of Zarahemla; but they could not find it, and they were lost in the wilderness.
>
> 26 Nevertheless, they did find a land which had been peopled; yea, a land which was covered with dry bones; yea, a land which had been peopled and which had been destroyed; and they, having supposed it to be the land of Zarahemla, returned to the land of Nephi, having arrived in the borders of the land not many days before the coming of Ammon.
>
> 27 And they brought a record with them, even a record of the people whose bones they had found; and it was engraven on plates of ore.
>
> 28 And now Limhi was again filled with joy on learning from the mouth of Ammon that king Mosiah had a gift from God, whereby he could interpret such engravings; yea, and Ammon also did rejoice.
>
> 29 Yet Ammon and his brethren were filled with sorrow because so many of their brethren had been slain;

I hesitate to place myself on the same list because I'm not one of the great prophets, but I was also given a book. On Tuesday, April 29, 2014, I

SECTION 18 - CONCLUSION

had the following dream:

I dreamed I was in the home of a man than I did not know, but that I had heard about. I saw something that reminded me of my father's business, a poster with the logo of his old company on it. I bent down to pick it up as instant nostalgia overflowed my being. As I was leaning down someone brushed by me and I turned to see my father standing there. He had been dead for over 9 years and I rushed to hug him. It felt so good to see him again!

Without saying a word he gently pushed me away with a somewhat stern look on his face that suggested he was here to deliver a serious message. I was confused and in my heart thought, "Dad, I haven't seen you in 9 years. Can't I hold on to you for a bit longer?" These are only thoughts in my mind and are not actual words, but there was no change in my father's face. He was very concerned that I get this message.

I turned to see a large book sitting on a coffee table and felt impressed to go pick it up. There were several other people in the room but I don't know who they were. The book was about 18 inches square and about 6 inches thick. The outside cover was red velvet and in the middle of the front was a cutout revealing a photograph or drawing, but I don't know what it was of. As I picked it up and tried to open it, and it instantly fell apart in my hands and pages fell out of it all over the table and floor. I was embarrassed that I had been given such a beautiful gift and was treating it so casually. I really had done nothing wrong as a profound message about to be revealed.

I quickly grabbed each of the pages and tried to find how they fit back into the book trying to determine what was the front, what was the back and which went in first. I didn't have time to look at much of the pictures as I was hurrying to get it all back together. I noticed that there were pictures of many things (mostly of very sickly animals that were almost dead) floating in the ocean. There were also many pictures of wars, earthquakes, tsunamis, riots, atomic bombs, plagues, floods, erupting volcanoes, hurricanes, etc. and they were all done in an unusual drawing style as they were not photos.

I did stop and look at one picture (or drawing) of a Duck. He looked terrible. He was not sitting on top of the water but was down in it a ways. His beak was broken, his eye was damaged, feathers were missing and he was covered in diseases. I inserted the page into the book and picked up another one of an Eagle in exactly the same situation.

My father then spoke for the first time saying, "Destruction is Imminent." I quickly turned and looked at him, rather alarmingly and questioning, "destruction is imminent?" He replied,

"Destruction is Imminent!"

I then gathered up the book with all of the pages loosely between the covers and all of the other items that were on the table. I bundled them all in my arms feeling so good that I knew this information. I then walked out of the door and promptly woke up."

-

The significance of this dream was that these calamities were imminent and not in any particular order. Every prophesied destruction in the world is coming, and they will be happening simultaneously all over the place. It will be impossible to try to put them on a timeline.

Mormon spent considerable time reviewing all of his nation's previous thousand-year history and compiled the Book of Mormon. Moroni compiled the history of the Jaredites giving a second witness to the destructions of those who fail to follow God's commands as they started and ended the same way. They were commanded by God to leave, they built ships to cross the ocean and they were destroyed by civil war. Inspired by the Lord, they hand-picked exactly which stories to include as they were preserved for our day.

The angel Moroni showed Joseph Smith the location of these plates. Through the power of God, he translated them into the Book of Mormon, which we have today. Thus, Joseph was another individual who received a book from God.

In every Temple of God built by the Church of Jesus Christ of Latter-day Saints, there is a baptismal font that is always below ground level and rests on the backs of 12 oxen. Each of the tribes of the House of Israel has a symbol associated with it; for instance, the tribe of Judah has a lion, and the tribe of Ephraim has an ox. Oxen are considered steady, strong, and useful creatures, and pioneers would always prefer an ox to nearly any other animal to pull their wagons. So what do they symbolize for us? What can we learn from this beautiful example?

I submit to you that, since the majority of the church today is part of the house of Ephraim, it is their responsibility to bear the burden of the entire restoration of the gospel and to save the rest of the House of Israel, both living and dead, bringing them back under the umbrella of the House of Israel. Yes, it is a burden, but God has provided us with the means to carry it. He has blessed us with a prosperous nation that enables us to send missionaries all over the world. It's truly inspiring to see these young men and women, with their bright eyes and youthful enthusiasm, under God's guidance, equipped with the power of His Spirit to teach anyone and everyone willing to listen.

What more can we do to share the gospel with our neighbors, friends, and acquaintances? What about the people we work with? What about the people who are our customers or vendors if we own a business? What about our example on social media and the invitation to anyone to join us for a church meeting, an emergency preparedness meeting, or a self reliance event? How about a Ward breakfast or dinner? A holiday celebration or just taking them a plate of cookies? There are so many things we can do, and I submit we can do more than what we are doing right now.

At a recent Stake Conference, a beautiful young woman stood up and shared her testimony, having just been baptized. I believe she was a junior in high school, but the unusual part of her story was that she laughingly criticized her friends, who eventually brought her into the church, for not inviting her to learn about it sooner! She had wanted this much earlier than the young men and women realized. I believe there are many more people who would accept an invitation to learn about their family history, attend a church picnic, or participate in some kind of event in the fall or spring that could spark their interest in the church.

And for those who have been offered that Book of Mormon—hopefully, you have received it! Through the marvelous Book of Mormon, the Lord is gathering the House of Israel and anyone who will listen to the voice of the Spirit and partake in the covenant offered to Abraham, Isaac, and Jacob. You can have the same opportunities as those given to the House of Israel through Moses and His prophets of the last days, through the res-

SECTION 18 - CONCLUSION

toration of the gospel of Jesus Christ!

Everything within it describes what will happen in the last days. It outlines the future by reflecting on past events. It reveals the reasons for these distractions and emphasizes our need to become part of Zion. Before Jesus Christ visited the Nephites, tremendous destruction swept across the land. The darkness, earthquakes, lightning, volcanic eruptions, horrific tornadoes, and the sinking of cities served as a type and shadow of what is likely to occur again in the near future.

You have been offered a Book of Mormon! If you don't have one, go to ChurchOfJesusChrist.org and have one sent to you for free!

God has provided this for you to achieve what every other prophet in the past has yearned for, if you choose to do so. You can embrace the message of this marvelous book and apply the atonement of Jesus Christ in your life. This book will transform the world and bring people into Zion. It is the book that will distinguish the righteous from the unrighteous. This book will guide people to Jesus Christ and His church, inviting them to flee Babylon. In the future, there will only be two churches: the Church of the Lamb and the Church of the Devil. Which one will you belong to?

This book was foretold to flood the Earth. It will reach every nation, language, and people, speaking to those who listen, read its pages, and recognize the power within. This remarkable book is offered to you!

What will you do with that book? Do you not recognize how much effort God has put into bringing this book into existence? Do you have any idea how many thousands of hours it took to create it over a 1,000-year period for the Nephites and an additional 1,500 years for the Jaredites? It's impossible to say enough good things—great things—about this book! It has brought millions of people to Jesus Christ. It contains the fullness of the gospel so that people may know the truth. It is the most correct book on earth.

No other book in all of history has faced as much scrutiny. It was criticized even before it was created! It has received more analysis than anything else. Now, don't get me wrong; we love the Bible; it is one of our standard works. It is the word of God. We cherish and teach it, and it remains a powerful tool. We've been discussing the entire book of Revelation here,

SECTION 18 - CONCLUSION

which comes from the Bible. Sadly, whether through intentional actions or mistakes, errors within it have caused the gentiles to stumble. There's a reason why there are thousands of Christian churches today: those mistakes.

The Book of Mormon addresses all of these issues. When read together, the two texts present two nations that testify that Jesus Christ lives. Both bear witness that He was resurrected from the dead and that if you accept His word delivered through His authorized servants, you can be forgiven of all your sins and live with Him for eternity. However, you must be baptized by someone who has the authority to perform your baptism.

I hope you not only take advantage of this book by reading it and applying its lessons to your life, as God wrote it specifically for you. He understands what we face today and knows the challenges you're encountering. Through this book, He can guide you on what to do and show you the way.

Our goal is to share this book with everyone we know. It will be the dividing factor in determining who is on God's side and who isn't.

Two years after the Book of Mormon was published, the Lord condemned the church for treating lightly what He had labored so hard to provide. That was in 1832. In 1986, President Nelson, the prophet of the church, stated during a General Conference, after reading that verse of condemnation, that this condemnation still rested upon the church. It had been 154 years, and the condemnation still rested upon the church!

Those words struck a chord with me, and as I mentioned before, I've read it almost every day for 39 years. I've had many experiences with this book, and I love it. The sad part is that I didn't always listen to what God taught me. Every mistake I've made in life is due to not heeding the spirit that spoke to me through its pages, guiding my actions. Sometimes, I'm as dense as a rock. Looking back now, I cringe at the choices I should have made, and I regret many consequences because I didn't listen.

This marvelous book has blessed, warned, uplifted, and enlightened me. At times, the pages seemed to shine a spotlight on my life. I could feel the words He spoke in my heart. Some days, I broke down in tears of gratitude for the incredible blessings He has given me. I thank my Heavenly Father for providing me with this book.

His revelation to me in December 2021 to read the Book of Revelation

SECTION 18 - CONCLUSION

did not halt my daily reading of the Book of Mormon; I read both. What I didn't realize at the time was just how many concepts in the Book of Mormon were also present in the Book of Revelation! You have encountered some of those concepts.

There's an amazing story at the beginning of the Book of Mormon about how Nephi obtained the brass plates from Laban. These brass plates were created by Joseph of Egypt and handed down for generations and contained the record of God's dealings with man since the creation of the earth. It had everything contained in the Bible up until Jeremiah and was needed to teach the Lehites the gospel. Many people have been highly critical of this story because Nephi beheads Laban to acquire these scriptures. They argue that this is not something God would do and claim that it serves as proof that this is false doctrine. The reality is quite different.

Laban was a member of the church in positions of power and authority. He was responsible for the records, the Scriptures, and the history of the people. This is a significant and important position. He had grown slothful and negligent in his duties. He had become drunken with not only with wine but with power. Additionally, he had turned wicked, having acquired the wealth of Lehi and his family through coercion, threatening to kill the four sons of Lehi.

Nephi stands over him, commanded by God to slay him because of his wickedness and to obtain these scriptures and records for their families for generations to come. Nephi hesitates, not wanting to bear the guilt of such an action. But God persuades him to fulfill this command, and he complies. He then obtains the plates with the servant Zoram, and carry everything to Lehi and Sariah in the desert (1 Ne 4).

The Sword of Laban is one of the artifacts found in the stone box alongside the Gold Plates, the Urim and Thummim, the Breastplate, and the Liahona. It was seen by the witnesses and is therefore deeply connected to the

SECTION 18 - CONCLUSION

Book of Mormon. I also propose that it serves as a prophetic symbol of the future.

The Sword of Laban represents the Word of God. The Sword of Justice that we are to wield in defense of the truth. This sword will serve as the dividing factor in the last days, separating the righteous from the wicked. It distinguishes those who belong to the church of the Lamb from those associated with the church of the devil whether they are a member of the church or not. God's word operates like a sword, dividing both joints and marrow. (D&C 11:2)

The members of the Church of Jesus Christ of Latter-day Saints hold a great responsibility to take the Book of Mormon and spread it across the Earth. They are to gather Israel and anyone else who seeks to keep the commandments of God and bring them to Zion. Many members have fallen away from the church and found themselves outside the covenant they had promised to uphold. Many of them oppose the church and have become significant obstacles to its growth. Essentially, they resemble Laban. They are slothful, drunken with iniquity, seek only worldly things, disobey the commandments, and resist the spirit. This is the great apostasy foretold in scripture and is happening right now. (2 The 2:3)

I submit that in the very near future, if they do not repent, this will bring to pass the fulfillment that the gospel was taken from them. Just as the House of Israel garnered the wrath of God and he cursed them never to be able to obtain the promised land because of their wickedness, the same will happen again to members of the church who have not repented and come back into the fold. The Sword of the Lord, the Book of Mormon, will essentially cut them off from the promised blessings they could have obtained.

This is a sobering proposition and situation they find themselves in. Some

SECTION 18 - CONCLUSION

of the greatest curses and warnings given in the scriptures are directed toward these people and the Christian Gentiles in America who reject the gospel offered to them. Christ says that he will bring fury upon them, such as upon the heathen, which they have never heard before; he's talking about them.

I pray wholeheartedly that those who have distanced themselves from the church will return. The sooner, the better, because the alternative is far more devastating and consequential than anyone understands while the blessings of being a part of Zion is greater than anyone realizes!

And if you are not a member of the Church of Jesus Christ of Latter-Day Saints, I would like to offer you that book—a book from God that contains His word. Will you accept it or reject it? The Book of Mormon teaches us that some people would trample upon Jesus Christ and regard Him as nothing. Similarly, individuals treat the Book of Mormon this way, and I've seen countless images on Twitter and Facebook of people who proudly burn it. They boastfully declare to the world that they want nothing to do with a "cult." It's astonishing how they try to brush aside all that God has done and all the good that has come to the world through the Church of Jesus Christ of Latter-Day Saints with one word. They may face God's one word Judgment in reply: condemned.

But I'm here to testify that this is God's church. It's the only one that has the authority to perform saving ordinances. Those who reject it, trample it underfoot, and fight against it will never receive the blessings that God wants to give them. Those blessings are eternal. But I also want to state that you do not have to be a member of the Church to be saved in the New Jerusalem! You just have to live righteously and not fight against the Church or the Book of Mormon.

While all churches contribute positively to the world and we support their efforts, we make just one claim. We do not assert that we are the only source of spiritual experiences or that we are the only ones doing good in the world. We are not the source of all truth, God is and He has revealed many things to many people throughout the ages. He has given them that which they were willing to receive. All churches I know (except the Church of the Devil) engage in positive acts that deserve support.

The Priesthood of God was restored to the Earth through John the Bap-

SECTION 18 - CONCLUSION

tist, as well as Peter, James, and John. Additionally, the priesthood was bestowed to seal families together through the restoration provided by the prophet Elijah. The authority to perform saving ordinances, such as baptism, is found solely in the Church of Jesus Christ of Latter-day Saints. All of these blessings are offered to you for your eternal salvation. You can be forgiven of your sins. You can receive the Holy Spirit to guide you daily. You can be sealed to your family for eternity. You can assist in bringing others to the truth. You can help redeem the dead and connect with your ancestors. You can do for them what they cannot do for themselves, but it all begins with a book:

The Book of Mormon.

I want to offer you that book.

To those who have it I recommend reading it and re-reading it.

What you do with this offer will determine your future.

It lies within your hands.

Please accept it!

I say these things in the name of Jesus Christ. Amen.

####

Thank you for reading my book. If you found it helpful and want to share it with others, you can join our affiliate program and earn a 30% commission on any PDF sales made through your link. Just scan the code here and sign up for free.

Endnotes

1 https://newsroom.churchofjesuschrist.org/article/latter-day-saint-prophet-wife-apostle-share-insights-global-ministry?lang=eng#churchofjesuschrist

2 https://www.churchofjesuschrist.org/study/manual/old-testament-student-manual-genesis-2-samuel/enrichment-section-g-hebrew-literary-styles?lang=eng

3 https://www.churchofjesuschrist.org/study/liahona/2024/08/come-follow-me/16-jesus-christ-the-center-of-our-faith?lang=eng#p15

4 https://www.churchofjesuschrist.org/study/manual/book-of-mormon-student-manual/chapter-31-alma-36-39?lang=eng#title4

5 https://revelation.biblicalblueprints.com/structure/explanation Wilber Pickering, Phillip Kayser, Josh Duff

6 Language of the Lord: New Discoveries of Chiasmus in the Doctrine and Covenants Hardcover – January 1, 1993 by H. Clay Gorton (Author)

7 https://www.churchofjesuschrist.org/study/general-conference/2022/10/14renlund?lang=eng#p5

8 W.W. Phelps's letter dated January 15, 1845, published in Times and Seasons (vol. 6, no. 1)

9 https://www.churchofjesuschrist.org/study/general-conference/2022/10/47nelson?lang=eng#p3

10 The Revelation 12 Sign in 5 Minutes! September 23 2017 Alignment Explained What you need to know - https://www.youtube.com/watch?v=ZSqPiR2EK2s

11 History of the Church, 6:318–319, 321, and eventually the entire earth (see Brigham Young, in Journal of Discourses, 9:138).

12 Methods of Operation and Control (Comprehensive List) of the Modern-Day Gadianton Robbers
1. Secrecy and Concealment
2. Censorship and Suppression
3. Manipulation of Power and Justice
4. Economic Exploitation
5. Cultural and Social Decay
6. Horrific Abortion Statistics
7. Faulty Science and Misleading Agendas
8. Health and Medical Control
9. Socialism and Communism as Tools of Enslavement
10. Climate Change and the New World Order
11. Economic Control through Digital Dependency
12. Technological Enslavement
13. Education and Indoctrination
14. The Promise of a Global Utopia

Overarching Goal:
All these strategies work toward establishing a global "beast system" modeled after the Gadianton robbers of old. This system removes individual freedoms, discourages righteousness, and perpetuates societal decay, leaving citizens dependent, controlled, and spiritually destitute. Only through divine intervention and the establishment of Zion can this tide be turned. (Compiled from Grok Prompt)

13 The President Makers: How Billionaires Control U.S. and Foreign Policy, Don Fotheringham, Paperback – January 1, 2014

14 The divine plan for redemption and the restoration of righteousness is centered on re-establishing the family as the core unit of society. The family, designed by God as the foundation for all human relationships, is the primary institution for nurturing, teaching, and fostering moral values. This restoration will bring profound changes to society, rooted in the principles

ENDNOTES

of freedom, unity, justice, and godliness.
1. Re-establishing the Family as Central to Society
2. The Freedoms Sought by the Founding Fathers
3. Economic Prosperity Through Unity
4. A Righteous Judicial System
5. Teaching God's Laws and Removing Hatred
6. A Society Aligned with God's Commandments
7. A World Transformed (Compiled from Grok Prompt)

15   https://onlinecoursesblog.hillsdale.edu/our-constitution-was-made-only-for-a-moral-and-religious-people/
16   Hyrum L. Andrus, "Joseph Smith and World Government," Deseret Book Company, 1958, p. 20
17   Image Source: https://www.tainoage.com/cosmic_coqui.html
18   https://youtu.be/ihwoIlx-HI3Q?si=NrxejJxG9VBLIs95
19   https://x.com/i/grok?conversation=1876076100557869269
20   Champions for Zion, Jesse Fisher pg 4
21   https://bookofmormon.online/jesus-expounds-the-prophets/redemption-through-christ-micah
22   https://i.dailymail.co.uk/i/newpix/2018/05/11/14/4C18E72000000578-5718129-image-a-71_1526046822076.jpg
23   Avraham Gileadi is an Isaiah scholar known for his work on what he calls the "Davidic Servant." To my knowledge, he has never connected that with anyone, in fact he claims outright that it is not Donald Trump but says he is a precursor to that Servant.

I purchased his first book on Isaiah in 1990, but never paid much attention to his teachings on the Davidic Servant. As his Isaiah Institute grew over the years, I attended some online Zoom meetings. During one of those meetings, I became frustrated by his insistence on the existence of a Davidic Servant. I felt that people were leaving the church because of this, and I questioned why none of the apostles, general authorities, or prophets ever discussed this servant. Why is it not taught more if it holds such significance? I admit I was a bit overbearing during that Zoom call, and I recently called him and apologized, and I want to publicly apologize for embarrassing him and being so insistent in my opposition.

Once I had my revelation about Donald Trump, I examined some of his work closely, but I disagreed with his conclusions regarding some of the symbols. I have found multiple references that mention or prophesy about the Davidic Servant, whom I believe to be Donald Trump, but I do not agree with everything Avraham has proposed. Perhaps someday he will be proven right again, but I'm sticking with what has been revealed to me.

Unless otherwise noted, nothing in my book has been taken from anyone else, including Avraham. Everything here comprises what I experienced during my three-year medical crisis and especially a four-month deluge of spiritual waters.

However, this raises an important question about why the general authorities do not address this topic. I believe it relates to the natural human tendency to seek answers beyond what God has revealed. Once people perceive something other than our Savior Jesus Christ to depend on, they will embrace it and exclude themselves from the kingdom. Personal salvation is fundamentally different from political salvation. It is also far more important.

ENDNOTES

If we begin to criticize our leaders or assert they have faltered, as mentioned in the section on One Mighty and Strong, we not only risk not being welcomed into Zion, we risk our eternal salvation. Pride can destroy anyone and we must unite as one. We must allow our leaders to do their calling, and refrain from demanding they act according to our wishes or beliefs.

This requires humility and submission to authority. I am confident that our current general authorities choose not to discuss this matter because it could create division, as many individuals are captivated by political power and frustrated with ecclesiastical authority, which requires much more faith, hope, and charity.

And no one will be allowed inside Zion without possessing a tremendous amount of faith, hope, and charity, all while living the law of consecration!

24   They Saw Our Day Audible Logo Audible Audiobook – Original recording -- Lance Richardson (Author, Narrator), American Family Publications (Publisher) https://amzn.to/4iTaPQB

25   Crown of Victory, Pg 62, Opening the Seven Seals, Richard D. Draper

26   https://www.churchofjesuschrist.org/study/general-conference/2002/04/hidden-wedges?lang=eng

INDEX

Symbols

2.555 billion years 30
3 ½ years 57, 204
5th seal 184, 206
6th seal 184
7,000 years 110
7th Seal 26, 27, 176
13 months 100
30 minutes 26, 84
81 million votes 178
144,000 18, 20, 26, 71, 78, 111, 184, 215, 216, 217, 218, 227, 248
1260 YEARS 57

A

Abaddon 22, 93, 97, 101, 107, 238, 245
Abominations 21, 42
abortions 197
Abrahamic Covenant 194
Adam 25, 30, 32, 54, 55, 57, 106, 110, 124, 125, 201
adon 167
a great city 43
aliens 90, 181
All world governments must come under his rule 176
Alma 32 35, 259
an army with banners 209
Antichrist 25, 58, 59, 67, 68, 69, 90, 179, 180, 210, 225
AntiChrist 68
Anti-Nephi-Lehi 40, 202
Apostasy 110
Approaching Zion 128
Archangel 55, 57
Ark of the Covenant 100, 105
Armageddon 19, 99, 102, 210, 226, 238
arm of the Lord 65, 182, 190, 191
artificial intelligence 11, 35, 68, 183, 224
asteroid 87, 89, 90
Avraham Gileadi 192, 292

B

Babylon (many pages)
Babylonian system 128, 225
Balaam or Balac 59
Barack Obama 177
bares his arm 244
Beast (many pages)
Beast System 34, 40, 55, 58, 59, 65, 66, 98, 102, 136, 179, 180, 183, 185, 186, 196, 245, 279
become like God 123, 125
Black Horse 24, 38., 111
blasphemy 42, 61, 64, 67, 123, 179, 239
bottomless pit 19, 22, 56, 57, 93, 95, 98, 99, 100, 107, 200, 237, 245, 248
Boy Scouts 123, 275
Brass Plates 140
Brother of Jared 29, 32, 33, 110, 141, 152, 201, 237, 280
bureaucracies 66
burning bush experience 170, 178, 183, 211
burning of the bosom 35

C

Caiaphas 174
cannibalism 79, 244
capitalism 131
cast his idols of silver 47
caught up 49, 90, 91, 166, 170
Celestial Kingdom 31, 126, 154
celestial marriage 122, 194
central verse 49, 158, 173
chemical 88, 89, 97
Chiasmus 14, 15, 16, 17, 160, 172, 185, 291
chiastic 14, 19, 20, 39, 49, 83, 93, 152
chiastically 50, 57, 73, 85
Christian bullies 192, 262
"Christ" is a title meaning "anointed one." 173
Church of the Devil 58, 68, 70, 239, 241, 249, 272, 285, 289
Church of the Firstborn 185, 214, 248
Church of the Lamb 68, 70, 79, 168, 239, 241, 247, 272, 285, 288
city of Zion 55, 210, 227
Civil War 56, 63, 66, 79, 93, 159, 180, 204, 209, 237, 240, 283
Columbus 12, 159, 238
Communism 68, 131, 223, 291
conquering and to conquer 47, 52, 225
consecrate properties 138
Constitution 63, 65, 66, 68, 179, 183, 185
continents to shift 102
covenant people of the Lord 79, 88, 201, 214, 229
covenant with death 181
COVID-19 134, 136, 137, 211
creation of the Earth 109
Creator 31, 46, 271
Cumorah 99
Cyrus 186, 188, 190, 192, 193, 195, 279

D

Daniel chapter 7 54
David 32, 65, 139, 141, 157, 174, 279
Davidic Servant 279, 292
day of vengeance and burning 138
deadly wound 61, 62, 63, 179, 279
Deep State 12, 63
Department of Education 121
destroying angel 94, 97, 99, 238, 245
Destruction is Imminent! 283
destruction of the family 122
Digital currencies 69
Dome of Protection 71, 88, 230
Donald Trump is the messenger of the covenant 167
Donald Trump is the modern-day Moses 172
Donald Trump is the political savior of the modern world 179
Donald Trump's name means "World Ruler who Tri-

INDEX

umphs." 172
Donald Trump will turn 80 on June 14, 2026 171
Dragon 17, 51, 52, 54, 55, 58, 65, 98, 99, 110
drones 40, 95, 97

E

Earth (many pages)
earthquakes 18, 19, 27, 31, 39, 40, 56, 83, 85, 87, 102, 103, 105, 107, 112. 141, 205, 206, 209, 220, 228, 229, 230, 237, 275, 282, 285
eclipses 27
economic collapse 24
economies 41, 210, 272
Elder Robert D. Hales 22
Enoch 25, 32, 110, 189, 190, 194, 216, 218, 219, 220, 221, 223, 253
enormous plasma display 77
Escape from Germany 217
Euphrates 98, 112, 195
Every child needs to be raised by both a father and a mother 123
Everything will be exposed 47
extortion 130, 131

F

face of God 28, 41
faith (many pages)
False Prophet 70, 99
famine 24, 28, 40, 43, 58, 66, 230
fifth beast 66, 67, 68, 69
fifth seal 24, 28, 38, 58, 84, 249
fight against Zion 53, 168, 214, 229, 230, 245, 246
filthy water 200, 237, 240, 241
financial 24, 53, 63, 103, 174, 178, 249, 276
fire down from heaven 67
First Born 168
First Horseman 19, 24, 47, 52, 58, 65, 71, 80, 105, 110, 117, 175, 176, 179, 196, 225, 246, 276, 278, 279
first seal 25, 28, 57, 59, 110

five months 95, 97, 100, 238
flaming sword 30, 124
flooding 55, 210, 228
flood of people 56
flood of water 55
food storage 103, 249
foreordained 117, 240, 273
Forgotten Wedges 264
Four Aspects of the Kingdom of God 116
Four Horsemen 24, 25, 47, 58, 79, 237
four seals 39
fourth beast 38, 40, 55, 66, 67, 69
Fourth Horseman 111
Fourth Seal 24
fourth world war 98
free people 148, 158, 175, 178, 179, 185, 248
free prisoners 243
frogs 98

G

Gadianton Robbers 12, 41, 52, 53, 58, 63, 159, 178, 185, 196, 199, 291
garments 99, 147, 264
gentile nation of America 181
George Washington 178, 195
Gethsemane 31, 32, 156, 175
get out of debt 104
Gidgiddoni 53
global government 70
Globalist 68
God's Army 91, 93, 95 99, 237
God's chosen political Savior 175
God's chosen servant 24, 58, 59, 80, 183, 211
God the Father 18, 225
God wants us to become like Him 125
God will help you 267
gold plates 29, 31, 140, 141, 161, 168, 200, 237, 251, 281, 287
Goshen 88
government, military, and media 69

great and abominable church 41, 42, 58, 168, 213, 238, 239, 240, 245, 248
great and a marvelous work 148, 179
great and spacious building 21, 44, 168, 177, 234, 236, 241, 245, 246, 250, 263
great apostasy 246, 262, 263, 266, 273, 288
great hail 105
Great mountain burning 88, 111
great pit 239
great sword 24, 38, 39, 40
Groves 59

H

hail 19, 87, 88, 105, 220
half an hour 25, 26, 83, 85, 90
have not instructed us to travel to Missouri 247
Heat of the Sun 260
Heavenly Parents 29
heaven on earth 52
heavens opening like a scroll 77
He does not know them 45
He will be healed 171, 211, 247
hidden 50, 94, 113, 126, 140, 188, 224, 293
Hidden Wedges 264
highway shall be cast up 80, 228
Holy Ghost 35, 36, 140, 146, 148, 166, 194, 207, 234, 236, 241, 262
Hugh Nibley 128
Hundreds of millions of people will join the church 161
hunters and fishers of men 215
hurricanes 83, 210, 282
husband and wife 118, 122, 241

I

ice flowing down 80
idols 46, 47, 59, 100

INDEX

image is marred 140, 157
image of the beast 62, 67
incense represents the prayers 86
iron rod 240, 241
islands to flee 102
I will bring the fulness of my gospel from among them 208
I will heal him 149, 160, 172, 211

J

Jesus Christ (many pages)
John Adams 65
John the Baptist 101, 173, 273, 278, 289
John the Revelator 101, 110, 152, 154, 165, 204, 211, 225, 246, 280
John Welch 15
join house to house 159
Joseph Biden 177
Joseph Smith never spoke before kings 161
Judgments of God 111
Justice of God 200

K

Key to open the bottomless pit 19
King David 32, 139, 174, 279
Kingdom of God (many pages)
kingdoms of our Lord 104
kingdoms of the Gentiles 238, 239
kingdoms of this world 104
King Herod 174
King James translators 87
King of kings 107
King of Righteousness 218, 225
Kings and Queens of the Gentiles 81, 168, 213, 214, 215, 217, 218, 223, 225, 227, 228, 244, 248, 279
kings of the earth 27, 39, 41, 42, 43, 99, 131
kings will shut their mouths 160
Kishkumen 64
Krakatoa 89

L

Laban 287, 288
Lachoneus 53
Laman and Lemuel 234, 241
Lawfare 195, 243
law of consecration 122, 126, 128, 129, 131, 160, 163, 164, 166, 168, 248, 293
leave the Church but can't leave it alone 266
Liahona 224, 241, 287
life of my servant shall be in my hand 149, 160, 172, 195
locusts 95, 96, 112
Lucifer 30, 54, 56, 105, 106, 139, 223, 224

M

magnetic poles 80
manchild 20, 50, 51, 56, 173, 225
Manifesto 136
Man of Sin 68, 225, 246, 263
Mark of the Beast 79, 83, 87, 88, 91, 94, 99, 111, 184, 186, 215, 238
Mark on their hand or forehead 67
marred servant 172, 173
martyrdom 66, 271
martyrs 24, 28, 40, 42, 54, 58, 84, 111, 184, 206, 237, 249
Marxism 223
Marxist 68
measure the temple 101
media 47, 52, 64, 69, 119, 135, 137, 157, 179, 180, 192, 276, 284, 292
Melchizedek 101, 216, 218, 219, 220, 223, 228, 253
merchants 21, 44, 46, 102, 189
meridian of Time 31
messenger before his face 163
meteor 19, 27, 41, 87, 88, 89, 107, 279
Michael 20, 32, 49, 54, 55, 57, 176, 225, 279
military-industrial complex 52
Millions of government workers 66
Millstone 45, 46
miracles 19, 21, 31, 35, 62, 67, 88, 99, 171, 174, 178, 205, 236, 279
misuse of the land 159
modern-day Cyrus, Donald Trump 190
modern-day pioneers 70
monopoly 159
moon becomes red 40
Moses (many pages)
most significant event in world history 248
Mother in Heaven 126
Mother of Harlots 21, 41, 42, 240, 248
Mount of Olives 193
Mount Sinai 170, 171, 172, 279
musicians 46
Mystery 42, 245

N

Nehor 242, 256
never truly free 104
New Jerusalem in Independence 52
new name 182, 224, 225
Noah 32, 110, 151, 189, 190, 194
None will He destroy who believe in Him 230
North Pole 41
Nostradamus 61
nova of the sun 41
No weapon that is formed 70, 151, 193
nuclear warfare 95
nursing fathers 80, 213, 244
nurturing and watering our Tree of Faith 250

O

One Mighty and Strong 134, 141, 142, 293

INDEX

one-party system 64
organize Zion 138, 139
Our only hope is Zion 182, 224
our only safety is in Zion 40

P

Pale Horse 24, 38, 111
Parable of the Sower 260
Patience of the Saints 204
patriarchal 118, 119, 120, 121, 126, 153, 277
patriarchs 118, 119, 121
Pella 236
perdition 225, 246, 251, 263
pillars of smoke 43, 95
pit is war 237
plagues 21, 24, 28, 43, 83, 85, 86, 88, 91, 98, 100, 102, 112, 170, 282
polar reversal 228
polished shaft in a quiver 243
Political Kingdom of God 39, 47, 118, 278, 279
pollution 141, 197, 205, 206
polygamy 135
power of his Christ 20, 50, 173
preparation 24, 103, 109, 117, 249
President Nelson 35, 135, 137, 229, 275, 276, 277, 286
pride 21, 44, 105, 106, 159, 160, 177, 205, 206, 208, 235, 236, 237, 246, 250, 256, 263, 265
priesthood keys 93
priesthood power 225, 277
Princes will bow down in worship 243
private jets 42, 242
profits 128
prophet Joseph Smith 18, 126, 136, 170, 191, 199, 206, 218, 239
prosperity gospel 42, 242

Q

questioned the science 135

R

Rahab 65
Red Horse 24, 110
Red Sea 28, 32, 80, 170, 184, 228, 243, 244, 279
red velvet book 226
reel to and fro 80
restoration 10, 28, 32, 116, 128, 206, 246, 275, 276, 277, 284, 290, 291
Restoration of the Gospel 110, 128
resurrection is a priesthood ordinance 220
Richard G. Scott 15
righteousness (many pages)
R-rated movies 59
rumors of wars 205, 206, 240, 248
Russell M. Nelson 10, 103, 135

S

Salt Lake Temple 103, 136, 210, 275
Satan (many pages)
Satanism 59
savior on Mount Zion 36
Savior's power 35
scorpions 95, 97
sealed book 29, 280
sealed plates 140
seal of God on their foreheads 93, 95
sea of glass 31, 85, 86
Second Horseman 39, 58, 59, 110
Second Seal 24, 90
second Woe 102
secret abominations 208
secret combinations 10, 42, 58, 59, 65, 179, 196, 205
secret societies 12
Self-justification 265
self-reliant 68, 127
Seven Angels 113
Seven Final Trumpets 113
seven heads represent the fact that it covers the entire earth 69
seven plagues 21, 86
seven seals 25, 29, 35, 39, 110, 111
Seven Sevens of God 29, 107, 109
seventh seal 18, 25, 34, 41, 83, 85, 90, 112, 140, 280
Seven Trumpets 112
Seven Vials 21, 42, 112
shaft of lightning 139
shall become gods 124
short season will last about 260 years 57
sign has been shown across the world 76
silence in heaven 85, 90
sing a new song 79
sing the song of Moses 85, 86, 176
six seals 18, 25, 83
sixth or seventh seal 25, 34
Sixth Seal 25
slaves 44, 159
Social credit scores 69
Socialism 129, 131, 223, 291
Socialist 68
social media 119, 135, 180, 192, 276, 284
Sodom and Gomorrah 43, 59
solar flare 19, 41, 92
sons of Levi 163, 167, 279
souls of men 44, 45
spiritual preparation 103, 249
sprinkle many nations 147, 156, 160, 183
stars fall from heaven 27, 41
stewards 127
stewardship 116, 117
Stout Horn 55, 58, 67, 225
Structure of the Book of Revelation 14
Suffering Servant 154, 156, 157, 158, 162, 166, 172, 279
sun blacken 27, 40
sun was smitten 91
supernova 19, 92
Sword of Justice 288
Sword of Laban 287, 288
Sword of the Lord 288

INDEX

T

Taliban 178
temple of God 19, 103, 105, 246, 263
ten horns 42, 49, 61, 69, 225
Ten Years After 223
Terrestrial 29, 30, 57, 84, 91, 95, 111, 113, 142, 168
The 10 Commandments 170
the Assyrian 55, 68, 69, 216, 225
the Church of Jesus Christ of Latter-day Saints (many pages)
the last president of the United States 211
the Man of Sin 68
the New Jerusalem 11, 33, 34, 52, 65, 66, 78, 81, 117, 150, 156, 161, 193, 210, 215, 220, 222, 223, 248, 252, 289
The Seven Seals 5, 18, 24, 110
the song of Moses 85, 86, 176, 279
they chose…poorly 201
They failed to nurture and water their tree of faith! 260
They Saw Our Day 211, 293
Third Horseman 111
Third Seal 24
third Woe 104
three eagle heads 69
Three Nephites 165
Three Witnesses 252
three woes 100
time frames 28
Time is running out 208
tithing 131, 163, 164, 167, 168, 180, 256, 264
toxic masculinity 119
trafficking 45, 46, 52, 178, 197
translated beings 95, 98, 184
translation ordinance 183
treason 64, 66, 179
tree of life 30, 101, 107, 124, 125, 233, 240, 245, 259, 263, 273
tribalism 66, 67, 95
trodden under foot 209
trumpets and vials 85
Trump is the Anointed One! 173
Trump's life is in God's hands 161
tsunamis 83, 89, 141, 209, 282
two angels above the Ark 105
two candlesticks 101
two churches 70, 239, 252, 272, 285
two hundred thousand thousand 100
two olive trees 101
Two Witnesses 19, 100, 101
tyrannical 52, 134, 135

U

United Order 117, 276
Urim and Thummim 280, 287
USGS 206
Utopian society 223

V

vapor of smoke 245
vengeance 40, 84, 138, 149, 181, 190, 196, 197, 200, 201, 202, 204
vials and trumpets 92
vial upon the sun 91
visage was so marred 147, 156, 183
Vision of the Brother of Jared 29
Vision of the Tree of Life 233
volcano 18, 89
volcanoes 83, 89, 209, 282

W

war in Heaven 106
war with the Saints 67
weak and simple 191, 192
White Horse 21, 24, 38, 110, 225
white stone 141, 224
whore 21, 42, 55, 235
Why people leave the Church 255
woe be unto the Gentiles 239
Woman is the Church 51
woman was arrayed in purple and scarlet 42
Wonder Woman 8, 119
Woodrow Wilson 63
Word of Wisdom 94, 164, 168, 256, 259
world lies in sin 129
world ruler who triumphs 139, 176
World War I 204, 211
World War II 204, 211, 217
World War III 24, 47, 66, 77, 79
Wormwood 19, 89, 111
wounding the head of the beast 177
wrath of the Lamb 27, 28, 39, 41, 46, 76

Y

year's supply of food 103, 131
year's supply of money 131
Yellowstone 89
your true potential 221

Z

Zion will eventually encompass all of North, Central, and South America 56

www.ingramcontent.com/pod-product-compliance
Lightning Source LLC
Chambersburg PA
CBHW050553170426
43201CB00011B/1679